CW00687695

PALGRAVE STUDIES IN CULTURAL

Series Editors

**Anthony J. La Vopa**, North Carolina State University.

**Suzanne Marchand**, Louisiana State University.

**Javed Majeed**, Queen Mary, University of London.

The Palgrave Studies in Cultural and Intellectual History series has three primary aims: to close divides between intellectual and cultural approaches, thus bringing them into mutually enriching interactions; to encourage interdisciplinarity in intellectual and cultural history; and to globalize the field, both in geographical scope and in subjects and methods. This series is open to work on a range of modes of intellectual inquiry, including social theory and the social sciences; the natural sciences; economic thought; literature; religion; gender and sexuality; philosophy; political and legal thought; psychology; and music and the arts. It encompasses not just North America but Africa, Asia, Eurasia, Europe, Latin America, and the Middle East. It includes both nationally focused studies and studies of intellectual and cultural exchanges between different nations and regions of the world, and encompasses research monographs, synthetic studies, edited collections, and broad works of reinterpretation. Regardless of methodology or geography, all books in the series are historical in the fundamental sense of undertaking rigorous contextual analysis.

Published by Palgrave Macmillan:

*Indian Mobilities in the West, 1900–1947: Gender, Performance, Embodiment*
By Shompa Lahiri

*The Shelley-Byron Circle and the Idea of Europe*
By Paul Stock

*Culture and Hegemony in the Colonial Middle East*
By Yaseen Noorani

*Recovering Bishop Berkeley: Virtue and Society in the Anglo-Irish Context*
By Scott Breuninger

*The Reading of Russian Literature in China: A Moral Example and Manual of Practice*
By Mark Gamsa

*Rammohun Roy and the Making of Victorian Britain*
By Lynn Zastoupil

# Benjamin Constant and the Birth of French Liberalism

K. Steven Vincent

BENJAMIN CONSTANT AND THE BIRTH OF FRENCH LIBERALISM
Copyright © K. Steven Vincent, 2011.
Softcover reprint of the hardcover 1st edition 2011 978-0-230-11009-0

First published in 2011 by
PALGRAVE MACMILLAN®
in the United States—a division of St. Martin's Press LLC,
175 Fifth Avenue, New York, NY 10010.

Where this book is distributed in the UK, Europe and the rest of the
world, this is by Palgrave Macmillan, a division of Macmillan Publishers
Limited, registered in England, company number 785998, of Houndmills,
Basingstoke, Hampshire RG21 6XS.

Palgrave Macmillan is the global academic imprint of the above companies
and has companies and representatives throughout the world.

Palgrave® and Macmillan® are registered trademarks in the United States,
the United Kingdom, Europe and other countries.

ISBN 978-1-349-29239-4     ISBN 978-0-230-11710-5 (eBook)
DOI 10.1057/9780230117105
Library of Congress Cataloging-in-Publication Data

Vincent, K. Steven.
    Benjamin Constant and the birth of French liberalism / K. Steven
Vincent.
        p. cm.—(Palgrave studies in cultural and intellectual history)
        1. Constant, Benjamin, 1767–1830—Political and social views.
    2. Liberalism—France—History—19th century. I. Title.

PQ2211.C24Z93 2010
320.5′1094409034—dc22                                    2010030931

A catalogue record of the book is available from the British Library.

Design by Newgen Imaging Systems (P) Ltd., Chennai, India.

First edition: February 2011

10 9 8 7 6 5 4 3 2 1
Transferred to Digital Printing in 2011

# Contents

# Acknowledgments

A work so long in the making (I count twelve years) inevitably means that its author has burdened many of his friends, colleagues, and students with discussions of its various themes. I thank them all for their patience, their encouragement, their assistance, their critical acumen, and their collegiality.

Portions of the argument have been presented at the Western Society for French History (1998 and 2007), the Triangle French Studies Seminar (1998 and 2008), the Triangle Intellectual History Seminar (1999 and 2009), the Stanford French Culture Workshop (2002), the Society for French Historical Studies (2002, 2003, and 2005), the seminar at Durham University on "Pluralism and the Idea of the Republic in France, 1789–2006" (2007), and the NCSU Department of History Works-In-Progress Seminar (2010). I'd like to thank the organizers and participants in all of these forums, and especially Susan Ashley, James Banker, Jonathan Beecher, Michael Behrent, Bob Blackman, Melissa Bullard, Aurelian Craiutu, David Gilmartin, Doris Goldstein, John Headley, Malachi Hacohen, Christine Haynes, Gerald Izenberg, Andrew Jainchill, Jeremy Jennings, Mimi Kim, Lloyd Kramer, John Christian Laursen, Keith Luria, Julie Mell, John Merriman, Martin Miller, Linda Orr, Thomas Ort, Don Reid, Joel Revill, Lou Roberts, Jerrold Seigel, Jay Smith, Anoush Terjanian, Ken Vickery, Cheryl Welch, Jim Winders, Mary-Ann Witt, Ron Witt, and Julian Wright.

I have a much deeper debt of gratitude to those who read, corrected, criticized, and sometimes reread major portions of the manuscript in its near-final form. Especially important here are Paul Hanson, Tony LaVopa, Helena Rosenblatt, Bernard Wishy, and the anonymous readers of the press. All of this reminds me, yet again, of how much I rely upon friendships and vibrant intellectual communities. They are what make scholarly work rewarding and, for me personally, possible. Thank you all.

Finally, my wife, companion, and colleague, Kimberly Bowler, took time off from her own scholarly endeavors to provide manuscript feedback, but more importantly has sustained me with her warm support and *joie de vivre*.

I wish to dedicate this book, however, to the scholars of a previous generation who, through their influence and example, have provided the greatest source of inspiration for my own work. I have had the immense good fortune to count them my mentors, supporters, interlocutors, and friends:

Richard Herr
Martin Malia (deceased 2004)
Stanley Mellon (deceased 2008)
Bernard Wishy

Early versions of the argument presented in this book, and selected paragraphs, appeared in the following publications:

"Benjamin Constant, the French Revolution, and the Origins of French Romantic Liberalism," *French Historical Studies*, 23.4. Copyright 2000, Society for French Historical Studies. Reprinted by permission of the publisher, Duke University Press.

"Character, *Sensibilité*, Sociability, and Politics in Benjamin Constant's *Adolphe*," *Historical Reflections/Réflexions Historiques*, 28.3 (2002): 361–83. Reprinted by permission.

"Benjamin Constant, the French Revolution, and the Problem of Modern Character," *History of European Ideas*, 30 (2004): 5–21. Reprinted by permission of the publisher, Elsevier.

Cover image: Benjamin Constant (1767–1830). Crayon, avec rehauts de craie blanche, attribué à Firmin Massot. Collection du château de Coppet. Photo: Alrège S.A., Lausanne/Impression: Filanosa, Nyon.

# Introduction

Liberalism has never been a unified movement following a common path. Liberals have defended different ideals, have based these ideals on incompatible epistemological foundations, and have defended these ideals with widely divergent arguments. Indeed, the central motifs of liberalism have often been in conflict. Does liberalism mean the unfettered market or the constitutional protection of rights? Is the core value individual liberty, or is this subordinate to providing equal opportunity for individual development? Is the center of liberalism legal, or is it rather political or economic?

Traditional scholarship on French liberalism frequently proceeded by defining the core issues and telling a story of their emergence and development. Kingsley Martin's book *French Liberal Thought in the Eighteenth Century* in 1929 hoped to provide "a better appreciation of the historical genesis" of his own liberal creed, one centered in beliefs in science, organization, and the popularization of knowledge. These, he claimed, were the "secular religion" at the center of "French liberal thought in the eighteenth century."[1] André Jardin also looked to the eighteenth century for the roots of French political liberalism, though he insisted on a broader relation among ideas, society, and institutions. He focused on "the common program of liberals"—respect for "rights" (freedoms of conscience, speech, press, and property); a judicial order that mediates the disputes between the individual and the state; government institutions that represent the will of the nation; and social pluralism. He traced how this "liberal program" developed in France from the 1680s to 1875.[2] More recently, Pierre Manent traced the origins of liberal thought to the endeavor of thinkers like Machiavelli and Hobbes to free political thought from the cosmology and pervasive influence of the Catholic Church.[3]

This book takes a different approach. Rather than apply the term liberal retrospectively to doctrines and historical eras before the word existed, it focuses on what self-proclaimed "liberal" thinkers

1

meant when they first used the term "liberal" to refer to a political stance. While the sources of liberalism may usefully be traced back into earlier eras of French (or, more broadly, European) history ["proto-liberalisms" can easily be identified in previous writings about religious tolerance, civil rights, and/or various forms of constitutionalism], the first calls for a "liberal" politics were offered in the 1790s. It was articulated by political moderates like Benjamin Constant and Germaine de Staël in the midst of the torrent unleashed by the French Revolution.[4]

In addition to this contrast with histories based on *a priori* definitions of liberalism, this book also differs from the thesis of Pierre Rosanvallon, who has recently identified early-nineteenth century French liberalism with rationality. Rosanvallon claims that French thinkers during the Restoration shared "a central preoccupation: to allow politics to leave behind the domain of the passions and to enter the Age of Reason, and to substitute for the vagaries of the will the regularities of a scientific order. From all quarters sounded a critique of the dogma of popular sovereignty, accusing it of having created the intellectual framework making the Terror possible."[5] While these claims are true of François Guizot and other Doctrinaire liberals of the Restoration (the focus of Rosanvallon's detailed scholarship[6]), it is not true of those who first used the term "liberal." Germaine de Staël and Benjamin Constant, as we shall see, advanced a liberal position during the late-1790s that defended popular sovereignty, will, and "sensibility." Rosanvallon, in short, reaches too quickly for a generalization that simplifies, and, therefore, distorts, the history of French liberalism. He ignores the emergence of the liberalism, which is the focus of this book: a generous liberalism that I call (somewhat anachronistically) "pluralist."[7]

Other recent scholars have examined a broader historical canvas that better captures the variety of early French liberalism. George Armstrong Kelley, in his posthumously published last book, focused on a cast of early-nineteenth century political writers who were intent on "putting liberty first."[8] Lucien Jaume, in his magisterial study *L'Individu effacé*, examined three currents of French liberalism in the nineteenth century: liberal Catholicism; state liberalism (referred to also as *"libéralisme notabiliaire"* and "elitist liberalism"); and, finally, a constitutional liberalism that put the individual before the state (referred to also as *"libéralisme du sujet"*).[9] Andrew Jainchill, in a recent study that follows Jaume's lead, distinguishes the emergence of "liberal authoritarianism" from "liberal republicanism" between 1794 and 1804.[10] Annelien de Dijn, in another recent book, suggests that nineteenth-century French liberalism split into three branches— *laissez-faire*, neo-republican, and aristocratic—and argues that the "aristocratic liberalism" deriving from Montesquieu was the main trunk.[11] The present book overlaps with these studies, but focuses on the strand of French liberalism that Jaume calls "constitutional liberalism," Jainchill labels "liberal republicanism," and Dijn "neo-republican liberalism." It draws freely from this earlier scholarship, but will argue that this liberalism emerged earlier than these scholars claim and, also, has distinguishing characteristics that have not been fully elucidated.

There are five contentions in this book. The first is that French liberalism first emerged in the 1790s in reaction to the Terror. Although it was refined during the Empire, when it was critical of Napoleon's despotism, the main themes of the "liberal" stance were developed in the late-1790s during the Directory and Consulate.[12] The second argument is that the institutional dimensions that concerned early French liberals were principally civil and political. Economic issues were not ignored (and came later to receive more attention), but initially these were less central than civil liberties and constitutional arrangements. The third contention is that social *moeurs* were considered as important as civil protections and political institutions. Although the protection of "rights" and the creation of representative institutions were important, these were viewed to be intertwined inextricably with the motives and sentiments of the wider political culture. The fourth thesis is that these first French liberals were "pluralists," viewing unified political sovereignty as inherently dangerous, and politics as ongoing negotiation among divergent groups and interests. The fifth point, finally, is that early French liberalism was socially and economically conservative. While economic issues were not central, early French liberalism was a movement of well-to-do elites who had, at best, little concern for the plight of the underclass. They did not take seriously enough the issue of class and the related problem of access to political power and economic achievement.

This book argues that a (perhaps *the*) central issue for early French liberals was the relationships among institutions, culture, and the "character" of citizens. They viewed these connections as complex and historically contingent. The sensitivity liberals showed concerning this complexity derived from their assessment of the political dilemmas created by the revolutionary torrent that engulfed France. In short, the cultural and institutional contours of early French liberalism were shaped as responses to the revolutionary conflict, and in particular to the difficulties of establishing, in the midst of revolutionary turmoil, a stable constitutional order that did not subvert the principles of the Revolution. This emerged starkly as the Terror was brought to a close.

What struck the early liberals was that there were no easy answers to the divisive theoretical issues thus revealed. Balancing issues of principle with a concern for institutional stability and/or economic reform was inherently complicated. Balancing all of these with an assessment of the social passions of the moment introduced added complexity. There was, for example, a tension between popular sovereignty and individual rights, and liberals recognized that the full realization of one of these would potentially undermine the other. There was another tension between adherence to strict legality and recognition that pragmatic action that violated legality was sometimes needed to protect the legal system. And, there was a tension between the protection of individual conscience and the perceived need for a shared moral belief to bind society together. What distinguished liberals from their opponents on the Left and Right was their conviction that however committed they were to principles (of, say, popular sovereignty and civil liberties), different contexts demanded different responses. It was impossible, in any concrete situation, to determine abstractly whether one principle or the other should prevail. Liberals recognized, in short, that these values *were* inevitably in tension, and, therefore, required constant vigilance.

I use the adjective "pluralist" to characterize this early liberalism because it captures something that is often overlooked in historical accounts of French liberalism, especially those that favor giving priority to the rationalizing and centralizing tendencies of the "state" liberalism of the Doctrinaires. Early French liberals recognized that incommensurable interests must be allowed to exist, and that the purpose of politics was to provide a structured location for dialogue and compromise. Closely associated with this was a conviction that the authority of the state must be carefully checked. They resisted the powerful *étatiste* and *dirigiste* tradition in France that insisted that the state should be strong, provide economic guidance, and control and harness private interests. Drawing from religious, political, and administrative traditions that opposed the excessive powers of kings and emperors, they insisted that the political and administrative functions of the state be restrained, and that some functions be returned to occupational and regional organizations. The institutional framework that they believed could contain excessive state authority and provide the arena for the peaceful resolution of differences was a constitutional system that separated and balanced sovereignty, provided for an independent judicial order, and guaranteed civil liberties and religious practice.[13]

## Benjamin Constant and Germaine de Staël

The book focuses on the life and writings of Benjamin Constant, and to a lesser extent Germaine de Staël, who were the first to use the term "liberal" to refer to their political stance. Germaine de Staël (1766–1817) is best known for her publications *Lettres sur les ouvrages et le caractère de J.-J. Rousseau* (1788), *De l'influence des passions sur le bonheur des individus et des nations* (1796), *De la littérature considérée dans ses rapports avec les institutions sociales* (1800), *De l'Allemagne* (1810/1813), and for her novels *Zulma* (1794), *Delphine* (1802), and *Corinne* (1807). In addition, she was an important and influential figure in the liberal opposition to Napoleon. Though Swiss, she was born in Paris, the daughter of Jacques Necker, an extremely wealthy Genevan banker who was a finance minister for Louis XVI (1777–81, 1788–90) and the author of important works on economic and political affairs. Her mother, Suzanne Curchod, presided over a fashionable salon in Paris in the final years of the Old Regime, and Germaine as a child thus met and delighted many of the luminaries of the late French Enlightenment. By all accounts, she was articulate, precociously brilliant, and self-centered to the point of grandiosity. Because of her father's connections with the French government, Germaine observed many of the dramatic early events of the Revolution, which she discussed with liberal commentary in her posthumously published *Considérations sur la Révolution française* (1818).[14] When in Paris, she presided over one of the most important salons of the era; when exiled from Paris (during much of the Directory, Consulate, and Empire), her château of Coppet in the *pays de Vaud* was a center of liberal culture and politics, with European cultural luminaries like August Wilhelm Schlegel and Jean-Charles-Léonard Sismondi regular *habitués*. She died in Paris in 1817, shortly after the defeat(s) of Napoleon and the restoration(s) to power of the Bourbon monarchy.

Benjamin Constant (1767–1830) was also Swiss, but from a more modest, though well-to-do, background. His mother, Henriette-Pauline de Chandieu died sixteen days after Benjamin's birth, and his father, Louis-Arnold-Juste de Constant de Rebecque, a professional soldier in the service of Holland, handed over the care and education of the young boy to family members and a string of itinerant tutors. Constant also briefly attended universities in Erlangen and Edinburgh, making him truly cosmopolitan. Until recently, he was best known for his short novel *Adolphe* (1816), which became part of the standard canon of French literature in the late-nineteenth century. In the past few decades, Constant has received renewed attention by historians and political theorists because of his political activities and writings. During the Directory, as we see below, he was an articulate and visible political moderate, hoping to help French politics find a way between a return to the Old Regime and, at the other extreme, a return to the authoritarianism of the Terror. Briefly a member of the *Tribunat* during the Consulate (he was purged in 1802), he went on to publish, during the last years of the Empire, highly regarded works critical of Napoleon: *De l'esprit de conquête et de l'usurpation* (1814), which attacked Napoleon's despotic rule; and *Principe de politique applicables à tous les gouvernements représentatifs et particuilèrement à la Constitution actuelle de la France* (1815), which outlined, as the title suggests, his political ideas. He returned to Paris during the Hundred Days, helping to draft, in a controversial move, *l'Acte additional aux Constitutions de l'Empire*. During the Restoration, he published numerous works, including the book he considered his most important, *De la religion considérée dans sa source, ses formes et ses développements* (5 volumes, 1824–31). During the 1820s, however, he was most famous for his leadership of the liberal opposition to the Bourbons in the Chamber of Deputies. He died shortly after the July Revolution of 1830.

## The Revolutionary Context

The immediate context for the emergence of French liberalism was the Thermidorian period of the French Revolution following the Terror, though how political issues were then conceived reached back to the Enlightenment and earlier. The Enlightenment, the political-fiscal crisis of the "pre-revolution," and the torrent of the Revolution itself—to point to the most obvious factors—deeply influenced the political thought of the early liberals. Equally important, however, was the effect these dramatic years had on the important role that emotions played in politics. The Revolution generated intense feelings, running from euphoria to red-hot anger, and these not infrequently spilled over into acts of both generosity and revenge. Experience and observing these passions strongly affected how liberals thought about political change and stability.

The intellectual inheritance of the Enlightenment framed political discussions of the revolutionary period, though the Enlightenment itself did not "cause" the Revolution. The revolutionary outbreak in 1789 was precipitated by the fiscal crisis of the monarchy, which was part of a more widespread economic slowdown that dated from at least the mid-1770s. The last, moreover, came on the heels of a crisis of political legitimacy that extended back to the 1750s. But, if the Enlightenment cannot be said to have "caused" the Revolution, the cultural envelope of the Enlightenment is all-important for understanding the nature of the calls for change. Without the Enlightenment's many versions of a rational society, people would not have believed it possible to create "new" legal and constitutional structures; without the Enlightenment, the break of 1789 could not have been perceived as a fresh beginning in which "men make their own history"; without it, revolutionaries could not have viewed the new regime as a culmination of natural and secular historical processes. *Les lumières* did not provide revolutionary actors with a unified political agenda or set of principles (there were many conflicting programs), but they did generate a common discourse—founded on sensationalist epistemology, a belief in English "liberties," and a faith in natural law and in progress—that deeply informed discussions of public affairs.

Equally important was the *passionate* politics generated by the crisis of the "pre-revolution" and by the traumatic events that followed. Beginning with the calling of the Estates-General in 1788, demands for reform—for votes by head rather than by order, for a "doubling" of the Third Estate, and so on—were brought forward with optimistic enthusiasm. Proponents of reform experienced fraternal compassion and utopian hopes for a more egalitarian order. In contrast, the same reformers expressed disgust for the privileges enjoyed by the upper two Estates, hatred of the haughtiness of nobles, and a desire for revenge for the humiliations they had endured. The abbé Sieyès' justly famous *Qu'est-ce que le tiers état?* (1788), to give just one example, is a text saturated with hope, but also with anger and desire for revenge.[15]

The radicalization of the Revolution heightened the stakes and sharpened the tenor of political debate. Attacks on the nobility, of course, continued. Heredity nobility, already eviscerated by the "elimination of feudalism" in August 1789, was officially abolished by the National Assembly on 19 June 1790. But this did not end anti-noble sentiment, which continued to spread as noble resistance to reform increased and the number of *émigrés* grew. Anti-noble sentiments frequently became fused with the idea that the Revolution was in danger. This was especially true after the attempted flight of the King in June 1791, widely believed to have been orchestrated by nobles.[16] The "flight to Varennes" precipitated a series of revolutionary laws that transformed any opposition to the Revolution into acts of conspiracy and treason against France. The law of 9 July 1791 declared that anyone who did not return to France within a month was a traitor. A law passed 9 November 1791 declared that all French citizens participating in assemblies outside of France were "suspects of conspiracy against France." On 9 February 1792, a new law sequestered the revenues of *émigrés*; on 27 July 1792, a law legalized the confiscation of their goods. Many of the laws that subsequently underpinned the Terror were passed by the Constituent and Legislative Assemblies before war and counter-revolution descended. They were emblematic of the anxiety that royalist anti-revolutionary conspiracies were forming, as indeed some were.

With the outbreak of the war against Austria in April 1792, manifestations of opposition were delegitimized and the distinction between opposition and treason was progressively effaced. It was the move from legal-theoretical exclusion of opponents and skeptics to their active persecution in the spring of 1793 that marked the opening of the Terror. The year of the Terror (1793–94) was marked by what Isser Woloch has termed, in a felicitous phrase, "the simultaneous expansion and contraction of democratic space." The expansion included the active participation of citizens in clubs and in the referendum on the new constitution in July 1793; the contraction, unfortunately, was more severe: "the suspension of elections and the increasing centralization of authority; the arrest of tens of thousands of citizens for allegedly subversive acts or opinions; the destructive

spasm of 'de-christianization,' with its church closings and persecution of constitutional priests; the power plays of urban paramili-
tary forces against peasants with grain surpluses."[17] The creation of
the Revolutionary Tribunal on 9 March 1793 was an early sign of
the contraction; the law of suspects of 17 September 1793, a more
troubling marker. The latter signals the beginning of what Patrice
Gueniffey has termed the "anarchic terror," when the Committee
of Public Safety could do almost anything it wished as long as it
defended its actions as celebrations of the "cult of the people."[18]

The law of 22 Prairial an II (10 June 1794) marked the ultimate
mutation of the Terror: persecutions and executions were no longer
justified because of the precarious situation in which the Revolution
found itself, but rather by appeal to the "Republic of Virtue" that
Robespierre wished to create. The Terror would thus not end when
the extraordinary situations of foreign war and domestic counter-
revolution were contained; it would need to continue until the moral
utopia of the Republic of Virtue was realized. In short, the Terror,
transformed into an "ideocracy," and directed toward a goal that was
impossible to achieve, would likely be permanent.

The Terror relied on the insecurity caused by the war and the
counter-revolution. It grew because of the climate of fear associated
with the rumors, denunciations, and chastisements that separated
the population into those believed to belong to the political community and those who were perceived to be not just the adversaries
of the community, but its enemies. It was a response to the desper-
ate circumstances in which the Republic found itself (as Left-wing
defenders of the Terror have claimed), but it also required decisions
by human beings who, of course, could have responded differently.
That they made the decisions they did speaks to their political-
ideological beliefs (as Right-wing critics of the Terror have claimed),
but also to the powerfully emotional context in which their decisions were made. What the Left-wing defenders of the Terror do
not appreciate sufficiently is that the ideology and passions of the
moment cannot be ignored—the circumstances did not *require* the
Terror. What Right-wing critics of the Terror do not appreciate sufficiently is that the revolutionary context cannot be ignored—revolutionary ideology, in itself, did not *inevitably* lead to the Terror.
As we see below, in the different context of 1794–95, revolutionary
principles would be adjusted to support a different political regime—
that of Thermidor and the Directory. Liberalism emerged only when

there was a significant ideological shift—a shift, moreover, that was in response to the markedly different conditions that defined the period following the Terror. What merits emphasis is the volatile and emotional nature of the revolutionary experience.[19] Early attacks and enthusiasms were only the first wave of a generation-long period of turmoil that never lost its passionate nature, though different emotions waxed and waned as the revolution spun through its different phases. And, needless to say, it was not just revolutionaries who experienced these phases. Members of the privileged orders felt the sting of attacks on their privileges and property, experiencing in turn cycles of emotion, ranging from anxiety and exhilaration to disgust and fear. The famous counter-revolutionary Joseph de Maistre, for example, referred to the Revolution as a "whirlwind which carries like a pile of straw everything that human force can oppose to it." He was appalled at the destructive nature of this "monster of power," this "frightful phenomenon," which he interpreted as a providentially ordained tempest that "bent all obstacles" before its terrifying force.[20] Not surprisingly, actors and thinkers, acutely cognizant of the emotional roller coaster that they were experiencing personally and observing in others, included analyses of sentiments and passions in their wider discussions of politics. This drew, as well, from Enlightenment thinkers (Montesquieu and Rousseau are only the most famous to insist on the *principes* that animated societies), but registering an urgency of an era marked by its political and social volatility.

### Thermidor and the Directory

The immediate context for the emergence of French liberalism was the period following the Terror. The symbols of the end of the Terror are familiar: the ninth of Thermidor, Year II [27 July 1794], the day Robespierre, Couthon, Lebas, and Saint-Just were arrested. During the following two days [28–29 July] Robespierre and eighty-seven Robespierrists were executed. Ending the Terror was not, however, as contained as this suggests. Ending the Terror, as Bronislaw Baczko has insisted, was a process, a transition.[21]

Transitions within revolutionary regimes are difficult in any situation. This particular transition was complicated by the fact that it was orchestrated by members of the Convention who had themselves supported the Terror during the previous year. Such continuity of political decision makers obviously complicated defining Thermidor as a definitive break with a vilified past. Some adopted the strategy of characterizing the Terror as Robespierre's work and, therefore, Robespierre's fault. The logic of this argument, obviously, was that with the monstrous tyrant dead, the Republic could be saved. Others focused on the circumstances of the Terror, especially the patriotic revolutionary struggle against the Republic's domestic and foreign enemies, and concluded that with the passing of the revolutionary crisis, the Terror with its lamentable excesses (represented by Robespierre) could now, thankfully, be brought to an end. Others, more ominously, suggested that the system of Terror had many sources, and that even with the execution of Robespierre and his immediate entourage, there were other agents who must be brought to justice. All of these raised, more or less directly, the issue of responsibility for the excesses of the Terror, which was clearly a sensitive issue given the high degree of continuity of personnel across the Thermidorian divide.

Another aspect of the transition was legal, marked by an endeavor to separate the "terrorist" laws and institutions, which needed to be condemned and removed, from the laws and institutions that were "revolutionary" but not "terrorist," and which needed to be retained. This was not an easy task, especially because the political principles that informed "terrorist" and "post-terrorist" were not clearly different in the minds of the legislators in the months following 9 Thermidor (more on this below). There were, nonetheless, a number of legal fronts on which the Convention moved. It repealed, on 1 August, the law of 22 Prairial that had marked the mutation into the "Great Terror." The Convention also purged and reorganized the revolutionary committees in the departments, eliminating the individuals who were most compromised by their actions during the Terror. It prosecuted individuals who were associated with the excesses of the Terror, most famously Jean-Baptiste Carrier and the members of the revolutionary committee of Nantes. It freed many of the citizens who had been detained and jailed during the Terror. It annulled the decree that had authorized the Committees to arrest representatives of the people without a hearing of the Assembly. It eliminated the prosecution and suppression of journals, effectively allowing again a free press and free expression. Finally, on 31 May 1795, it eliminated the Revolutionary Tribunal.[22]

Overlapping with this legal transition were institutional reforms. There was, first of all, an insistence that power be taken from the

Committees and returned to the body of the Convention, viewed as the clearest acceptable place where popular sovereignty was expressed. And, there was a simultaneous removal of legitimacy of the Jacobin Club.[23] This *de facto* shift of power would later support an *ideological* shift in perceptions of where political sovereignty was to reside. But the immediate effect was a dramatic shift in the relationship of institutions. During the Terror, Robespierre's stature and ability enabled him to assume political and moral authority in two institutions simultaneously, and at the same time to embody two principles of legitimacy. On the one hand, as one of the most effective leaders of the Jacobins, he was seen to represent the *direct* voice of the people. At the same time, as the most powerful member of the Committee of Public Safety, he was the most obvious embodiment of the *representative* voice of the people. Such representative power was officially situated in the institution of the Convention, but during the Terror it was expressed by the Legislative Committees, to which the Convention had given authority. In a significant shift, after 9 Thermidor neither the Jacobins nor the Legislative Committees were viewed as seats of political sovereignty. *Direct* sovereignty was delegitimized (except, perhaps, as expressed by "public opinion" via the press). *Representative* sovereignty was still legitimate, but it was now carefully restricted to the decisions of the Convention itself. The Jacobins resisted this change, attempting to derail the dismantling of the institutions created by the Terror and the authority they exerted through them, but they were unsuccessful. Instead, they found themselves on the defensive; indeed, they symbolized for many the excesses of the Terror.

In the context of these legal and institutional shifts, the debate about political sovereignty was renewed. There was still widespread agreement that sovereignty belonged to the people, but there was a discussion concerning who, exactly, constituted the "sovereign people" and, even more contentious, how *le peuple* [in French the noun is singular] was to exercise its authority. Was it to be exercised uniquely through its representative institutions or, alternately, were there legitimate forms of direct democracy, and if so what were they?[24] Such debates about the *exercise* of sovereignty, and about the appropriate laws and institutions for the exercise of sovereignty, continued during the late-1790s, as we see in the following chapters. Deeply informed by the memory of the Terror, these debates initially showed considerable continuity with earlier revolutionary concepts.

For example, the language utilized against Robespierre by the members of the Convention who brought the Terror to an end was very much like the language used by Robespierre and his associates before 9 Thermidor. Robespierre was charged with conspiracy and acting as a traitor to the *patrie*. These were identical to the charges brought against those executed *during* the Terror. Moreover, as during the Terror, it was assumed that all right-thinking people would recognize obvious political truths; the difference was that after 9 Thermidor this included the "obvious" characterization of Robespierre's actions as conspiratorial and tyrannical.[25] That is, the language of politics and the expected behavior of the sovereign people, which were characteristic of the Terror—what we might term the "social imagination" that informed the politics of the Terror—was largely unchanged. Part of the struggle of the Thermidorians, as they formed the post-Terror order in France, was to shed the tainted language, behavior, and assumptions that had informed the Terror and continued to resonate in the body politic. On this level, the transition was about creating a new political language to legitimate the new political order and to distinguish it from what was being left behind.

How to conceptualize the sovereign nation was one of the major issues. One strong view was that the sovereign nation must be viewed as a unified entity. This had deep roots in French thought, going back, at least, to defenses of the monarchy's indivisible and inalienable authority as expressed, for example, in the works of Jean Bodin. It survived in antimonarchical form in the thought of Rousseau, who wished to transfer the power of the unified sovereign king to the unified sovereign people. What is striking is that revolutionaries across the political spectrum, for all their differences on the issue of the *location* of sovereign authority, shared this conception of a unified political voice.[26]

One indication of the strength of this "unanimist outlook"[27] was the emergence during the Revolution of fluid categories to identify those who were not part of the "nation." After the outbreak of the war in 1792, and especially during the Terror, it became common, for example, to speak not just of the foreign "barbarians" threatening *la patrie*, but also of the "barbarian" elements within France. The "barbarians" were by definition not part of the nation; they were external and internal outsiders. Here, 9 Thermidor was not a watershed. Expressions of the unified will of the nation voiced by individuals and groups *before* and *during* the Terror were paralleled by similar expressions voiced by individuals and groups *after* Thermidor. The only change was that the category of "barbarian" now included those who were labeled as Terrorists. It was a vicious cycle: charges and countercharges identifying those who were "barbarians" and/ or who had betrayed the Revolution reinforced the pervasive sense of suspicion that was such a fundamental part of the revolutionary mentality. And, it led to cycles of revenge.

It is telling in this regard that even at the end of Year II (September 1794), when it was clear that members of the Convention were more and more divided on significant political and theoretical issues (when "unity" obviously did not exist) that the pervasive general ideology of sovereign national unity remained in force.[28] It would take months before political writers began to argue that divisions of opinion were acceptable. It would take months before political opponents could be seen, not as "barbarians," but simply as political opponents. As we shall see, Constant and Staël were important voices making this argument, which is one aspect of what I have termed their political "pluralism."

## Organization of the Book

The emergence and development of a liberal politics that emerged in the late-1790s was a response to the aforementioned complex legal, institutional, and cultural conditions of post-Terror revolutionary France. Study of these responses will focus on Benjamin Constant and (to a lesser extent) on Germaine de Staël, and on their role in the first articulation of French liberalism. The methodological orientation of the book is a densely contextualized intellectual biography, but one that privileges political issues over those of family and personal relations. Both central figures left extensive manuscripts and correspondence (and, in Constant's case, journals) that permit a detailed view of the evolution of their political views. These also provide insight into their responses to events and into their agreements and disagreements with contemporaries. These sources also provide a window into the controversial personal lives of Constant and Staël. We touch on this dimension when it helps our analysis of the evolution of their respective political thought, though it is not the primary focus of this book.[29]

Constant and Staël's liberalism was born, as we see in the first two chapters, of their firsthand experience of the magnificence and barbarisms associated with the French Revolution and, especially, of what they perceived to be the unfortunate consequences of ideological excess combined with governmental power. Their response was what, in another context, Judith Shklar has termed "the liberalism of fear," a moderate stance that insisted that the overriding aim of politics should be securing the conditions necessary for the protection of rights and the exercise of personal freedom.[30] Constant and Staël believed that this would require the creation of a constitutional order with public laws and representative institutions and, also, the encouragement of a tolerant political culture. They were hopeful that, together, these would contain the passions of fanaticism and revenge that the revolutionary torrent had spawned, permit more positive human sentiments to flourish, and be enabling of human progress.

Constant's political thought was refined during the Directory and Consulate, the focus of chapter 3. He developed a sophisticated constitutional theory that provided for the separation of powers and for what we would call "checks and balances." He also argued, while a member of the *Tribunat* (1800–1802), for the importance of civil freedoms, regular judicial procedures, and an articulate legislative opposition. All of these were related to what I refer to as his "political pluralism." Constant insisted that national sovereignty be viewed in its sociopolitical embodiment as plural, residing in different bodies with opposing interests. He argued for the rights of individuals and groups, hoping to provide them with the security necessary for the free articulation of their divergent interests—interests that he never assumed would be definitively resolved. His constitutional proposal was designed to provide a close connection between representatives and constituents, to encourage negotiation and compromise at all levels of government, and to prevent the monopolization of power by any individual, party, or region.

The final two chapters focus on Constant's reactions to the Napoleonic Empire and his political maneuverings during the First Restoration and Hundred Days. They analyze his famous novel *Adolphe* and his well-known political writings of 1814–15. More broadly, they situate his thought in the wider intellectual traditions of *sensibilité* and "pluralism," traditions that framed his distinctive contribution to liberal political thought.

# 1
# Benjamin Constant: The Early Years (1767–95)

Benjamin Constant's reputation as a liberal political thinker has been growing during the past thirty years. He is now widely recognized as one of the most articulate and influential exponents of classic liberalism of the nineteenth century, sharing this honor with Alexis de Tocqueville, John Stuart Mill, Lord Acton, and Thomas Hill Green, among others. During the last decade of his life—that is, during the 1820s—Constant's reputation among his contemporaries paralleled this current assessment. He was a prominent liberal opponent of the restored Bourbon monarchy that, in his estimation, was not respecting the constitutional reforms introduced by the Charter of 1814 and was sliding back into the absolutist ways of the monarchy of the Old Regime. Though governments could rightly intervene, according to Constant, especially in the struggle against religious persecution, and though they had an obligation to protect the nation against foreign invasion and internal subversion, the inclination of the administrations appointed by Louis XVIII and especially Charles X was to monopolize power and progressively to expand prerogatives of the executive branch to new areas.

Constant's preference during the Restoration was for a constitutional regime on what he took to be the English model, with free press, a well-informed public opinion, an impartial judiciary, and religious toleration. Such a liberal politics had the best chance of protecting liberty and allowing individuality to flourish. This was the institutional underpinning of his famous testament of 1829.

> For forty years I have defended the same principle, liberty in everything, in religion, in philosophy, in industry, and in politics: and by liberty I mean the triumph of individuality, as much over the authority which would wish to govern by despotism, as over the masses which claim the right to subject the minority to the majority.[1]

This liberalism developed from a more radical position Constant had adopted as a young man, and suggests a constant political position that the evidence does not support.

Traditional scholarship on Constant's political thought has emphasized the importance of the years of the late-Empire and the Restoration, when he was the famous liberal journalist and prominent Deputy. New manuscripts, which became available in 1961 and 1974, forced reassessments of this chronology.[2] First came works in the 1960s by Paul Bastid and Olivier Pozzo di Borgo.[3] These were followed in 1980 by Marcel Gauchet's new edition of Constant's political writings[4] and Etienne Hofmann's path-breaking study of the genesis of Constant's political thought, in which he argues that the "center of gravity" of Constant's political *oeuvre* must be pushed back from the Restoration toward the Consulate and Empire.[5]

In contrast, I argue that the critical formative period of the development of Constant distinctive political position was the Revolution, especially the years of the Directory and Consulate (1795–1802). This reevaluation of the chronology and content of Constant's liberalism would not have been possible were it not for the ongoing publication of the new scholarly edition of Constant's writings and correspondence.[6]

Before turning to these early political writings, we must introduce the young Constant and discuss the controversial issue of his character.

## Constant's Family and Education: The Making of a Cosmopolitan

Benjamin Constant's early life was marked by personal loss and frequent changes of residence. His father, Louis-Arnold-Juste de Constant (1726–1812), was a military officer in the service of the Dutch. His mother Henriette-Pauline de Chandieu (1742–67) was of a Swiss Protestant family that traced its roots back to the Dauphiné region of France. She gave birth to Benjamin when she was twenty-five; tragically, she died sixteen days later. Benjamin's father was crushed— indeed suffered a seizure—but he survived and returned to his professional post as the commander of a Swiss regiment in Holland. As a consequence, young Benjamin was sent to his relatives for care: first to his maternal grandmother, Françoise de Chandieu; then to his paternal grandmother, "la Générale" Rose-Susanne de Constant.[7]

At the age of four, Constant was moved to the care of Jeanne-Suzanne-Marie Magnin (1752–1820), a young woman of twenty years, who cared for the young child between 1772 and 1774. There is a curious history associated with this. At the age of nine, Marianne Magnin (as she was called) had been kidnapped from her peasant family by Constant's father Juste, who took charge of raising and educating her. After the death of Benjamin's mother, Marianne Magnin became Juste's mistress and, subsequently (probably in 1792), his wife. Marianne Magnin gave birth to a son Charles in 1784 and a daughter Louise in 1792. Until 1798, Constant was unaware of the second marriage, and, therefore, of the fact that he had half-siblings.[8] When Constant's father died in 1812, there was a dispute over inheritance, but cordial relations between Constant and Marianne Magnin remained.[9]

There were two other important members of Constant's family who deserve mention: his maternal aunt, Anne-Marie-Pauline-Andrienne comtesse de Nassau (1744–1814), with whom Constant corresponded until her death; and his cousin Rosalie-Marguerite de Constant (1758–1834). Rosalie never married, and she remained the "dear cousin" who Constant could rely upon for kindness and support.[10] A testimony to the importance of both of these women is the voluminous correspondence Constant carried on with each of them.[11]

Constant's education, following the years with Marianne Magnin, was conducted by a series of six tutors between 1772 and 1782 and brief stays at educational institutions. The tutors generally were kept for only short periods, because his father found them inadequate, or because the Constants were moving to a new location. For a short period in 1782 (four-and-a-half months) Benjamin was enrolled at the University of Erlangen. More significant was his matriculation in the University of Edinburgh from July 1783 to April 1785. While the specific content of his reading in Edinburgh is a mystery, we do know that he heard the lectures by Alexander Fraser Tytler on Egyptian *moeurs*, Greek mythology, and the origins of Western Civilization. He also established friendships with James Macintosh and John Wilde, and participated in a discussion at the so-called Speculative Society on the topic "The Influence of Pagan Mythology on Manners and Character."[12] Again, precise information is lacking, but Constant was probably at this time introduced to the theories of the Scottish economists.[13] Upon leaving Scotland, Constant made his first extended trip to Paris, staying with the family of Jean-Baptiste Suard from May to August 1785. Constant's early travels and education made him truly cosmopolitan. He was seventeen years old when he left Paris in 1785 to join his father in Brussels, and by then he had spent time—in addition to years in his native Switzerland—in London, Oxford, The Hague, Brussels, Erlangen, Edinburgh, and Paris. He had read widely in several languages, and spoke French, English, and some German.

## Early Infatuations and the Issue of Constant's "Character"

Dennis Wood, in the best recent biography of Constant, draws from the clinical work of John Bowlby and Ian Suttie to suggest that Constant's character was largely the result of the traumas he experienced as a boy and adolescent: the early death of his mother; a father who was aloof, vain, secretive, stern, and emotionally unavailable for his son; a string of caretakers—relatives and itinerant and sometimes abusive tutors—who left him feeling unloved and abandoned. These factors, Wood persuasively argues, provide a key to understanding Constant's fear of rejection, his depressions, and his difficulty sustaining a long-term intimate relationship. Constant, on this reading, remained psychologically locked in an inner world that revolved around the tyranny of his early deprivations.[14] While it is easy to exaggerate the long-term significance of any individual's upbringing, there seems little doubt that the emotional and relational cycles of Constant's life, and many of his inner demons, resulted from his early history.[15]

The most telling evidence of Constant's impulsiveness and insecurities comes from what we know of the series of flirtations and engrossing infatuations he had as an adolescent and young man. These affairs were less important than his later connections with Isabelle de Charrière, Germaine de Staël, and Charlotte von Hardenberg, but they are illustrative of lifelong characteristics of Constant's psychological makeup. About these amorous affairs, we have an unusually large quantity of information, most of it from Constant's own hand.

The first occurred in 1781, when Constant was thirteen years old. He recounts in his memoir, the so-called *Le Cahier rouge* written in 1811, that at this time he "fell in love, for the first time" with the daughter of a friend of his father while living in the garrison town of Geertruidenberg.[16] He composed love letters, but never sent them. The next year, while at school in Erlangen, he made what he describes as some clumsy attempts to attract a mistress, which led to his disgrace at court and departure from the school. More important was his infatuation, while in Brussels in 1785 (he is now eighteen years old), with Marie-Charlotte Johannot, the wife of a Genevan cloth merchant who later became a member of the National Convention. Marie-Charlotte swept the young Benjamin off his feet, but she was prudent enough to insist on some distance, apparently recognizing that the relationship could not succeed. Constant remained deeply attached to her, as indicated by a poignant passage in his memoir.

> In this coterie [of Genevans in Brussels] there was a woman of about twenty-six or twenty-eight, with a very seductive figure and very distinguished intelligence. I felt drawn towards her, without clearly admitting it to myself, when, by a few words that at first surprised me more than they delighted me, she allowed me to discover that she loved me....
>
> Madame Johannot—such was her name—is set apart in my memory from all the other women I have known: my liaison with her was very brief, and reduced to a few things. But she never made me pay for the sweetness she gave me with any mixture of agitation or grief; and at forty-four years old I remain grateful for the happiness that I enjoyed with her when I was eighteen.
>
> The poor woman came to a very sad end....I was myself in Paris [when she poisoned herself years later]...and I have never been able to pronounce her name without being moved to the bottom of my soul.[17]

Mme. Johannot was clearly more important than the next focus of Constant's attention, Harriet Trevor (1751–1829), the wife of the English Ambassador in Turin. Constant met Harriet in 1786 at her house on the outskirts of Lausanne, where Constant went to gamble. There is an extremely entertaining description of his obsessive infatuation in *Le Cahier rouge*, one that would find a strong echo in his later novel *Adolphe*. Constant remembers how he convinced himself that he was deeply in love with her.

> I took it into my head to win her favor. I wrote her an eloquent letter in which I declared my love for her. I handed her this letter

one evening, and returned the following day for her answer. Agitation due to uncertainty about the result of my overture had put me in a kind of fever, which resembled the passion that at first I had only wanted to feign. Madame Trevor replied to me in writing, as the circumstances demanded. She spoke of her obligations, and offered me a tender friendship .... I thought that the adroit thing to do was to show the most violent despair because she offered me only friendship in return for my love. The poor woman, who probably had had affairs previously with men of more experience, did not know how to act in this scene, which was the more embarrassing for her because I made no movement that might have put her in a position to terminate it in a manner agreeable to us both.

I kept myself ten steps away from her, and whenever she approached to calm or console me I retreated, repeating that, since she had for me only friendship, there was nothing left for me but to die. For four hours she could get nothing else out of me, and I departed leaving her, I suspect, very annoyed with a suitor who would dispute about a synonym.[18]

Constant recounts that he continued his pursuit for months, "becoming each day more and more in love, because each day I ran up against difficulties that I myself had created." She responded with patience and became more attentive, but she resisted becoming his lover. *Le Cahier rouge* provides a hilarious description of his foolish actions. Jealous of a rival Englishman, he challenged him to a duel, even though, as it turned out, "he took not the least interest in Mrs. Trevor."

With the hopes of appeasing me, he declared to me that, far from wishing to take the wind out of my sails, he did not even find Mrs. Trevor attractive. I then wanted to fight him because he did not sufficiently respect the woman I loved. Our pistols were already loaded when my Englishman, who had no desire for so ridiculous a duel, got out of it very cleverly. He demanded seconds, and informed me that he would tell them why I had picked a quarrel with him. When I told him that it was his duty to keep such a matter secret, he laughed at me, and I had to renounce my brilliant enterprise....[19]

The episode ended when Benjamin's father took him to Paris, where he quickly lost interest in Mrs. Trevor. He was unmoved, he tells us, when he saw her three months later.

In Paris, there was a somewhat similar episode, with another desperately unsuccessful resolution, though the object of Constant's affection was not a mature woman in her mid-thirties, but a young woman of seventeen years. In May 1787, Constant met Jeanne-Jacqueline-Henriette "Jenny" Pourrat, the daughter of Augustine-Magedeleine Pourrat (ca. 1740–1818) who ran a Parisian salon that Constant frequented. Constant, with his father's encouragement, declared his love and proposed marriage. When he was rebuffed and confronted by the lover of Madame Pourrat (Jenny's mother), he impulsively staged an attempted suicide. "I repeated without ceasing that I wanted to kill myself, and by saying it I almost came to believe it, although at bottom I had not the least desire to do so."[20] He made a clumsy attempt to do so, but failed, and was barred (not surprisingly) from the house.

These affairs suggest that Constant was craving, even more than the average libidinous adolescent, intimacy and connection, and that he would act in extreme ways to pursue the immediate object of his attention. His correspondence provides insight into other elements of his character. These early letters reveal a stance of worldly skepticism, articulated as pessimism, moral indifference, and a critical regard toward everything. Kurt Kloocke has suggested that Constant was a member of the proto-romantic generation that first experienced the modern malaise of *ennui*, apathy, extravagance, and immoral egoism.[21] Whether this explains sufficiently Constant's despair is open to question. But the characterization is apt. Constant often lamented that he could find no firm foundations for belief; and his early correspondence is peppered with pessimism and the general hopelessness of life. "I feel more than ever the nothingness of all things," he wrote in June 1790; "how everything seems so promising and nothing lasts; how our capacities are above our achievements; how this disproportion ought to make us unhappy."[22] In January 1791, he was, if possible, even more despairing:

I am not, shall never be, am not able to be happy. I have had, as everyone, my periods of illusion; this has passed....Unable to believe in the mysterious and unproven promises of a religion which is in many respects absurd, and seeing no reason for hope in a philosophy which consists merely of words, I see here on earth only a great deal of unavoidable suffering..., very few pleasures..., and at the end of it all, sooner or later, nothingness.[23]

This bleak outlook would abate in later years, but Constant always accepted the absurdity of human existence, sensed the vanity of everything, and experienced a morbid fascination with death. His correspondence indicates that Constant was plagued by "melancholy," the term used in this period for what we now would probably term "depression." Jean Starobinski has suggested that Germain de Staël, who was also preoccupied with melancholy and with thoughts of suicide, struggled with such dark thoughts because she believed in the possibility of total sentimental intimacy. She believed in the possibility of a state of intimacy that was animated by the spontaneous, natural, nonreflexive form of communication that Rousseau had termed "transparency." The inevitable frustration resulting from such an unreasonable expectation, according to Starobinski, was one source of Staël's melancholy.[24] A similar dynamic is appropriate for understanding Constant. Constant had longings for transparency, and he experienced similar frustrations.

Constant's melancholy, combined with the revelations of his early infatuations, in part account for the adverse characterization of Constant often encountered in the secondary literature. Constant's character is frequently judged wanting, even by scholars who are attracted to his political views and who might discount the importance of his early upbringing. During the nineteenth century, in spite of being a political celebrity at the time of his death in 1830, he was often depicted as slightly disreputable. Critics noted his gambling (he often was unable to pay his gambling debts), his political past (especially his cooperation with Napoleon during the Hundred Days), his being of Swiss birth (and, therefore, in the eyes of some, non-French), and his being a Protestant divorcée married, during his final years, to a German divorcée. This negative reputation was reinforced by critical characterizations of Constant disseminated by descendants of Germaine de Staël (especially the Broglie family) after she and Constant had separated. There was also the unflattering portrait penned by Sainte-Beuve.[25]

With the publication of an abridged version of Constant's *Journaux intimes* in 1887, more information became available, especially concerning Constant's perception of his emotional and intellectual needs, and the important place of women for his needs.[26] He reveals himself to be sexually promiscuous, continually in pursuit of women for physical satisfaction, emotional warmth, social respectability, and apparent security, and at the same time chronically anxious and indecisive. He analyzes his need to find a relationship that would promise him some comfort and security, but recognizes that, once in a relationship, he was longing for freedom from its constraints. The journals indicate that Constant was saddened by the fragility of relationships and the difficulty of maintaining them, and that he was obsessed by the tragedy of their failure and the emotional suffering that this entailed. Much of this analysis drawing from personal experience informed *Adolphe*—"that most quietly disruptive of all French novels," in the words of Alison Fairlie[27]—which is about the failure of a relationship and, more broadly, about the tragic incompatibility of certain character traits with the structure and mores of modern society.

Twentieth-century analyses have generally been less censorious of Constant, though, arguably, this has as much to do with changing mores as anything else. Again, the issue of "character" has been central. Modern scholars comment on Constant's chronic anxiety and tendency to melancholia, his fear of ending relationships but his inability to sustain them. Gustave Rudler and Georges Poulet have noted his obsession with death; his uncertainty about the future; his detachment; his tendency to indecision; his oscillation between one quality and its opposite.[28] Etienne Hofmann points to doubt and moderation as the essence of Constant's personality, and notes how these cohere uneasily with his desire for stability and certitude, and with his fear of *ennui*.[29] Kurt Kloocke, as mentioned above, also stresses the importance of Constant's *ennui*, linking this predisposition to the destructive nihilism in the romantic sensibility.[30] Other scholars, more critically, see Constant as a spoiled, self-centered misfit. C.P. Courtney, for example, describes the young Constant in 1787 as "a mixture of shyness and aggressiveness, intellectually brilliant but emotionally immature." He was "a conceited monster and cosmopolitan *déraciné* constantly at odds with his milieu and family (including his well-meaning father)."[31] Harold Nicolson, noting Constant's "variations between egoism and remorse," judges that Constant "remained temperamentally adolescent to the day of his death."[32]

What is impressive, of course, is how successful and productive Constant was in spite of his unfortunate early life history, and in spite of the emotional turmoil left in its wake.[33] Many secondary accounts, I believe, have overstated the degree to which Constant was a weak plaything of stronger forces. Constant's *Journaux intimes* reveal, as Tzvetan Todorov has pointed out, his emotional weaknesses with "a pitiless lucidity,"[34] but they also disclose an unusually acute and critical mind. As one would expect from the private daily ruminations of someone as perceptive as Constant, the *journaux* read a bit like life as it might feel to live it—a mixture of confusion, surges of power, cross-currents of frustration, moments of triumph, recognition that things are not as they previously had appeared, and belated realization that in fact things *are* as they previously had appeared. Constant's strength—which accounts for the continuing appeal of the diaries—was his persistent endeavor to see his emotional weaknesses as clearly as possible, to analyze the ways in which various character traits played a role in his personal life and in the affairs of the wider world, and to chart a course that would promote improvement. Constant's vulnerabilities were expressive of his sensitivity to the many and varied forces and settings in constant flux around him. Even his novel *Adolphe* is evidence of this. While it obviously "reflected" his experiences (something arguably true of all novels), it was a self-conscious literary construction of immense introspective power. It grew out of Constant's coruscating attempt at self-understanding.

### Isabelle de Charrière, Minna von Cramm, and the Court of Brunswick

Two women played important roles in Constant's early life, though in dramatically contrasting ways. The first was Isabelle de Charrière, who Constant first encountered in early March 1787 at the Paris salon of the Jean-Baptiste Suard. Isabelle de Charrière was an accomplished writer whose literary output included novels, short stories, plays, essays, verses, and operatic libretti. Born into a prominent family in Holland in 1740, she had known many famous suitors, including James Boswell, and had carried on, as a young woman, a voluminous correspondence with Constant's uncle, Constant d'Hermenches.[35] Following her marriage to Charles-Emmanuel de Charrière in 1771, she moved to Le Pontet in Colombier, Switzerland. She was forty-six when she met the nineteen-year-old Constant in Paris. Constant was enthralled by this older woman, twenty-seven years his senior. He recounted in *Le Cahier rouge* that "it was during this epoch that I made the acquaintance of the first woman of superior intelligence whom I have known, one who had the most intelligence of all those whom I have encountered.... We passed some days and nights together. She was very severe in her judgments on all those she saw. I was by nature given to mockery. We suited each other perfectly"[36]

Whether or not the relationship was physical remains a mystery.[37] What is not in doubt, however, is how deeply attracted they were to each other and how profoundly important this connection remained for Constant for the next eighteen years, until Isabelle de Charrière's death in 1805. No doubt, there were some obvious similarities of background and experience that brought them together: both were non-French by birth, but both wrote in French; both were highly intelligent and extraordinarily gifted; both felt (or *had* felt in the case of Isabelle) hemmed in by the constraints of their families. But the real commonality seems to have been their caustically skeptical view of the world, a deeply felt unhappiness with their environments, and a strong desire for friendship, connection, and intimacy. It is difficult to resist a clinical interpretation: at forty-six, Isabelle must have seen Benjamin as the intelligent articulate son she never had; Benjamin must have seen Isabelle as the warm nurturing mother he never had.

Gustave Rudler attributes to Isabelle de Charrière a large responsibility for the growth of Constant's skepticism, pessimism, and rebelliousness.[38] Most modern scholars see her influence as benign or positive. Cecil Courtney suggests that Isabelle understood Constant's rebelliousness, but that she did not encourage his unbridled individualism and anarchic behavior.[39] Dennis Wood sees the influence of Isabelle de Charrière as "a tonic" for Constant, a practical sustaining influence during Constant's years as a young man. She was the first woman in Constant's adult life to give him the stable affection that permitted him to accept without guilt his own perceptions: for example, his sense that all things and people are complex and mutable. She played a critical role in Constant's development as a novelist. And, she helped him find the strength to rebel against his obtuse and difficult father.[40]

What is beyond dispute is the important role Isabelle de Charrière played in Constant's life during the next few years. He referred to Colombier, where Isabelle lived in her house at Le Pontet, as the

haven to which he could always return.[41] In person or via correspondence, Isabelle was his principal confidant and advisor during
this early period of his life. The correspondence between the two is
justly famous for its literary quality, for its intellectual power, and for
its political perspicuity.[42]

There would be considerable strain in the relationship, as we shall
see, due to contrasting views of the French Revolution, but the relationship survived. It was only when Constant fell under the spell
of Germaine de Staël that Isabelle de Charrière distanced herself.
Perhaps Isabelle was jealous of losing Constant to a younger rival
or found the rival an affront to and rejection of the way of life and
set of values (so different from those of Germaine de Staël) that she
assumed she and Constant shared.[43] The distancing probably had
elements of both. Shortly after their break, she referred to Constant's
political positions as driven by his "desire to make a sensation."[44]
Constant, nonetheless, remained immensely attached, and he was
devastated when she died in 1805.

The other important woman in Constant's life before meeting
Germaine de Staël was Wilhemine Luise Johanne (Minna) von
Cramm. Following one of his youthful acts of rebellion against his
father—a "ridiculous escape" to London and Scotland in 1787[45]—
Constant was sent to take up a position at the court of Duke Karl
Wilhelm Ferdinand in Braunschweig (Brunswick). Benjamin arrived
in Brunswick in 1788, and in December was given the position of a
*conseiller de Légation* at the court.[46] All the available evidence indicates that he developed an intense and enduring dislike for this
small northern German town. He was alternately amused at what
he viewed to be the pettiness of court rituals, bored with the bland-
ness of the available diversions in provincial society, and depressed
because of his frequent ill health and his isolation. He clearly missed
the companionship of his close friend Isabelle de Charrière, with
whom he carried on an intimate epistolary dialogue.[47] Periodically,
he traveled. He took an extended trip to Holland to help his father in
a protracted legal struggle (September 1789–May 1790), and he went
to Switzerland to conduct his father's business (September–December
1791) and to visit friends (July 1793 and December 1793–April 1794).
Excepting these excursions, he lived in Brunswick from March 2,
1788, the date of his arrival, until his departure on August 8, 1794.

At the Brunswick court, Constant met Minna von Cramm, a lady-
in-waiting to the Duchess. Constant became enamored and, equally
significant, saw her as a wife who would bring him financial stability

and independence from his father. They were married on May 8, 1789. Constant took Minna to Switzerland in July of the same year to present her to his family. He seems to have been very happy in the first two years of the marriage.

At the end of 1791, however, his correspondence with Isabelle de Charrière indicates there were difficulties in the marriage and that his dissatisfactions were growing. There were a number of enmeshed events that together led to his frustration and depression. There was, first of all, his boredom with life in Brunswick; he found the people at court tedious and stupid. Second, there was his sympathy for the French Revolution, which contributed to his isolation (more about this below). Third, there was the deterioration of his relationship with his wife Minna. In December 1791, they struggled over the fact that Minna, while Constant was away, had taken as a lover a young Russian prince named Gallitzine.[48] This led to a scandal at court. And, finally, there were the legal and financial difficulties of his father, a consequence of a mutiny of the officers in Juste de Constant's battalion that had taken place on October 29, 1787. Juste lost the initial legal battle before the military court in Amsterdam on August 25, 1788, and Constant spent an impressive amount of time during the next few years working to save his father's reputation and wealth. Juste was eventually rehabilitated in 1796, but, as C.P. Courtney has noted, it was "a hollow victory, for by this time Juste was completely ruined."[49] It also was about this time, probably in January 1793, that Constant first met Charlotte von Hardenberg (about whom more information is given in chapter 4). The result for Benjamin, of all of these converging events, was despondency and melancholy, expressed forcefully in his letters to Isabelle de Charrière.

Constant and Minna agreed to a separation on March 20, 1793. Though the divorce did not become final until November 18, 1795, Constant left Brunswick for several month beginning in June 1793, and definitively departed from the court in August 1794. Years later, he reflected acerbically on his marriage:

> I…married her without much thought, she had no money, she was ugly and was two years older than me. I was entwined in the affair like a fool. If I had been 30 instead of 21, I would have been able to control her because she was as weak and timid as she was violent and capricious in her emotions. But I was governed by her and those around her from the very beginning. How I suffered![50]

## Early Political Ruminations

From his earliest writings, Benjamin Constant was interested in social and political issues. We know, for example, that in 1784, while studying in Edinburgh, Constant discussed with the so-called Speculative Society the topic "The Influence of Pagan Mythology on Manners and Character."[51] Two years later, at the age of nineteen, he wrote an essay about Roman military discipline, which is partly about character and mores. It makes the point that in the move from Republic to Empire, the Romans had to intensify the severity of punishments within the military because of the corruption of *moeurs*, the growth of indiscipline, and the progressive enfeeblement of the state.[52] We also are able to consult a translation Constant made in 1787 of a chapter of John Gillies' *The History of Ancient Greece*, entitled "Essai sur les moeurs des tems héröiques de la Grèce."[53] This chapter is about Greek courage, charity, and hospitality, as well as Greek religion and the strong sentiments for conjugal union and love of children. It recommends the civic spirit of the ancients and faults modern commercial society for fostering imaginary wants and dissipated pleasures (this, of course, in stark contrast to the valorization of commercial society found in *doux commerce* theories of the late-eighteenth century). Greek society, the chapter claims, was a model of moderation. It had avoided, on the one hand, the barbarism of savage societies, and, on the other, the perverted pleasures and artificial refinements of modern polished societies. The Greeks "had emerged from the melancholy gloom of the first situation, and had not yet declined into the foul vapors of the second."[54] The Greeks had "domestic virtues," an "excessive sensibility, which interested them so deeply in the affairs of their community, their tribe, their family, and their friends, and which even connected them by the feelings of gratitude with the inanimate objects of nature." They had, we are told in the final paragraph of the translation, "a certain elevation of character which will be forever remembered and admired."[55]

Constant's continuing liaison with Isabelle de Charrière in 1787 brought new refinements to his considerations of human nature and their relation to sociopolitical issues. While visiting Charrière in Neuchâtel in the last months of this year, Constant helped edit a collection of her essays, "Observations et conjectures politiques," first published in 1788.[56] Many of the essays are concerned with Dutch politics, but others focused on the importance of morals, sentiments, and *moeurs*, and their relationship to politics. The third essay, for example, is about "generosity," "this magnificence of soul and conduct which forces hearts to enthusiasm."[57] In Charrière's opinion, it is a virtue that, unfortunately, most political leaders do not possess.

Charrière criticized the arbitrary nature of French absolutism, especially the "cruel and revolting" practice of issuing *lettres de cachet*.[58] She wanted, like many reform-minded thinkers of the age, a monarchy oriented toward reform and sensitive to the opinions of the enlightened public. She encouraged sovereign rulers like the French king to be open, accessible, and willing to engage in conversations, suggesting that this would lead to well-considered reforms and create a nation "more flourishing and more respected than ever."[59]

Charrière's political preference was for a monarchy animated by what she called "Republican robustness." "We do not want to live without a chief, but we do not want to live under a despot, that is to say, without energy, without glory.... We want a relationship in which the Nation is unable to undertake anything without the King, and in which the King is unable to consummate anything without the Nation: to Republican vigor we want to join promptness, dignity, and the unity of a Monarchy."[60] She was critical of the Parlements and the disrespectful tone with which they addressed the King in 1787.[61] Constant echoed with a criticism of the "imperious air, full of haughtiness and a cold and precious insolence, which characterize Parlementary representations."[62]

Constant was equally critical of the mores of court society, especially of the court of Brunswick. "You do not have an adequate idea of the boredom of this town," he wrote Isabelle de Charrière in March 1788. "There is something so dismal in its appearance, something so cold in its inhabitants, something so listless in their intercourse together, something so unsociable in their attitude."[63] He lamented the lack of the two sentiments—gratitude [*reconnaissance*] and friendship [*amitié*]—which he referred to as the most gentle of the human heart.[64]

Overall, what strikes the reader of Constant's early works and correspondence is the highly developed critical abilities of this sensitive young man. He took pleasure attacking the pretensions of nobles and the stuffiness and arbitrariness of court life, especially the relatively subdued court life of Brunswick. Everywhere he traveled, he searched for the warm embrace of friends—*reconnaissance et amitié*—and the stimulating intellectual interchange of a cultivated elite.

## Reactions to the French Revolution

Constant's long residence in Brunswick meant that he viewed revolutionary events in France only vicariously. He would argue later in life that this provided him with a more neutral position than that available to those who participated directly in the Revolution.

> In order to be judged, the Revolution demands minds that are not so burdened by embarrassing memories, those who...are not blinded by rancor or forced to apologize....Only those whose later appearance on the scene of the world has preserved them from the necessity [of partisanship] can take on the role of judge with the moral independence required for that function.[65]

We unfortunately have very little evidence of Constant's political reactions to the early stages of the Revolution. Mostly, he was shocked at what he would come to call the "devastating torrent" of the Revolution, at how it overwhelmed peoples' lives in unforeseen and often tragic ways.[66] He took an early stance in support of the radical political transformation brought by the Revolution, which alienated him from many in the court in Brunswick. He was clearly happy to see the overturn of the Old Regime in France, with its feudal remnants, its hostility to liberty, and its intolerance of Protestantism. And, he was obviously in favor of the civil and political reforms instituted during what we now refer to as the "liberal" phase of the Revolution (1789–92). The first evidence of Constant's reaction to the Revolution was in a 1790 letter to Isabelle de Charrière, where he poked fun at the misguided rulers of Europe who dismissed the Revolution as "the result of the innate sinfulness of mankind."[67] A few months later, he referred to reading Edmund Burke's *Reflections on the Revolution in France*:

> I occupy myself at present with reading and refuting the book of Burke against the French levelers. There are as many absurdities as lines in this famous book....He defends the nobility, the exclusion of parties, and the establishment of a dominant religion, and others things of this nature.[68]

During these early years of the Revolution, as these references indicate, Constant focused more on the inequalities of the Old Regime than on the positive elements of the new revolutionary order. Unlike many of his contemporaries, he did not place exaggerated hopes in the new regime, largely because of his chronic cynicism. In the same letter in which he referred to Burke, for example, he categorized the human race, in general, as "born stupid and led by rogues," though he also made clear his political preferences. "I prefer the kind of double-dealing and frenzied passions that topple fortresses and get rid of titles and other stupidities of this kind [and] that put on an equal footing all forms of religious day-dreaming" to the double-dealing that would preserve the "freaks" of the Old Regime. "The human race is born stupid and led by rogues, that is the rule: but if I must chose between rogues, I give my vote to Mirabeau and Barnave rather than to Sartine and Breteuil."[69]

Constant referred to himself as a "democrat" during these years,[70] suggesting to Isabelle de Charrière that "common sense is clearly against any other system."[71] The use of "democrat" at this time was in contrast to "aristocrat": it did not imply that Constant favored full political equality. As he put it to his uncle in August 1790, "I do not know if universal equality is a chimera, but I do know that aristocratic inequality is the most horrible of realities."[72]

Constant remained a strong supporter of the Revolution into 1794. This did not prevent him from voicing some criticisms. He became disenchanted, for example, with the squabbling among political factions that emerged in the summer of 1792. In July 1792, he wrote that some of the revolutionary leaders were "demagogues who betray the people. This infamous excess...inspires me with such distaste that I can no longer hear the words humanity, liberty, country, without having the desire to vomit."[73] He was also disgusted by the massacres in Paris in 1793 and by the actions in Paris of le peuple, singing and dancing near the guillotine when the Girondins were excluded from the government.[74] "So many talented individuals," he lamented in November 1793, "massacred by the most cowardly and beastly of men."[75] But in spite of his growing reservations, Constant refused to give up on the Revolution; his dislike of some revolutionary leaders and his distaste for some revolutionary episodes did not erode his belief in democracy. He complained, in fact, that public criticism of aspects of the Revolution would undermine the positive accomplishments that had already been achieved.

Pressed by friends like Isabelle de Charrière who were more critical of the Revolution after August 1792, Constant even defended Robespierre, preferring to defer criticism until he saw what turn events would take. Exerting pressure in the opposite direction, and clearly an important influence on Constant during these years, was Jakob Mauvillon (1743–94), a radical figure of the German *Aufklärung* who Constant befriended in Brunswick at this time. Mauvillon had translated into German the ten volumes of the abbé Raynal's *Histoire des deux Indes* (a vehemently anticolonial work) and Turgot's *Réflexions sur la formation et la distribution des richesses* (a physiocratic work). When Constant met him, Mauvillon was working with Mirabeau on a work criticizing absolutism and despotism, entitled *De la monarchie prussienne sous Frédéric le Grand* (published in Paris, 1788). Mauvillon's radical enlightenment perspective reinforced Constant's early favorable attitude toward the Revolution; they shared radical views that set them apart from most of polite society in Brunswick. When Mauvillon died in January 1794, Constant was devastated. He wrote to his aunt that Mauvillon had been "a friend of liberty and enlightenment," a man whose "high opinions in morals, politics, religion, accord on all points with mine."[76]

In the months following Mauvillon's death, Constant remained a supporter of the radical revolution. He wrote to Isabelle de Charrière in June 1794 that one was either for or against the Revolution: "To occupy the middle ground is to take up a worthless position; at this juncture it is more worthless than ever. That is my profession of faith."[77] In this same letter, Constant reflected on extending the suffrage and on the problematic relationship between an educated elite and the masses.

> Our doubts, our vacillation, all this mobility which comes, I believe, from the fact that we have more *esprit* than others, all of these are great obstacles to happiness in relationships and to happiness in regards to the consideration in question.…
> What is the consideration? [T]he suffrage of a number of individuals who, each taken separately, do not appear to us to be worth any effort to please. I agree with you about this, but these are the individuals with whom we have to live. It is necessary perhaps to scorn them, but it is necessary to lead them…if one is able, and it is necessary for this to reunite with those who most share our views.…We are in a stormy time, and when the wind is powerful the role of the reed is not agreeable.[78]

Though he clearly has reservations about the intelligence of the masses, given the purposes of the Revolution he supported extending the suffrage.

In such letters, Constant shows himself to be a "democrat" who worried about the excesses of the Revolution, but unwilling to oppose its momentum. In November 1793, he employed the metaphor of a rock rolling down a hill to refer to the demands of *le peuple* during the Revolution, reflecting that "one is able to make it roll, but it is always necessary to run ahead of this rock to avoid being crushed."[79] The momentum of the Revolution sometimes worried Constant—he was shocked by the executions of Desmoulins and Philippeaux in the spring of 1794[80]—but he believed that the attainment of peace would allow any excesses to be moderated.[81] And, on balance, the changes introduced by the Revolution were worth the price. As he put it succinctly in June 1794, "Whoever seeks the goal consents to the means."[82]

With the onset of the Terror in France, Constant's relationship with Charrière was tested by diverging assessments of the Revolution. Isabelle, who always disliked abstract systems and favored moderate reform, became more and more critical of the Revolution following the events of August 1792. By late-1793, she was expressing sympathies for the counter-revolutionary views of Antoine Ferrand (author of *Rétablissement de la monarchie*) and of Mallet Du Pan (author of *Considérations sur la nature de la Révolution de France*). Constant had some criticisms of the Terror, but he remained a supporter of the Revolution. In a letter of 9 September 1794, he told Isabelle that

> You were wrong, if you believed that I doubted the possibility of a Republic without a tyrant like Robespierre, and consequently with liberty. I believed that compression, in that moment of crisis [during the Terror], to be absolutely necessary. I believe it still, but I think that a time will come, a time that is not far off, when this compression will no longer be needed and when the Republic will be only liberty.... I am like a man who, obliged to travel on a very bad road, tired of hearing his fellow travelers complain about the rocks, the mud, the potholes, the chaos, plugs his ears, and fixes his eyes on the tower of the village that is his destination.[83]

Isabelle found this "ends justifies the means" attitude offensive, and she could not resist making fun of his metaphor. "It is very good not to complain of a bad road, but it is equally bad, that is to say it is a shame, for an intelligent person to take for the tower of the village that is one's destination a stick illuminated by the moon."[84]

Constant's stance was modified by the end of 1794. On October 14, 1794, he wrote to Isabelle de Charrière in a more moderate tone.

> The French political scene has mellowed to an astonishing degree.... I see with pleasure the moderates taking a clear ascendancy over the Jacobins.... I can feel myself growing more moderate, and that it would be necessary for you to propose an innocuous little counter-revolution for me to return to the high ground of republican principles.[85]

There were so many possible causes for this ideological transition that the shift is, for all practical purposes, overdetermined. There was the influence of Isabelle de Charrière, who had been critical of Constant's support of the Terror. There was the influence of Germain de Staël, whom Constant met in Switzerland on 18 September 1794, the beginning of their long and tempestuous relationship. There was the moderate turn the Revolution had taken. There was the new possibility of Constant actually playing a role on the stage of French politics. Before proceeding to an analysis of this transition—a transition that represents the formation of Constant's distinctive political identity as a "liberal"—it is necessary to consider Constant's relationship with Germaine de Staël.

### Germaine de Staël

Constant's richest intellectual collaboration, but also the most troubled emotional connection, was with Germaine de Staël (1766–1817).[86] Staël was a supporter of the monarchy during the early years of the revolution, and she had published in 1793 a work, *Réflexions sur le procès de la reine*, that attempted to convince the government not to prosecute the former queen, Marie-Antoinette. Constant severely criticized this work in a letter to Isabelle de Charrière.[87] By the time Constant met Stael, in September 1794, she had concluded that the Republic should be supported, a position that she stated publicly in her *Réflexions sur la paix adressées à M. Pitt et aux Français*.

The relationship between Germaine de Staël and Benjamin Constant is enormously fascinating because of the prominence of the participants, the drama of the historical period on which both made their mark, and the passionate and turbulent nature of the relationship itself. When Staël and Constant met, both had had numerous liaisons and both were married. Germaine had had affairs with Hippolyte de Guibert and the future power broker Charles-Maurice de Talleyrand. In 1786, she had married Eric Magnus de Staël Holstein, the Swedish ambassador to France. It was a marriage of convenience for both parties, and they lived virtually separate lives. When Constant and Staël met, she already had given birth to two children as a result of her passionate relationship with Louis de Narbonne, a liaison that lasted, roughly, from 1788 to 1794; and she was in the throes of an amorous attachment to Adolf von Ribbing. As we have seen, Benjamin also had experienced numerous early romantic episodes and an unsuccessful marriage to Minna von Cramm.

When Staël and Constant met, therefore, they were far from being sentimental neophytes. They were both in their late-twenties and, though both were legally married (Constant's divorce did not become final until November 1795), they were not in any important ways emotionally encumbered, with the exception of Germaine's attachment to Ribbing. From their first meeting, Constant was dazzled with Germaine's mind, wit, and enthusiasm. He was immediately infatuated and soon very much in love. Staël, on the other hand, was not swept off her feet, though she was attracted to Constant's energy, sensibility, and generosity, and found great pleasure in their intellectual exchange. Constant became part of Staël's entourage, but not her lover, in February 1795 when he moved into a room in her house in Mézery. Distraught that they were not lovers, Constant staged some dramatic scenes, including a threatened/attempted suicide in late-March 1795. Staël was touched by his devotion, but found him physically unappealing and experienced at most what Béatrice Jasinksi has called "amused compassion."[88]

Staël and Constant returned to Paris together on May 25, 1795, and became embroiled in post-Thermidorian politics. They became lovers in late-January 1796, signing in mid-April an "engagement" that declared their intention to remain "indissolubly joined together" and "to devote our lives to each other."[89] Because of her political activities and reputation, Staël was frequently forced to live outside of France during the Directory. There was a decree for her expulsion from France dated October 15, 1795, for example, and she left Paris for her father's château Coppet on 20 December. She was in and out of France during the next few years and, as the political leaders permitted, in Paris.[90] Constant was torn between pursuing his ambition to play a role in French politics and being with Germaine. As a consequence, he was often on the move between Paris, his residence outside Paris at Hérivaux, where Germaine often stayed when she was allowed to reside in France, and the Staël château in Switzerland. On June 8, 1797, Germaine, in Paris, gave birth to Albertine de Staël, Constant's only child.

The beginnings of the relationship with Germaine de Staël in 1794 corresponded with Constant's increasing involvement in politics, and these together corresponded with a noticeable shift in Constant's emotional state. His correspondence with Isabelle de Charrière before this time noted the corruption of Europe and the artificiality of social interactions, and these same letters expressed the hope for escape— escape physically to the New World, and escape emotionally to an intimate unconditional "transparent" relationship. As Constant's connection with Staël thickened, and his interest and engagement with revolutionary politics grew, he distanced himself from this stance of cynicism and skepticism.[91] He would still, in future periods of his life, fall into deep despair when personal connections were strained. He would still hope for the intensity of a personal relationship that would provide a temporary safe harbor against the storms of his emotions; he would again feel the pull, the attraction, the hope of a total merging with another. But he now seemed to appreciate that there was another arena for intense activity—politics—that could assuage the pain of *ennui* and partially satisfy his emotional needs. Politics joined personal intimacy as therapy against melancholy and against the despair of facing "nothingness."[92]

The connection between Constant and Staël was buttressed, from the beginning, by similar political and intellectual concerns. They read and corrected each other's works; some, like Staël's unpublished manuscript *Des circonstances actuelles qui peuvent terminer la Révolution et des principes qui doivent fonder la République en France*, were in essence collaborative projects.[93] Their politics were deeply influenced by the constitutional ideas of Germaine's father, Jacques Necker.[94] Both embraced a middling "liberal" politics that recommended the protection of "rights," called for a constitutional and representative system that would ensure the separation and balance of power, and insisted that energetic public involvement was necessary for republican survival. Constant published his first political pamphlets during their time together, and he worked on a large manuscript, *Fragments d'un ouvrage abandonné sur la possibilité d'une constitution républicaine dans un grand pays*, unpublished until 1991, that contained many of the political ideas that would emerge in his later works.[95] These early important works mark the emergence of French liberalism.

# 2
# The Emergence of Liberalism (1795–97)

## Constant and Staël in Paris

Staël and Constant returned to Paris together on 25 May 1795, and quickly became embroiled in post-Thermidorian politics. They both supported the Constitution of 1795 and worried about the restoration of the Bourbons, whose leader Provence (the future Louis XVIII) made it clear in his Declaration of Verona (24 June 1795) that a royalist restoration was synonymous with a return to the Old Regime and revenge against republicans associated with the Revolution. They also opposed the Jacobin Left, whose defenders called for continued ascendancy of the Montagnards and their allies among the *sansculottes*, and who insisted on the application of the (never utilized) Constitution of 1793.

Staël's salon at the Swedish embassy on the rue du Bac became a central meeting place of moderate republicans and constitutional monarchists who hoped to see the post-Terror Republic stabilized. Working to find a middle way, they recognized that this would require both institutional and cultural change. Staël herself, perhaps due to Constant's influence, only recently had come to embrace the Republic. During the early months of the Revolution, witnessing many of the famous events at the side of her father, she had favored a constitutional monarchy.[1] Like her father, Jacques Necker, she had believed that the most stable political solution for France was a sharing of power between the Assembly and the King. They advocated a separation of powers, but not too much separation, fearing that without some union between the branches of government there would be too much intergovernmental struggle. The executive (i.e., the monarch) should have a role in discussing laws; he should have a suspensive, but not an absolute, veto.[2]

39

Shocked by the violence of the October Days, 1789, Staël had worried about the stability of the new regime and sympathized with the plight of the royal family. In July 1792, she even contacted the King and Queen with an elaborate plan (which they rejected) for a second attempted escape from the country. Following the outbreak of the war and the radicalization of the Revolution in late-1792, she continued to be concerned about the personal safety of Louis XVI and Marie-Antoinette. After the establishment of the Republic (in September 1792) and the subsequent trial and execution of the King (in January 1793), she published, in August 1793, *Réflexions sur le procès de la reine*, which attempted to convince the Committee of Public Safety that the interests of the new Republic would be severely damaged if the Queen were condemned. The Queen, she wrote, had always had sentiments "favorable to true liberty" and "had constantly opposed projects hostile to France."[3] Moreover, further suffering and/or the death of the Queen would give the forces fighting against France a new cause and renewed enthusiasm.

Staël was appalled by the violence of the Terror, which she read about from the relative safety of the Necker château in Switzerland, and did all she could to help individuals facing imprisonment and execution. By 1795, however, she had come to believe that many of the political changes of the revolution were irreversible. This meant that the Republic needed to be supported. She articulated this position in her *Réflexions sur la paix adressées à M. Pitt et aux Français*, published in late-1794, and in *Réflexions sur la paix intérieure*, written and printed in 1795 but never offered for sale.

In the former work, Staël appealed to moderates inside and outside of France to avoid the "spirit of party" that animated the extremes on Left and Right, and encouraged all sides to adopt a policy of peace. She was especially critical of *émigrés* who "fall back on prejudices of the fourteenth century," "treat political questions as principles of faith," and "reject as heresies considerations drawn from what is useful, sage, and possible."[4] Reasonable royalists, she argued, would separate themselves from feudalism and unite around the interests of property and peace, which in France at this moment were identified with the moderate Republic. Reasonable French republicans, she cautioned, must substitute peace and justice for the furies and enthusiasms that had been associated with Robespierre and the Terror, and which were easily stirred up in periods of warfare.

In *Réflexions sur la paix intérieure*, Staël was even more determined to separate herself from the Bourbon pretenders to the throne and to rally support for the republican government. In her estimation, all the surviving Bourbons were "enemies of liberty," and moderate aristocrats who imagined that a Bourbon restoration would lead to a constitutional monarchy were badly mistaken. Moderate royalists, if they attempted to install the system established in 1791, would gain the temporary support of the monarchist extremists, she argued, but the real agenda of the latter would be absolutism. And, given the weakness of moderates, the extremists would almost assuredly carry the day. In short, attempts by moderate royalists to restore the monarchy "would lead necessarily to absolute power."[5] Moreover, any attempted restoration would radicalize the republican Left, meaning that if the monarchists failed in their attempted restoration, the Republic would again be controlled by Jacobin extremists, an equally troubling scenario.[6] What was needed, Staël argued, was to close ranks around the current Republic. This would avoid another revolutionary upheaval, and this would help contain the reinvigoration of extreme, unpractical ideas. Staël's reflections were informed by a moderate pragmatism that insisted on the acceptance of the constraints of circumstance.

> It is obvious that there is no absolute system of government that does not need to be modified by circumstances. And what circumstance is more influential than a revolution?...This boiling fermentation produces a new world; one day is able to render impossible the plan of the previous day; and for those who advance always toward the same goal of liberty, the means continuously change.[7]

In a passage that seems prophetic given later historical developments, Staël judged that "France is able to come to a halt as a republic; but to arrive at a mixed monarchy, it is necessary to pass though a period of military government."[8]

In what is arguably Staël's most impressive political writing of this era, *Des circonstances actuelles qui peuvent terminer la Révolution* (written between 1795 and 1798 but unpublished until 1906), she expressed regret that she had continued to support the monarchy after the June 1791 Flight to Varennes, arguing that if the Assembly had had the courage to suppress the monarchy at this time, in 1791, then France would have been spared some of the subsequent traumas, like those of August and September 1792, and perhaps even the subsequent Terror.[9] By the time she returned to Paris in May 1795, in short, she was a firm advocate of a moderate republic.

The late-1790s were also defining years for Constant. Personally, of course, he had finally extricated himself in November 1795 from his unhappy marriage with Minna von Cramm, and, on a positive note, he and Staël became lovers in January 1796. Politically, he had left behind his more radical views of the early-1790s and was developing the more moderate stance for which he was to become famous. Constant fondly remembered these years as the period during which he worked to conceive the appropriate political regime intellectually and, simultaneously, to impose the appropriate regime concretely. It was an exciting confrontation of the world of ideas and the world of action. As he put it in *Cécile*, "In the springtime of 1795, I followed her [Germaine de Staël] to France....I was overwhelmed with ambition. I saw in the world only two desirable things, to be citizen of a republic, and to be at the head of a party."[10]

Following the May 1795 return to Paris, Constant spent most of the next seven years in the region of the French capital, though he traveled often to Switzerland to be with Staël during her periods of exile. He would leave the Paris region for an extended period only after his exclusion from the Napoleonic *Tribunat* in March 1802. Initially, he was tied to the world of the Thermidorians and close to the circle of Staël. In her salon, Constant met important political figures like Paul Barras and Emmanuel-Joseph Sieyès. He also began attending sittings of the Convention. Constant became one of the important spokespersons for moderates who hoped to unify moderate republicans and constitutional monarchists into a centrist party.

Constant had high hopes of playing an active role in French politics. To do this he needed to become a French citizen, reside in France, and own property. Constant petitioned for French citizenship during 1797, taking advantage of a new law that allowed descendants of Huguenot exiles to become citizens.[11] His ancestors were Huguenots, but in fact they had left France before the revocation of the Edict of Nantes; nonetheless Constant was granted citizenship on 21 March 1797. Often, in subsequent years, Constant would be accused of being Swiss, not French, and the problem of his nationality would frequently plague him. The other qualification for public office was property. To secure this, he bought several properties during 1795: the farm of Vaux close to Gisors (sold in 1798); the farm of Coquereaumont close to Rouen (sold in 1797); the farm of Saint-Denis de Moronval close to Dreux (sold in 1796–97). And then in November 1796, after borrowing money from Germaine de Staël's father Jacques Necker, he purchased for 50,000 F Hérivaux, a ruined abbey and estate near the town of Luzarches, in Seine-et-Oise twenty miles north of Paris.[12] Constant translated his new status into political office. On 30 March 1797, he was elected chairman of the municipal administrative body of Luzarches. There was a temporary complication, when Constant's election was declared null and void due to the fact that he had not been a resident of Luzarches for a full year. But, on 5 November 1797, a year after his purchase of Hérivaux, Constant succeeded in having himself reinstated as president of the municipal administration of Luzarches. He carried out the duties of this office during the next few years, including organizing festivals celebrating the Republic.[13] Other, more important political positions eluded his grasp. It looked briefly as though he would be named Secretary of the Ministry for Foreign Affairs in July 1797, following Talleyrand's appointment as Minister for Foreign Affairs, but it fell through. He also hoped to get elected to a seat in the legislature in 1797, 1798, and 1799; he was not successful.

The relevant political context of Constant's actions and writings was the instability of the post-Thermidorian period (July 1794–November 1799) and the precariousness of the Constitution of August 1795, which was adopted just three months after Constant and Staël arrived in Paris. The months following the fall of Robespierre and the Committee of Public Safety in July 1794 were difficult ones, especially for moderates who sought to establish a liberal constitutional regime in France. They did not wish to compromise with the royalists, nor did they wish to compromise with the Left, identified with the excesses of the Terror. The republican regime, attempting to find a path between these extremes, faced difficult conditions and trials. The most pressing conditions were continuing economic crisis, civil war, and war with Austria and England. The economic crisis was a result of the inflation that had begun soon after the outbreak of war in 1792; by mid-1795 this inflation was beyond control, with the *assignat* of 100 francs worth less than twenty *sous* and the expenses of the government at least ten times revenues. Moreover, the harvest of 1795 was poor, and the difficulty of provisioning the cities kept the popular classes at near starvation levels during the winter of 1795–96. This economic mess was aggravated by the expenses of fighting against the rebellions in the West and Rhône Valley, where taxes went unpaid and brigandage was rampant. And, finally, there were the even greater expenses of the campaigns of the French Armies along the Rhine and in Northern Italy. Though France had concluded treaties with many of its adversaries—with Prussia on 5 April 1795, with Holland on 16 May, and with Spain on 22 July—the military campaigns against Austria and Britain continued to put severe financial strains on the government.

Political stability was also tested by a series of uprisings and attempted coups. One of the most dramatic occurred immediately preceding Constant and Staël's return to Paris in late-May 1795. On 20 May (1 Prairial, an III), the last of the great popular uprisings of the Revolution began, with popular crowds from the old revolutionary faubourgs, Saint-Antoine and Saint-Marcel, converging on the Tuileries and, for a brief period, forcing the National Convention to accept reforms, including the release of imprisoned "patriots" and the creation of an Emergency Food Committee. Loyal National Guard detachments arrived to protect the Convention and to arrest several of the compromised Montagnard deputies, but an even larger demonstration occurred the following day, 21 May, when large armed contingents faced each other around the Place du Carrousel. As on the previous day, the insurrection failed, and the result was the beginning of a repression of the Left that some have viewed as the ending of the Revolution. During the next few days, the Faubourgs were forced to surrender their leaders and their cannons; a military commission was established to deal with "rebels"; and forty additional Montagnard deputies were arrested or proscribed from the Convention. The repression effectively eliminated the political role of the Parisian population; and the masses of Paris did not again rise in arms until the revolutionary *journées* of the nineteenth century. This repression in Paris was joined, as well, by even more ruthless actions in other parts of the country, especially in the southeast where scores of so-called terrorists were slaughtered. In the words of M.J. Sydenham, these events "undoubtedly mark the final stage in the destruction of the social-democratic movement in the Revolution."[14]

This crisis was quickly followed by the threat of counter-revolution in the form of the landing of a royalist army, assisted by a British

fleet, on 27 June and 15 July 1795 at Quiberon on the south coast
of Brittany. The royalist troops were trapped and captured on 20–21
July, but it was a potent reminder—hardly needed, given the continuing activity of *chouans* in Britany, counter-revolutionaries in the
Vendée, and royalists in Lyons—that there was a serious threat from
the royalist Right.

Constant was not sympathetic to either of these insurrectionary
groups. In his correspondence, he referred to the participants in the
Prairial uprising as "anarchists and *buveurs de sang*."[15] He also mentioned the latter royalists as "abominable," though initially he incorrectly identified the group of French émigré royalists descending on
Quiberon as English.[16] He identified the enemies of the new regime
as "the extremes, Royalists or Terrorists."[17]

## "Ending the Revolution" and
## the Constitution of 1795

For the next few years, political and social power was in the hands
of men of position and property who were Republicans, a group
among whom Constant felt much at home. Their first major act was
to write a Constitution—the Constitution of 1795. This Constitution
has traditionally been viewed as a selfish act of the "haves" against
the "have-nots"; that is, it is viewed as the moment when the egalitarian aspects of the radical revolution were overturned in favor of
the self-interested actions of a social and economic elite.[18] This view
has been effectively challenged by those who insist that the political
context following the Terror must be given greater attention and,
further, that the focus should be more on the politics and ideology
of the Thermidorians than on their economic interests.[19]

The Constitution was drawn up by a "Commission des Onze" of
the Convention.[20] It was presented to the Convention on 23 June
1795 by Boissy d'Anglas, debated during the summer, and accepted
on 22 August 1795 (5 Fructidor, an III). It was then approved by
plebiscite (941,853 votes in favor versus 41,892 votes against), proclaimed the fundamental law of the Republic on 23 September 1795
(1 Vendémiaire, an IV), and finally put into effect on 26 October
1795. Its implementation marked the end of the Convention and the
beginning of the Directory. The Constitution retained the fundamental features of the Revolution (civil liberty, popular sovereignty,

political authority exercised by elected officials, independent judiciary, rule by law, sanctity of property), but attempted to avoid the evil of dictatorship by one committee, and the more general danger of concentrating political power in a single institution. To guard against this, the Constitution provided the executive branch more power over the administration than had been the case in the Constitution of 1791, but still kept the executive subordinate to the legislature. Also new was a rigorous separation of church and state. The pay of the constitutional "juring" clergy was eliminated; public displays of religious dress or symbols, including the ringing of church bells, were prohibited.[21]

The heart of the new government was the *Corps législatif* in Paris. Elected indirectly by property owners, it was divided into two bodies. The Council of Five Hundred, composed of 500 deputies of at least 30 years of age, was responsible for proposing laws and taxation. The Council of Ancients, composed of 250 deputies of at least 40 years of age, was responsible for accepting or rejecting these proposals. One-third of the Deputies were to be elected each year. This bicameral legislature suggested the influence of England and the United States, but in fact the Council of Ancients was different from either the British House of Lords or the American Senate. A French body like the House of Lords would have reinstituted an aristocratic assembly too reminiscent of Old Regime nobility. A Senate-like body would implicitly have introduced a federalism seen by most in France as too threatening to the unity of the nation. The new Constitution specified that both the Council of Five Hundred and the Council of Ancients were to be elected by department electoral assemblies, with members of the Council of Ancients distinguished only by their more advanced age.[22]

The executive was to be composed of a five-man Directory, chosen by the Council of Ancients from a list of fifty names submitted by the Council of Five Hundred. The Directors were important in that they were the heart of the executive branch: they named and revoked ministers; directed the administration of the country; and were responsible for diplomacy and the direction of military operations. However, they were confined in their actions by elaborate rules. They did not have the right to declare peace and war, for example, which was left to the Councils. Nor did the Directors have control of finances, which were left to a five-member Treasury Commission that was elected in the same way that the Directors were elected.

Moreover, the chairmanship of the Directory was to be rotated; and, one Director would retire each year, in accordance with the outcome of a drawing. Finally, none of the Directors was to go abroad. The Constitution of 1795 has been controversial. Necker and Staël both lamented that there were not more provisions in the Constitution for coordination and checks between the executive and legislative bodies.[23] Some subsequent scholars, following their lead, have criticized the excessive separation of powers prescribed by the Constitution, especially the lack of executive authority to veto legislation and to dissolve the Councils. The Constitution of 1795, in sum, provided for less "balance of power" than the Constitution of 1791, both because the 1795 document gave the Councils exclusive authority over the passage of legislation, and because it confined the legislative role of the Directors to the execution of the laws. Recent scholars, however, have been less critical, noting that the bicameral legislature was an advance over the unicameral predecessors of 1791 and 1793, and that the strengthening of the executive vis-à-vis the administration addressed some problems encountered during the Convention.[24] The implication of this new scholarship is that the serious issues faced by the Directory were as much sociopolitical and cultural as institutional. It was not only the rigorous "separation of powers" that led to the various coups of the late-1790s. In addition, the instability was due to other factors: the difficulties of overcoming a political culture that still expected the national will to be unified; the dilemma of founding a new constitutional order when some of the individuals elected to office desired to subvert the system. Faced with royalists and Jacobins, moderate republicans opted for a defensive centrism.[25]

The Constitution of 1795 provided much of the focus for political discussion during the first months of the new government. The most controversial aspect of the new order, however, was the so-called Two-Thirds Law that was approved at the same time as the Constitution.[26] It specified that two-thirds of the deputies in the new legislative bodies be held by departing members of the Convention until the elections of 1797. This obviously allowed the men who had written the Constitution to remain in political control, even of the executive branch, since the Directors were to be chosen by the legislature. The Commission des Onze defended the Two-Thirds Law with claims that it would restore stability and allow the country to leave behind the revolutionary cycles of radicalization. The specter they raised was the potential renewal of the tyranny of factions: resurgent royalism on the one extreme; resurgent terrorism on the other. Only the experience of those who had ended the Terror, but were devoted to the Revolution, would safely lead the country to a new era of peace and repose.

Constant wrote articles concerning this law that were his first published political interventions. They illustrate the political maneuverings of the era, and the difficulty of finding a middle way between the Left and the Right. In the first three articles, "lettres à un député à la Convention" published in Suard's journal *Nouvelles politiques* (24–26 June 1795), he argued that the Two-Thirds Law was a mistake: "In no imaginable case is it useful to public affairs to decree that a part of the Convention has a right to be seated in the legislature."[27] As Constant recounted thirty years later, the articles created an uproar— in his own words, a *"bruit de diable."*[28] He found himself celebrated by those on the Right, who interpreted the articles as indicating that Constant hoped for a return of the monarchy, and attacked by moderates for "his naive impudence and royalist *effronterie."*[29] In fact, he was appalled by the association with the royalists and wished, above all, to demonstrate his support for the Republic. Therefore, he published an article in *Le Républicain français* (24 July 1795) in which he appealed to returning moderate *émigrés* to renounce the counter-revolution and to support the Republic. Constant warned all those who had some connection with the Revolution that a rejection of this law could lead to a restoration of monarchy, and this in turn would lead to reactionary vengeance.

> You, therefore, who have loved the Revolution, you who, for a day, for an hour, have had hope in the Revolution, would be struck with an equal excommunication [if the counter-revolutionaries take power]. Constituents, legislators, members of the Convention, monarchists, feuillants, ministers, magistrates, administrators, municipal office holders, generals, officers, soldiers, philosophers, journalists, constitutional priests, purchasers of *biens nationaux*, holders of *assignats*, creditors of the Republic, you criminals of acclamation, you guilty of silence, all of you who have not served under Condé, or in the Vendée, open yourselves up to these insane libels, astonishing monuments of the frenzy of vengeance.[30]

The danger of reaction meant that all must accept the Two-Thirds Law and close ranks with the Thermidorians.[31]

It was a tense time for all moderates, and especially for those who had had any connection with *émigrés*. Constant addressed the issue of *émigrés* in the same public letter of 24 July 1795. He argued that it was necessary to make a clear distinction between those who had emigrated because they hated the revolution and those who had left France because they feared for their safety. He identified the first group as those who had fled before the crisis of August–September 1792 (the symbolic date is 2 September, the date of the bloody prison massacres of political detainees). He wished to encourage the latter group to return to France to support the Republic, while he warned the former, even if they had already returned to France, that they were identified as the enemies of the Republic. Constant was here publicly emphasizing his strong support for the Republic and attempting to convince people that he was bitterly opposed to the counter-revolutionary Right.[32]

Staël had more difficulty shedding these associations, because of her earlier support of the monarchy, and because her background and activities connected her closely with returning *émigrés*. In fact, she was viewed by both political extremes, the royalist Right and the Jacobin Left, as a dangerous organizer of political intrigues, and she quickly found herself under a cloud of suspicion. Most troubling, perhaps, was an attack that occurred in the *séance* of the Convention of 18 August 1795. While Staël and her husband were observing the proceedings, she was attacked from the Left by Louis Legendre, who accused her of being a "correspondent of *émigrés*" and one of their "greatest protectors." During this same period, as we have seen, Constant was also suspected by some of royalist sympathies, largely because of his initial opposition to the Two-Thirds Law. They were even briefly worried about their security. In early-September, when the Constitution and the Two-Thirds Law were under consideration, and when there also was potential conflict between the Parisian sections and the Convention, they left Paris for Mathieu de Montmorency's château at Ormesson. Staël also decided at the beginning of October to stop the sale of her *Réflexions sur la paix intérieur*, probably because in it she had pleaded for a policy of allowing *émigrés* to return to France.

These political maneuverings created some tension between Constant and Staël. Constant's revised position moved him close to Jean-Baptiste Louvet and his journal *Le Sentinelle*, which was controlled by the partisans of the government. He even helped, in August

1795, to draft three speeches that Louvet gave on the floor of the Convention.[33] Staël, on the other hand, was closer to the journal of Pierre-Louis Roederer, *Le Journal de Paris*. This journal was supportive of the Republic, but critical of the government: it advocated finding an honorable peace to end the external wars; called for a forging of national reconciliation by allowing nobles to return and participate in politics; and hoped that the "dictatorship" of the Convention would end. Both groups wished to forge an alliance of the political center in support of the Republic, but the group around Roederer was more closely identified with the old nobility and not tied directly to the group in power.[34] During 1795, in another indication of the different political inclinations of Constant and Staël, Constant spent time at the salon of Julie Talma, an ardent republican and atheist, more radical in her views than Staël.[35]

On the eve of the transition to the Directory in October 1795, there was another serious political crisis: the monarchist uprising of 13 Vendémiaire (5 October 1795). Conservatives, fearful that the government was being too lenient on former "terrorists," combined with monarchists in an attempt to overthrow the government by force of arms. They were repelled by cannon-fire—in an exchange that became an important moment in Napoleon's rise to prominence—and the constitutional Republic was saved. This led to the government closing ranks with the Jacobins: it allowed the reopening of the Jacobin Club and pushed through the appointment of some Jacobins to local administrative bodies. It also initiated, with the military occupation of Paris, the intervention of the army as arbiter of political conflicts.

Constant and Staël followed events in Paris closely, even though they were staying at Ormesson. Constant returned to Paris during the Vendémiaire crisis to observe two all-night sittings of the Convention (26–27 September and 3–4 October 1795). Ironically, immediately following the uprising, on 7 October, Constant and a friend, François de Pange, were arrested at the Palais-Royal on suspicion of supporting the monarchists.[36] Constant spent the night of 7–8 October in prison, a turn of events that had a deep impact, not least because it seemed to suggest that many still questioned his republican convictions.[37]

In the weeks surrounding the installation of the new government in late-October, Constant was extremely anxious about the stability of the Republic. He worried about the rearming of the Jacobins following the Vendémaire crisis, was unhappy to see the military reentering domestic politics, and sensed that the country was "almost in the midst of a civil war."[38] On 21 October, he wrote to his aunt:

Nothing has been decided, nothing is able to be, nothing is yet ready to be decided, and in this uncertainty we move ahead with difficulty....Each day some new clouds appear; we barge into some reef, but so far the ship has not broken apart. However, the man most endowed with the faculty of hope, the most enthusiastic optimist, cannot deny that we are in a situation much more critical than that in which we found ourselves one month ago.[39]

He hoped that the Republic would hold on, and believed that each day it avoided being overturned would strengthen its position. "We have some terrible days to survive. Each hour that passes without revolution is a benefit, each quiet day is a day gained."[40] On 29 October, he noted the presence of numerous dangers: the inflation that was causing the value of *assignats* "to go to the devil"; the maneuverings of the Jacobins who wished to "plunge again the country into anarchy." But, he was hopeful that the new constitutional structure, especially "the division of the *corps législatif* into two chambers, [would] prevent decrees of enthusiasm, [and be] a guarantee of stability."[41]

The persecution of Staël (but not Constant) continued during the following months. On 16 October 1795 (ten days after the crushing of the Vendémiaire uprising) a royalist agent named Lamaître was arrested, and in his possession was a letter that suggested some complicity of Staël with royalists. The Committee of Public Safety responded by issuing a formal *ordonnant* for Staël to leave France within ten days. She in fact postponed her exit from the country, but she left Paris quickly and, subsequently, in mid-December arrived at Coppet. Constant followed her. Henri Grange is probably correct to suggest that this was a case of "love over politics."[42] Staël and Constant in fact became lovers while at Coppet in the following month.

Constant's political maneuverings during 1795 are the first solid indication of his political pragmatism. As his first published articles indicate, he would have preferred a straight-forward electoral system, without protection for those already in office. However, he subsequently became convinced that, given the context, such a path would risk a monarchist takeover. This made it necessary to protect the legal system represented by the Constitution, and this explains his shift to support of the Two-Thirds Law. This law, in his mind, would assure that the elected officials of the Republic would not subvert the Constitution, which he viewed as a dike against a return to the Old Regime. This is an early example of one of the important dimensions of Constant's "liberal" stance: the refusal to embrace any principle absolutely. He would always consider the impact on principles of the surrounding context.

He was a proponent of the Republic that the revolution had created, but recognized that it required not only a constitutional structure to prevent new excesses, but also careful nurturing to prevent passions of the moment from tearing it asunder. By December 1795, he was more hopeful concerning its survival. As he put it in a reflective passage to his Aunt,

> I do not doubt that all will come to terms [with the new order], and that this Republic that I have adored since its birth, although in its first years its interior has not been without flaws, and while its cradle was bloodstained, will take root in spite of the passions of its projects, and above all in spite of the lack of enlightenment of the majority of its agents. The Revolution has always existed despite individual men; it will proceed yet, and conduct us to true liberty, and to the repose that is inseparable from it. The important point is to conceive that liberty is a thing in the present, and not the future, that it is a thing for all time, and not of a particular epoch...that it is finally a route and not a goal.[43]

## Constant's Political Writings, 1796–97

The agenda in 1795 for moderates like Constant was to retain and consolidate the "democratic" institutions that had been created during the revolution, and to prevent a return to the Old Regime. This was arguably the objective of the Constitution of 1791 as much as the Constitution of 1795. Both situated popular sovereignty in the representatives of the people in the Assembly; and both were dedicated to the protection of individual liberties. Moreover, both contained articles that made revisions extremely difficult, which was one way of "ending" the revolutionary change (at least in institutions), and indicative of the anxiety that more rapid change would not be salutary. The Constitution of 1795 was different from that of 1791, however, in that it had to digest the lessons of the Terror. Its goal, as a consequence, was to consolidate the gains of the revolution, to avoid a return to the Old Regime, *and* to avoid a return to the Terror, which was seen as equally threatening to the gains of the revolution. The structure of the legislative branch in the 1795 Constitution, and the careful balancing of power between the legislative, executive, and judicial branches, was one of the ways that its creators had adjusted the specifics of the earlier Constitution, attempting thereby to avoid a slide into tyranny.

Constant's writings of the next few years strongly supported the moderate republican position whose goal was to "end the revolution" and protect the constitutional order represented by the Constitution of 1795. He wished to find a *via media* between Old Regime and Terror. He left behind his more extreme views of the early-1790s, and eschewed violence and revolutionary turmoil. His 1795 articles on the Two-Thirds Law were followed by two important extended pamphlets: *De la force du gouvernement actuel de la France et de la nécessité de s'y rallier* (published in April 1796) and *Des réactions politiques* (published in March or April 1797).[44] These, along with his addresses and other briefer public interventions, established Constant's reputation as an articulate defender of political moderation.

In the preface to *De la force du gouvernement actuel*, Constant indicated his new moderate stance:

> I ardently desire to see the Revolution closed [*se terminer la Révolution*], because its continuation can only be fatal for liberty; and this is one of the reasons that I ardently desire the affirmation of the Republic, to which it seems to me all that is noble and grand in human destiny is attached.[45]

Given the historical juncture at which France found itself, Constant was convinced that the Republic needed to be defended. The current legislative assembly, he wrote, "has marched towards liberty, though strongly urged to pursue the path of tyranny; has respected the barriers that itself has raised;...and has remained constitutional and moderate, though encouraged to become revolutionary and all-powerful."[46]

He criticized those who spent their time focusing on the past injuries of the old regime or of the revolutionary period. "The Republic is a goal, the revolution was a route; it is time to turn our view away from this route, in order finally to see where we have arrived."[47] What was needed was an assessment of the present, which entailed bringing the revolution to a close and supporting the Republic. Constant argued that any restoration of the monarchy would weaken France internationally and further destabilize France internally. It would undermine the war effort, would have no impact on the weakness of the French navy *vis-à-vis* the English navy, would not reinvigorate commerce or lead to solutions to the monetary and credit crises. Moreover, it would lead to civil war.[48]

As this indicates, Constant was not an advocate of revolutionary change per se, recognizing that changes of government inevitably involved "convulsions, anarchy, massacres."[49] He characterized the turmoil in France since 1789 as "a devastating torrent."[50] In the preface, he declared that it was not his intention "to write against any type of government," and repeated later in the work that he "did not write against any form of government, but against all species of new revolution."[51] This suggests a support of the French Republic primarily for anti-revolutionary reasons, which was certainly an important element of his moderate stance (and one that would continue to inform his thought in subsequent years). But, in fact, he was also supportive of the Republic because it was a legal representative government, a regime that was in principle more defensible than the hereditary system of the monarchy. He strongly supported the institutional reforms issuing from the Revolution: equality of all before the law; and political power based on popular sovereignty. He insisted that governments should respect free thought and private property, and resist interfering in commerce. And, he was a firm defender of legal regularity against arbitrary action, arguing that historical experience had demonstrated that such regularity prevented the arbitrariness that denatured governments.

I believe that I have proven that I do not fail to recognize the importance of circumstances. But one ought not to forget how in this area abuse is easy. If one is not careful, there will always be circumstances to invoke against principles. Factions advance from circumstance to circumstance, always outside the law, sometimes with pure intentions, sometimes with dreadful ones, always demanding that they are pursuing great measures in the name of the people, liberty, and the nation.

It is up to the government to uproot this habit [of allowing circumstances to trump legality], which perpetuates the revolution. It has the means, and it has the interest to doing so. In everything that public safety demands, there are two manners of proceeding, one legal, one arbitrary. In the long run, it is always by following the first, even when it will be slower, that the government will find itself better off. It alone gives it permanent dignity and force.[52]

Constant supported the French Republic, in short, for reasons of principle *and* because it was the extant system that provided a bulwark against radical change generally, and against anarchy and despotism specifically.

Constant argued that the Republic, as consolidated by the Constitution of 1795, stood for order, peace, liberty, and legal regularity. And, he believed that any attempt to return to the *ancien régime* monarchy would not reestablish a pre-revolutionary order, but would initiate another period of disruptive revolution.

Those who want to reverse the Republic are strangely the dupes of words. They see that a Revolution was a terrible and disastrous thing, and they conclude from this that what they call a counter-revolution will be a happy event. They are not aware that this counter-revolution will itself only be a new revolution.[53]

This indicates that Constant was a moderate. He believed that in the current situation, France would be best served by defending the existing constitutional system. More broadly, he suggested that, with the acceptance of the reforms of the Revolution and the current system of legal regularity, humanity could progress to a higher level with more equality—in his own words, *'que l'espèce humaine s'égalise et s'élève.'*[54]

The French Republic issuing from the Revolution was additionally to be recommended, however, because it accorded with the interests of the vast majority of the French people. "The people pass judgment by its acts. On July 14th, it declared for liberty; on August 10th, for the Republic; on 9th Thermidor and 4th Prairial, against anarchy."[55] Any attempt to return to the Old Regime would lead catastrophically to civil war and anarchy; and if the monarchists prevailed, there would be repression and retribution. As we have seen, Constant was intent upon defending the Republic against its adversaries, even if this meant defending curious legislation like the Two-Thirds Law. His wider objective was to outline an open, tolerant republic that would appeal to the majority of French citizens, and that would eliminate exceptional laws and terrorist decrees—it would exclude "only the degraded partisans of pure despotism [and] the ferocious sectarians of crime."[56]

Constant's first political pamphlet, *De la force du govrnernement actuel*, was greeted warmly by the government's supporters, who saw Constant as an important new political voice. The royalists, on the other hand, disliked it.[57] The most interesting response was from those who supported the Republic and the Constitution, but who were prepared to criticize the government in ways that Constant believed to be dangerous. They reminded their readers that Constant's stance ran the risk of confusing those who criticized the government with those who were enemies of the Republic.[58] In June, 1796, for example, Adrien de Lezay-Marnésia (1769–1814), a journalist close to Roederer, attacked Constant's defense of the government.[59] Lezay-Marnésia made the argument that if a government found itself in an "exceptional situation," then it should not look to the assembly but to "public opinion" as the true expression of the "general will." Constant took a contrary position, arguing in his article that while the people were the ultimate source of sovereignty, it was reasonable to have reservations about the wisdom of public opinion in times of crisis.

> It is necessary, in order to appreciate it [public opinion], to have seen it exhibited in the sections of Paris, at the bar of the Convention, at the heart of the primary assemblies; demanding, and at the same time violating, all the forms; ceaselessly unjust because of its impatience, but also constantly pursuing with sincerity what it believes to be right; never acknowledging its own tyrannical and impetuous inconsistencies, abusing the institutions that it disapproves; and trampling under foot those very laws which it itself had demanded. Arbitrary and mysterious power, it always has a commendable goal, but it always passes it by.[60]

Constant's carefully worded passages showed an extreme sensitivity to the potential conflict between the momentary excitements of popular will and the measured deliberations of the elected represent-atives of the people, both of which derived their ultimate authority from *le peuple*. "It is necessary to support the majority in its assumed invariability. It is necessary to recall to it that which it wanted, to instruct it concerning that which it wants, and to help it find hap-piness and tranquility under the protection of the laws."[61] Constant obviously worried about the mercurial nature of public opinion. "The mind of man [*l'esprit de l'homme*] is changeable," he wrote, therefore "it is necessary that institutions be stable."[62]

More ominous than the disagreements with other moderates, Constant found himself, in June–July 1796, attacked by the jour-nalist Louis-François Bertin de Vaux for being a "discourteous little Swiss" (*ce petit Suisse incivil*) and a Jacobin terrorist.[63] He responded by challenging Bertin to a duel. Fortunately, after arriving on the field of combat in the Bois de Boulogne (on 14 or 15 July), a mutual friend mediated and Bertin promised to publish an apology, which he subsequently did. Bloodshed, therefore, was avoided, and in fact, Bertin and Constant subsequently became good friends.[64]

In general, however, Constant viewed the growing stability of the Republic in 1796 as a very positive development. On 11 June, he wrote to his uncle that "all is tranquil, the fermentation is muffled, and the government is vigilant."[65] On the same day, he happily reported to his aunt that "the resurgent conspiracies of the anarchists [perhaps referring to the repression of the Conspiracy of Equals on 10 May] and the royalists... have run aground."[66] In subsequent months, he noted in his correspondence that there were attempts by the Jacobin Left and Royalist Right to destabilize the Republic, but he remained relatively optimistic.[67]

## *Moeurs:* Between Vengeance and Fatigue/Between Rebelliousness and Resignation

Constant's moderate political stance was closely connected to his relatively pessimistic view of human nature and to his assessment that unstable historical periods were dangerous for what we might term "political culture." Constant did not have an optimistic view of the character of political actors or the populace in general. As we have seen above, in a letter to Isabelle de Charrière in 1790 he cat-egorized the human race as "born stupid" and referred to political leaders as "rogues." "The human race is born stupid and led by rogues, that is the rule: but if I must choose between rogues, I give my vote to Mirabeau and Barnave rather than to Sartine and Breteuil."[68] Constant could believe that some individuals were generous and altruistic, motivated by kindness and concern for their follow citizens. But, too often, individuals were driven by darker emotions and moved in clouds of ignorance and ill-will.

Constant's growing concern about human nature was related to his perception that unstable eras like the Revolution reinforced negative sentiments. This was clearly expressed in his correspondence, but also in *De la force du gouvernement actuel* and his later pamphlet *Des réactions politiques*. He pointed out that when dangerous situations combined with extraordinary effort, violent passions often resulted. And when violent passions were mixed with uneasiness, the result was often "la fureur"—fits of rage.[69] Sensitive to the complex interactions of human nature, social mores, and politics, he looked back with horror at the violence and factionalism of the Revolution, which, he reasoned, had led everyone to put a premium on intemperate criticism of government institutions and current leaders, with little concern for the effect this had on political stability. He was especially critical of men in 1795–97 who, because of their vanity and discontent, devoted all of their energies to attacking people for past transgressions and/or reproaching a government for its inadequacies. These natural impulses and weaknesses were disruptive enough in peaceful times, according to Constant, but during a revolution or during a period when a government was in its infancy (the situation in France in 1795–96), such discontent was socially and politically unsettling. At such times, there was a great danger of "memories and hatred" undermining stable politics. And, there was a tendency for weaker shades of opinion giving way to "rage." Passion too often prevailed over reason; rejection of ideas over the examination of ideas; the settling of accounts over legal judgment. Constant, in a memorable passage, referred to these angry people as capable of defining themselves only in terms of past battles; "marching towards the future with back turned, they contemplated only the past."[70]

This culture of impatience, discontent, and ridicule, he believed, undermined not only a specific government "but the general idea of order." The resentments of the past combined with the vanity of orators to reinforce the "rebellious disposition" of mankind. While the masses in normal times look primarily for repose, the volatile political culture of the Revolution had increased impatience for change, as well as the suspicion of those in government. The government, in turn, responded with its own "withering criticism" of the opposition.[71] Constant pointed out that while in normal times a government tended to be satisfied with retaining the status quo, when attacked it often acted on the innate institutional propensity to expand its power. All of this undermined political stability. It was a culture that "confirm[ed] people in the habit of discontent, and ma[de] the government feel the necessity of arbitrary action."[72] Impatience and intolerance, unfortunately, were becoming the characteristic orientations of both the government and the opposition.[73]

France was especially prone to the dangers of violent passions and rage because there had been limited participation in public life during the Old Regime. In September 1797, he analyzed the history of French mores in the following terms:

> A monarchical education, monarchical customs, monarchical souvenirs, monarchical castes besiege us from all sides. Fourteen centuries of royalism have narrowed most souls; enlightenment has gone ahead of sentiment, ideas are too strong for the sensations, characters too small for the human minds. Liberty, which is sliding toward us between anarchy and royalism, encounters a mutilated, fatigued, faded generation....[74]

But, if the Old Regime provided a weak apprenticeship for a public-spirited citizenry, it was the Terror that, more than any other period of the Revolution, had damaged French mores and character. Constant attacked the Terror on many levels, not least for the misguided principles upon which it purported to situate politics and for the arbitrariness of its actions. It was a reprehensible system that had undermined the commendable ideals of the Revolution. But, equally unfortunate for French society, it had led to the emergence of a new type of political personality:

> These men [the terrorists], or rather beings, are of a species unknown before our time: phenomena created by the Revolution, at the same time fickle and ferocious, irritable and hard-hearted, unmerciful and passionate. They unite everything which has hitherto been considered contradictory: courage and cruelty; the love of liberty and the thirst for despotism; the pride which elevates and the criminality

which degrades....This new race...seems to have emerged from the abyss to deliver and devastate the earth, to break all the yokes and all the laws, to make liberty triumph and to dishonor it, to crush those who attack liberty and those who defend it....[75]

The Terror had engendered an all-pervasive fear that made citizens "indifferent to liberty." "It bent heads but it degraded spirits and withered hearts." "It is to the Terror that it is necessary to attribute the decline of public spirit, the fanaticism that undermines all principle of liberty, the opprobrium spread over all republicans, on the purest and most enlightened men."[76]

During the Directory, Constant was especially worried about the rancor of those who had been forced to emigrate. In 1795, he warned that the most dangerous actions would likely result from a return to power of *émigrés*: he disagreed with their politics; he worried about their desire for vengeance.

The hope of victory inspires in them no plan of generosity: the school of unhappiness has given them no lesson in wisdom. Entering the plains of Champagne,[77] they desired only vengeance: pushed back by the republican armies, vengeance alone was what they regretted losing the opportunity to achieve. Of all the physical forces, of all the moral faculties, they seemed to have conserved only the power to hate.[78]

For five years, they had lived "between denunciation and hate."[79] In 1797, Constant described the character of former aristocrats who desired a restoration of the absolute monarchy in the following terms: "Prejudice, arrogance, greed, vengefulness, superstition, all the base and furious passions have rallied around the idea of a King."[80]

Constant argued that it was unlikely that the royalists would succeed in retaking power. And, if the threat became serious, he believed the government would have no choice but to turn to Terrorists for support. The unfortunate outcome of this would be a further degeneration of French political culture.

The victory [of the government party] would not be in doubt; but who can calculate the consequences? Who can claim that the government would have sufficient power to restrain its conquering allies? Who can foresee where the excesses of victory will lead? Who can calculate the misfortunes that would be caused by so many new motives, so many memories, so many humiliations, so much rage![81]

Constant believed that the revolution had already created a political culture that pushed many virtuous people out of politics. In August 1797, Constant published an article in memory of Jean-Baptiste Louvet, recently deceased, that castigated the lamentable degeneration of French politics, which had forced Louvet out of public life. Constant was especially critical of French journalism, which had become a major cause of "this drying out of the soul, of this moral shrinking that discolors all that passes under our eyes, and blackens sensations that we ourselves experience."[82] In 1799, Constant lamented the destructive effects on French political culture of faction and denunciation. "Fragments of resuscitated factions fill the air with confused denunciations. The slander that for ten years has covered this vast empire...exercises without interruption its destructive influence."[83]

At the opposite extreme from the impatience and intolerance characteristic of the furies unleashed by the Revolution, Constant perceived another tendency among his French contemporaries that was to be lamented—the penchant for self-absorption and passivity. This trait had been encouraged under the Old Regime monarchy, when ambition, in his words, "was always driven back upon itself.... [O]ne bows down before the thanks of a master. One feels oneself made smaller by the surrounding narrowness. Disgraceful *ennui* marks with its seal all that is not degraded by servitude, distracted by ignoble pleasures, or preserved from contagion by study and isolation."[84] This propensity toward inactivity, motivated by fear, had resurfaced in the late-1790s, when individuals who had enthusiastically entered politics in the first years of the Revolution retreated from public life. After the Terror, France was filled with "those egoistic and timid souls who demand only rest, and who do not feel, in their senseless calculations, that repose under despotism is only helplessness in despair."[85]

There was a growing propensity to focus on narrow self-interest, which in a striking passage in *De la force du gouvernement actuel*, Constant describes in the following terms:

[t]his arid and burning sentiment [of inactivity] consumes our existence, discolors all objects, and, similar to the burning winds of Africa, dries out and withers everything that it encounters. This

sentiment, which is not to be found in ancient languages or in the languages of free people…was born principally of this privation of goal, of interests, of hopes other than those that are narrow and personal.…One is not able to forget oneself, one is not able to be carried away with enthusiasm, one is not electrified by the recognition of equals.…Characters are still too small for the spirits, they are worn down, as the body, by the habit of inaction or by the excess of pleasures.[86]

Constant's recurring fear, in sum, was that the Revolution had reinforced French character traits—fanaticism, on the one hand, and self-interested passivity, on the other—that undermined stable liberal politics. This does not imply that Constant imagined another political system to be better. He suggested, in fact, that any return of the old regime monarchy would be even more damaging of *moeurs*. This was because a monarchy tended to reduce ambitions to restricted goals. Monarchy, in his own words, "displaces ambition more than it extinguishes it:…it reduces hope to mere personal interest, thus degrading, even as it intoxicates, what popular ambition elevates."[87] He continued to hope that the Republic would encourage positive sentiments, and in some passages he is hopeful. "The Republic is not able to subsist without certain kinds of morality; but, as everything in nature tends to preserve itself, it restores the very species of morality which is necessary for its own existence."[88] More frequently, however, he is troubled by the effect of the revolutionary torrent on the dispositions of the French population.

At the beginning of his most famous pamphlet of the revolutionary period, *Des effets de la Terreur* (published in June 1797 as an addition to *Des réactions politiques*), Constant referred to the dangerous politics that issued from a population alternating between the search for repose and the impulse for vengeance. The doctrine supporting the Terror, according to Constant, was accepted because the French population was permitted at the same time "the repose which seven years of jolts has made a need for fatigued souls, and the vengeance which seven years of suffering have made a need for bitter hearts."[89] Fatigue led to self-regard and inactivity; the desire for vengeance led to fanaticism. Both were corrosive of liberal politics.

In a review of Germaine De Staël's *De l'influence des passions* published a few months earlier (in October 1796), Constant recommended a view of the passions that responded to the twin dangers of fanaticism and passivity. He wrote that it was necessary to find a path between "passions that become dangerous" and passions that are "compressed" [*comprimées*]. That is, he believed that, on the one hand, it was necessary to avoid passions that were overexcited, because these could lead to fanaticism. But it was equally important, on the other hand, to avoid the denial of all passions, because passions that were "compressed" led to a debilitating passivity.[90] He recommended Staël's book because she had searched "the means to conciliate the advantages of two species of government, that is to say, the order that prevents the passions from becoming dangerous, and the liberty which allows the necessary flight to the most beautiful faculties of mankind."[91] As he put it in *De la force du gouvernement actuel*, what was needed was the path between rebelliousness and resignation.[92]

In short, Constant's analysis of the Revolution in 1796–97 heightened his anxiety about the political resonance of sentiment and character. Constant's particular view of the classic problem of the relationship of political institutions to social *moeurs* drew, of course, from a rich cultural tradition (Montaigne, Montesquieu, Rousseau, etc.) that insisted that politics was as much about "the spirit" of society as about institutions. Constant's stance, however, has most in common with later participants in this tradition. There are marked similarities, for example, between Contant's stance and that of his famous successor Alexis de Tocqueville. One of Tocqueville's main points, in volume two of *De la démocratie en Amérique*, is how to accept and defend the self-oriented propensity of modern individuals while at the same time finding ways to encourage civic commitment. The problem, in Constant's mind, was especially acute in France because the revolution had fostered political fanaticism and individual isolation—vengeance and fatigue.

## Liberal Opposition to Revenge and Exclusion

Defending the Republic entailed, in Constant's view, a new tolerant politics. With recent events clearly before his mind, he argued that "public opinion" needed to be channeled by a legal structure and moderated by reasoned deliberation. It was necessary for critics of the government to be cognizant of the damage of intemperate criticism, which undermined confidence in the government without offering any reasonable alternative. And the government, in its turn, must immediately put an end to "the withering politics," which punished out of revenge and weakness.[93] The greatest present danger to the Republic, according to Constant, came not from enemies of the Republic, but from "certain revolutionary habits" that led to precipitous actions and unreasonable expectations. "That which has done France the most harm, the harm most difficult to repair, has been precisely the impatience to do good."[94]

Constant viewed the degeneration of French "political culture" as one of the most unfortunate legacies of the years of revolutionary instability. Because the revolution had implemented radical laws during the Terror, it led naturally to a desire to retract some of these. The danger was that this attempt to adjust legislation and to restore order was often taken to exaggerated lengths—a movement that Constant labeled "reaction."

> I do not call reaction the just punishment of the guilty, nor the return to reasonable ideas. These things belong to law and to reason. Those things, on the other hand, which essentially distinguish reactions, are the replacement of law by arbitrary action, and the replacement of reason by passion: in place of judging men, one prescribes them; in place of examining ideas, one rejects them.
>
> Reactions against men perpetuate revolutions, because they perpetuate oppression, which is the germ of revolution. Reactions against ideas render revolutions unfruitful, because such reactions recall all the abuses [suffered before and during the Revolution]. Revolutions devastate the generation which experiences them; reactions weigh on all generations. The first kill individuals; the second stupefy the entire species.[95]

Reaction, in short, would create new oppressions and resentments that, in turn, would lead to a new swing of the pendulum in the opposite direction. "When this happens, the causes of unhappiness accumulate, all the brakes are shattered, all the parties become equally culpable, all the borders are passed; criminals are punished by criminals; the sentiment of innocence, that which makes the past the guarantee of the future, no longer exists."[96]

Constant's concern about the growing strength of "reaction," especially in 1797, led him to view with special concern the actions of intellectuals and journalists. The revolution, according to Constant, had led to the creation of numerous groups of writers who were motivated primarily by resentments and memories of past injustices. As we have seen, Constant worried about the intemperate criticism that this led to. He was conscious of the important role that "intellectuals" played in the formation of "public opinion," and he insisted that governments allow the free play of critical and independent opinion. But he was conscious of the potential negative social and political consequences of a radical skepticism. "Deliver us from your doubts, do not fatigue us with your skepticism, aid us to consolidate liberty, to make the Republic prosper." And if you cannot do that, then "close yourself in the schools, where you can make your arguments reverberate, intoxicate yourself with your abstractions, and above all never come to trouble our realities."[97]

While Constant clearly had the royalist reaction in mind, he was also concerned about the strength of the Jacobin Left. In the second edition of *Des réactions politiques*, published in June 1797, Constant published a new essay, *Des effets de la Terreur*, critical of the Jacobins and the radical phase of the Revolution, and of those who looked back on this period as the source of revolutionary values. In 1793, we must remember, Constant had viewed the Terror as an objective necessity that could not be avoided. Now, he argued that the Terror "produced nothing good.... The Terror was neither a necessary attendant of liberty, nor a necessary *reinforcement* of the Revolution.... It only exist[ed] when crime [was] the system of government."[98] He wished "to prove that the Terror was not necessary to save the Republic, that the Republic was saved in spite of the Terror,..., that the Terror did nothing but harm, and that its legacy to the Republic of today is all the perils which threaten the Republic even now."[99]

Constant's new attack on the Terror was a response to those who had accused him of being a Jacobin,[100] and it was also a new chapter in the intellectual confrontation that he was having at this time with Adrien de Lezay-Marnésia.[101] As we saw above, Lezay attacked Constant's *De la force du gouvernement actuel* with a pamphlet entitled *De la foiblesse d'un gouvernement qui commence*. Constant explicitly referred to this publication in *Des réactions politiques*. Moreover, simultaneous with the appearance of Constant's *Des réactions politiques*, Lezay published a new brochure entitled *Des causes de la Révolution et de ses résultats*. This book made two arguments, both of which Constant explicitly criticized in *Des effets de la Terreur*.

Lezay argued, first of all, that the Revolution had to be defended in its entirety because of its positive results, even if this entailed accepting, as necessary parts of the Revolution, certain calamitous episodes. Constant, on the contrary, was unwilling to countenance what he viewed as the excesses of the Terror, and he believed that the defense of the ideals of the Revolution—ideals like popular sovereignty and liberty—would be compromised if they were implicated in the extreme policies of 1793–94. Lezay also argued that the first revolutionaries of 1792, the Girondins, were "brigands." Constant again took a contrary position, arguing that the Girondins should not be confused with other actors during the Revolution, and especially not confused with the Jacobins associated with the Terror.

One of the things that makes this interchange so fascinating is that it displays the depth of tension among moderates. Lezay-Marnésia, for all of his seeming defenses of the Terror, was sympathetic to a restoration of the monarchy, though he would have distanced himself from the absolute monarchists around the pretender; that is, he was a member of the constitutional opposition, on the Right-Center of the political spectrum. Constant was not sympathetic to a restoration of the monarchy, and he believed that the government needed to be protected from all reactionary forces; that is, he was a member of constitutional governing party, on the Left-Center of the political spectrum. Part of the purpose of *Des effets de la Terreur* was no doubt to display a critique of the Terror and to separate himself from the position of Lezay-Marnésia. Constant's position was to insist that the principles of the revolution were not implicated in the Terror, and to insist that the dynamic of the revolution, which he favored, did not lead in any inevitable way to excesses like those of the Terror.

*Des effets de la Terreur* also contained elements that would remain central to Constant's liberal stance. He specified, for example, that unlimited power was never admissible, nor was it necessary.[102] Sovereignty should be divided among different institutional bodies; power should never be concentrated in one location. The government must have coercive power—that is, it must have the power to force citizens to respect the laws and decisions of the government—but this coercive power must be limited by legal restrictions that protect individual rights and by constitutional procedures that allow different voices to be heard. Constant's insistence on tolerance was an early articulation of his liberal pluralism. The French government during the Terror was the antithesis of this: it had elevated coercive power into a system of government; it had eliminated the legal and procedural checks that constrain the exercise of governmental power.

Specific disorders, frightful, momentary, illegal calamities, do not add up to terror. Terror exists only when crime is the system of government, not when crime is the enemy of the government; it exists when the government orders crime, not when it combats it; when it organizes the fury of scoundrels, not when it invokes the support of good men.... It is therefore necessary not to confound the republic with the terror, the republicans with their executioners.[103]

## Germaine de Staël's Politics

Staël found her exile from Paris, forced upon her in 1795 by the government of the Directory, very difficult. She spent much of this time in Coppet, entertaining and writing, as was her habit. She tried desperately to get the Directory government to lift the ban on her residence in France, but she remained under a cloud of suspicion and was not allowed to return. On 22 April 1796 (3 Floréal, an IV), there was even a government decree issued that stated that Staël should be arrested, interrogated, and imprisoned if she returned to France. This was abrogated, but the ban against her residing in France remained in effect. There were various attempts, by both Staël and Constant, to have this ban lifted, but to no avail until mid-1797.[104] Part of the legal complication concerning her status was related to her Swiss family background and to her marriage when she was a minor to a Swedish subject (and, therefore, before she could declare her allegiance to France). She fulfilled other conditions, however, like birth in France and length of residency, so it is difficult not to conclude that the problem was largely due to her political reputation.[105]

Staël's political writings of these years, like Constant's, focused on both institutions and culture, and were informed by a deeply pragmatic judgment of what was possible given the state of French and European affairs. As we have seen above, during 1794 Staël shed her monarchist leanings and became a strong supporter of the French Republic. Just after her arrival in Paris in 1795, she made public her support of the Republic: "I sincerely desire the establishment of the French Republic on the sacred bases of justice and humanity, because it has been demonstrated to me that, in the current circumstances, only the republican government is able to give repose and liberty to France."[106] In *Réflexions sur la paix intérieure* (1795), she argued that while the Republic had been "impossible" in 1789, it had become essential after the Terror. Because of the unyieldingly reactionary actions of the surviving Bourbons and the actions of *émigrés*,[107] the monarchy was no longer an option for France. Moreover, the Republic was the regime that best united people with different sentiments and motives. "The hate of despotism, the enthusiasm for the Republic, the fear of vengeance, and the ambition of the talented all speak with the same voice."[108] She appealed to moderate monarchists by pointing out that the Constitution of 1795 provided the institutional provisions they desired, like the independence of the executive power and the restriction of political power to the propertied class. They had only one bad idea that needed to be given up: *hereditary* monarchy. She appealed to moderate republicans, similarly, by pointing out that the regime had all the essentials of an enlightened and liberal order, like the division of the *corps législative* into two bodies and the important political role of property owners. They had only one idea that needed to be sacrificed in the interests of public order: democracy. To both groups, she made the point that any revolt against the current order would lead to the strengthening of extreme ideas and the loss of liberty.

Staël had some reservations concerning the Constitution of 1795, but on the whole she was pleased and astonished that the Convention, which had emerged during the radical phase of the revolution, had accepted the reasonable constitutional proposals of the Commission of Eleven. She attributed this to the lucky result of circumstance—the ending of the Terror and the pressures of external and internal opposition—and she warned that radical action against the system would lead the government to turn to the Jacobins for support, and thereby return France to the Terror. Constantly lurking was the danger of fanaticism, which Staël defined as the "singular passion...that unites the power of crime and the exaltation of virtue."[109]

Closely connected with her anxiety over the power of fanaticism was her more general insistence on the need for calm and the avoidance of vengeance.[110] To stabilize politics, heated passions must be put in abeyance.

> This unhappy country, persecuted by so many diverse factions, has less need to punish all the crimes which have torn the country

apart, than to remove death from its fatal shores; to make the people less familiar (*désaccoutumer*) with the blood of the guilty, which is so near to that shed by the innocent. Take us away from, reject, this revolutionary dross.[111]

What was needed above all was the reconciliation of opposing forces, and political and social calm. "Never has there existed a moment which commands more imperiously the need to push aside all principles of division.... If one reopens no wounds, if one is devoted to the idea of mending divisions, if one advances without reversing course, the Republic will be consolidated.... It is necessary to calm and to console; this simple idea is the secret of this moment."[112]

Staël returned to these themes in *De l'influence des passions sur le bonheur des individus et des nations*, written between 1793 and 1796 and published in Lausanne in October 1796. Though it is a work that deals with many things—philosophical, aesthetic, moral, and social—it was in part intended to demonstrate that she was strongly in support of the Republic, but not in favor of further revolutions. As she stated at the beginning of the work, she intended her reflections about the passions

to conduct us to a principal object of current debates, the manner of constituting a great nation with order and liberty, of reuniting thus the splendors of the arts, sciences, and letters, so much valued in monarchies, with the independence of republics. It will be necessary to create a government that encourages the emulation of genius and constrains factious passions; a government that is able to offer a great man a dignified goal, and to discourage the ambition of usurpers.[113]

She made clear in this work that it was necessary to focus on the dangerous passions aroused by the revolution. What she most worried about was the corrosive nature of hatred, and the closely related desire for revenge. Vengeance, she reasoned, was a contagious passion that was difficult to assuage, and unchecked it would quickly poison social relations. It needed to be contained if social and political stability were to be achieved. Uncontained, it would undermine the possibility of the emergence of a stable *esprit publique* that would allow discussion and reason to prevail. How was this to be done? Staël recommended encouraging generosity and, especially, compassion (*pitié*), the sentiment that grows from identification with the suffering of others. That is, she recommended the cultivation of positive sentiments, and more specifically of the "sentiment prior to reason" that Rousseau had recognized as the basis of all morals.[114] Staël consciously turned to this moral-sentimental theme in hopes of countering the passion for revenge, which she believed infused the counter-revolutionary forces that wished to return to the Old Regime, and to counter the stern sentiments of sacrifice and virtue that had underpinned the revolution during the Terror. "It is in the milieu of a revolution that *la pitié*, this involuntary movement in all other circumstances, ought to be the rule of conduct."[115] More that ever, she reasoned, France in 1795–96 needed *pitié* and *générosité*.[116]

Staël also opposed the exclusion of revolutionaries or nobles from politics; either exclusion, she reasoned, would lead to bitter resentment, and this in turn would fuel the cycle of revenge. The danger was that "Each step of injustice renders the second step necessary," as she wrote in *Des circonstances actuelles*. "A dominating party in a nation which comes by degrees to proscribe the entire nation will create each day a new enemy.... The number of those seeking revenge grows in proportion to the number of victims and, in order to finish the war, it is necessary to give to the victims conditions which attach them to life."[117] Staël recommended a *héroïque oubli*, the willed forgetting of past injuries and injustices.[118] The conflicts and injuries of the revolution were so fresh and severe, so strongly experienced, that only such an agenda would help heal social divisions. Without such effort, the negative passions of resentment and vengeance would prevail.

As we have seen above, Constant and Staël had slightly differing political stances in 1795–96. Staël was a moderate republican; Constant was a radical republican. This tension is expressed clearly by Constant in his article about Staël's *De l'influence des passions*, published on 26 October 1796.[119] But, the similarities are more notable than the differences. Like Constant, Staël supported the Republic, and she hoped that all of the moderate factions could achieve a reconciliation of sentiments and passions, though she feared that many royalists were haunted with the idea of revenge. She pointed out that with the Republic established and consolidated, any dramatic institutional, legal, and/or political change would be itself a revolution. Like other Thermidorians who argued "in the counter-revolution, there is a revolution," Staël believed that any attempt to reinstall the

Bourbon monarchy would lead to a civil war that would launch a new revolution—a "revolution" in opposition to the true revolution that had already been achieved.

## Salons

It is difficult not to view Stael's recommendation of cultural reconciliation of opposing sentiments as related to her close association with salon culture. For her, salons were the model for meetings of people who might disagree about political, scientific, and aesthetic issues, but who related to each other without rancor or physical conflict. Her nostalgia for the salon world of the recent past—for the elegance and grace of the "worldly" culture of the salons of the late–Old Regime, and for the intensity, sensibility, and refinement of the salons of the early stage of the revolution—was frequently expressed. Salons provided, in Staël's mind, the *locus classicus* of an open communication of ideas, in which an intelligent elite could discuss and mediate their differences. In salons, refined sociability joined reasoned deliberation. As she recounted in a famous passage of her *Considérations sur la Révolution française*,

> Foreigners are not able to conceive the charm and brilliance of Parisian society, if they have not seen France twenty years ago. One is able to say with truth that never has a society been at the same time as brilliant and serious as during the three or four first years of the revolution, running from 1788 to the end of 1791. As public affairs were still in the hands of the best people, all vigor, liberty, and grace of the old politesse, were united in the same individuals. Men of the Third Estate, distinguished by their enlightenment and talents, were joined by gentlemen who relied more on their merit than on the privileges of their estate, and as a consequence the most important questions that the social order has ever given birth to were treated by the minds most capable of discussing and understanding them.[120]

Of course, salons were not universally viewed in such a positive light. Jacobins favored clubs, rather than salons, as the appropriate locus for the sociability that would generate enlightened political interchange.[121] Some important intellectuals, including Rousseau, viewed salons as privileged places where "insiders" intrigued to protect their wealth and influence, and where brilliant conversation was designed less to illuminate the truth about important issues than to exhibit the pretensions and puffed-up *amour propre* of notables. From such a perspective, salons were a glittering façade that hid a disgusting *ennui* and encouraged a stifling conformism.

Salons had a long pedigree, dating back to the intimate conversations that took place after 1618 in the "Blue Room" of the Marquise de Rambouillet. But the seventeenth and eighteenth centuries produced the most famous salons: those of Madame de Sablé, Mademoiselle de Montpensier, Madame de Scudéry, Madame de Sévigné, and Madame de Lafayette in the seventeenth century; those of the Marquise de Lambert, Madame de Tencin, Madame Geoffrin, Madame de Deffand, Mademoiselle de Lespinasse, Madame d'Epinay, and Madame Necker (Germaine de Staël's mother) in the eighteenth century. What characterized them all, and distinguished them from other forms of elite sociability, was the mixing of the sexes in the home of a wealthy *salonnière*. As this suggests, a salon was an intimate society of men and women of the leisure class meeting for elegant conversation. It was designed to facilitate an amicable and open conversation among culturally compatible participants who desired, through the charms and delicate intimacies of polite interchange, to hear the latest news, encounter cultural luminaries of the moment, make social and political connections, experience intellectual stimulation, and find amusement.As this indicates, salons had a wide variety of uses. In the Old Regime, salons liberated discussion from the constraints and influence of the court, and they were instrumental in eliminating the identification of the sociability of nobles with the crude and brutal manners of the military camp or with the pedantic stuffiness of scholastic schoolmen. More relaxed than the court, but associated with *honnêteté* and the refined communication of the nobility, salons were attractive to people beyond this group, and they showed remarkable resiliency even after the legal privileges of the nobility were eliminated during the Revolution.[122]

Staël's own salon in the early period of the Revolution, especially during the winter of 1791–92, was one of the most famous and influential. Prominent Feuillants like Barnave rubbed shoulders with Girondins like Condorcet, and with Staël's lover at the time, Louis de Narbonne, briefly Minister of War in 1791–92. Like other salons at this time, Staël's was more overtly political than the majority of salons of the eighteenth century, which is scarcely surprising given the intensely politicized nature of culture and society during the Revolutionary era. One historian has recently referred to Staël's salon in 1791–92 as "un véritable centre du pouvoir."[123] The Revolution, of course, was not kind to "associations," and many were specifically prohibited by legislation like the Le Chapelier Law of 1791. Salons, however, were not legally proscribed; nonetheless, they largely disappeared during the years of the Jacobin dictatorship, no doubt because of their connection with the elitist aristocratic society and culture that radical revolutionaries loathed, and because, simply, many aristocrats left Paris. After Thermidor, as *émigrés* returned and upper-class sociability reemerged, salons were revived, and again took on a marked political coloration. There seems little doubt that Staël, coming back to Paris in mid-1795, hoped to exert an influence at least as great as she had exerted before the fall of the monarchy. Her salon at the Swedish embassy during 1795 quickly became an immensely influential gathering place for moderates. It was not, however, to last.

As we have seen, Staël went into exile in December 1795 because of persecution by the government. This was followed by even more threatening actions by the authorities. On 22 April 1796, a secret arrest warrant was issued for Staël, but when it was made public it raised such an uproar that it was annulled, replaced by a warrant prohibiting her from entering France. As a result, she did not return to France until mid-December 1796, after a year's absence, and even then she had to stay the first five months in Hérivaux, Constant's residence outside the capital. She would move into and out of Paris during the next years, as the authorities permitted, but found herself constantly under suspicion. And her salon, so influential in 1791–92, and again briefly in 1795, for all practical purposes ceased to exist. The context of this was the politics of the immediate post-Terror period.

What role did Staël imagine for her salon? She hoped that it would be the location where an enlightened sociability, under her direction, would facilitate the intelligent discussion of important public issues, leading to benefits for the public good. Her ideal salon would combine the sociability and worldliness of salons of the Old Regime, but now with a political orientation that incorporated the significant changes that had been introduced by the Revolution. It would be the primary setting for liberal republican politics. Bronislaw Baczko recently has argued that, for Staël, the salon was a utopian space where aesthetics and politics made a perfect mix. It was the private space in which she imagined it was possible to detach the urbanity, good taste, and sociability—that is, the *moeurs*—of the old regime, and to transfer them to the republican post-revolutionary era. In short, it was the privileged location for a melding of republican politics and aristocratic culture.

The transplantation of aristocratic culture would not be easy, however. Staël recognized that originally the emergence of the manners and *esprit* of the French salon derived from the historical convergence of a stable monarchy, which had obtained the tacit consent of nobles, and a cultured aristocracy, which received privileges and honors from the monarchy in return for its support. Reminiscent of Montesquieu, she wrote of the culture of grace that infused the court, and the mores of finesse, civility, and urbanity of the nobles who surrounded the monarchy.[124] The Terror had destroyed this world. Staël was not restrained when she discussed this period of the revolution, denouncing it for its "detestable literary and political effects, the audacity without measure, the gaiety without grace, and the debasing vulgarity."[125] French culture and sociability had suffered along with its institutions. The Terror had profoundly undermined ancient forms of French culture, replacing these with bad manners, vulgarity, and fanaticism.

As we have seen, Staël returned to Paris after the end of the Terror, in 1795, hoping to reestablish herself as a political force, closely connected with becoming a prominent *salonnière* in the French capital. But with the exile of 1795–96, her hopes were frustrated yet again, and her consideration of the importance of salons was qualified. It is not surprising that Staël's view of the *moeurs* and sociability of the salons of the late–Old Regime and early years of the Revolution assumes a tone of nostalgic affection. At times, she writes as though the cultivated *moeurs* were inextricably entwined with the salons of the Old Regime and the early years of the Revolution; she seemed to suggest that the loss was irrevocable.

But, a new culture—a culture appropriate for the new Republic—could and must be nurtured. However idealist and nostalgic, this is the message of Staël's writings. The narrow *esprit de parti* must be replaced with a dialogue across political boundaries. Vengeance and hate must be replaced by conversation and sympathy. "By degrees, this profound aversion that one feels for the man one has attacked, this aversion weakens with conversation, with regard, with consideration, which reanimates sympathy, and leads to finding an equal (a fellow-creature) in one who previously was considered an enemy."[126] The *moeurs* of the aristocracy cannot be recreated, but they must be restored as a deeply buried vein of French culture. Staël's hopes for salons declined as the years passed. She herself pointed out that under Napoleon, salons were largely replaced by grand official ceremonies—judged by many, especially Staël, as intellectually deadening. And the salons that remained, unfortunately, had become miserable spectacles where suspicion, careerism, and venal passions prevailed. As she put it in a letter to Constant, high society had become "a labyrinth of interests and ambitions."[127] And though salons continued to exist, they no longer provided the forums for open reflection about the common good, the constitutional order, or the nature of the state that Staël considered their most important function. Stael may still have considered the salon—reinvigorated from its unfortunate decline during the years of Napoleon—as a potential center of intelligent sociability. But, she did not have the faith in them that she once had had.

Constant's faith in salons declined earlier than Staël's. He had known the Paris Salon of the Suards before the Revolution. It was there that he had first observed Enlightenment luminaries like Condorcet and Morellet, and where, in 1787, he met Isabelle de Charrière. His real introduction into the world of the Paris salon, however, took place when he returned to Paris with Staël in May 1795. In 1828, he recounted to Jean-Jacques Coulmann (in his characteristic ironic manner) the confusing interactions among the competing political groups in Stael's salon.

> The salon of Mme de Staël [in 1795] was frequented by four or five different tribes: some members of the current government, whose confidence she [Staël] hoped to gain; some remnants of the past government, displeasing to their successors; all the returning nobles, who she was at the same time gratified and embarrassed to receive; some writers who since the 9th of Thermidor had regained some influence; and some members of the diplomatic corps who were abjectly obsequious towards [*aux pieds du*] the Committee of Public Safety while conspiring against it. In the midst of the conversations, acts, and intrigues of these different groups, my naïve republicanism was greatly encumbered. When I talked with the victorious republican faction, I heard them say

that it was necessary to cut off the heads of anarchists and to shoot the émigrés without trial. When I talked with the small number of disguised terrorists who had survived, I heard them say that it was necessary to exterminate the new government, the émigrés, and foreigners. When I allowed myself to be seduced by the moderate and gentle opinions or the writers who preached a return to morality and justice..., they insinuated that France would not be able to do without a king, an opinion which I found singularly shocking. I did not know what to say, or above all what to do, with my enthusiasm for the republic.[128]

He did not share Staël's hope that the salon was the arena from which a sensible and reasonable politics would emerge.

By 1797, Constant was suggesting that salons were frequented by reactionary intellectuals who attacked the government.

These beings...who have only an artificial existence, some imitating motions, some rallying words, these burlesque disguised beings dispensing glory, wanting to resuscitate the empire of the salons, the fashionable tribunal, this powerful legislator of vanity, indestructible as it is, dear to all who are nobody, because in gathering together it seems to reunite, at the same time, *l'amour-propre* and fear, reassures ridicule and renders it general, and aggrandizes pygmies, by reducing the rest of the world to their diminutive stature.[129]

He repeated these reservations in his address of 16 September 1797 when he attacked the depraved *moeurs* of the aristocracy, the frivolity of their conspiracies, the *coquetterie* of some noble women, the *fatuité* of idle adolescents, and the *ennui* of the entire lazy crowd. Salons were unfortunately one of the places where people were charmed into arming themselves against republican institutions.[130]

## Liberalism

Constant first labeled his position "liberal" in 1795. He and Germaine de Staël were the first in France to use this term to define a political stance.[131] Liberals, he wrote, "must accept neither despotism, nor a mitigated royalty, which will soon cease to be mitigated, nor an arbitrary republic, which will not be less vexatious than royalty."[132]

Liberalism was to protect liberty and constitutionalism while avoiding a return to royalism or Jacobinism. As other commentators have pointed out, this "centrist" position is one of the distinguishing characteristics of modern French liberalism, which was markedly different from the English liberal tradition that assumed the existence of opposing parties committed to the peaceful alternation of political power.[133] One legacy of the French Revolution was a more unstable political culture, a bipolarization of the political landscape, situating Directory liberals in the center between groups that were not committed to representative parliamentary institutions. I have termed this a "liberalism of fear" because of the constant vigilance they believed was required to avoid the dangers on both extremes.[134]

French liberalism was also pragmatic in that it was centrally concerned with negotiating the tension between popular sovereignty and civil liberties, and with balancing concerns like the protection of the Republic with analysis of social *moeurs* and the broader culture. This pragmatic "liberal" stance emerged during the early years of the Directory. Kurt Kloocke has argued that there was an essential continuity in Constant's political stance during the entire Revolutionary period. He claims that Constant remained committed during all of these years to the "democratic" ideal, and was equally sensitive to the need for political compromise because of concrete conditions. "Constant possessed already, in the Summer of 1790, not only the essential elements of a political ideology that he never would abandon, but also this astonishing faculty of analyzing political play which makes him such a cunning political tactician."[135] In contrast, I believe that Constant lacked this pragmatism in 1790, but found it during the early years of the Directory.

Other scholars have insisted that Constant's liberalism was not fully formed until the early years of the Empire. Etienne Hofmann, for example, in his magisterial study of Constant's early works, has argued that Constant is naive and opportunistic during the Directory, and largely neglected constitutional questions until the early-1800s.[136] According to Hofmann, Constant did not embrace "pure liberalism" until he separated the issue of protecting individual liberty from a commitment to any specific form of government, something that is evident only in his 1806 manuscript *Principes de politique*.[137] Helena Rosenblatt, similarly, has argued that during the Directory, "Constant's liberalism was only embryonic." "Constant was not yet a liberal in the true meaning of the word. His political principles were 'germinating.'" "Constant's transformation into a truly liberal political thinker," she claims, came only in 1806, when he attacked Rousseau's conception of sovereignty and compared ancient and modern liberty.[138] The essential elements of Constant's liberalism, however, were present in these earliest political writings. He favored the principles of civil liberties and popular sovereignty, but recognized that making absolute either of these principles ran the risk of undermining the other. He favored religious toleration, but worried that a population without any common beliefs would potentially lack solidarity. He worried about passionate politics during unsettled times, and cautioned that the emotions of revenge would eviscerate any hopes of political stability. Politics was always the difficult process of balancing conflicting ideals, including the complex issues of human character. As we shall see, he refined these liberal positions in his writings during the Consulate and Empire, as he gave more attention to the difficult constitutional issue of institutional checks and balances, and articulated more concisely his rejection of a unified conception of sovereignty. But, already in 1795–96, he had outlined the central components of a "liberal" politics.

An indication of the pragmatism of Constant's "liberalism of fear" was his reaction to a legal debate that was taking place in Paris in early-October 1796. On 11 October, Constant returned to Paris from Coppet, where he had been from mid-September until 7 October, and where Staël was still in exile. The legal issue at the center of the debate was the law of 3 Brumaire, an IV (25 October 1795). This law, passed following the royalist uprising of Vendémaire, had eliminated from the voting roster relations of *émigrés*. Royalists and the constitutional opposition were critical of the law, not surprisingly, and argued that it was a violation of the spirit of the Constitution. The supporters of the government argued that this exclusion continued to be necessary because it was important to keep royalists from undermining the Republic; it was necessary to "defend the citadel under siege." Constant supported the government republicans.[139] The contentious debate over this law was rejoined in 1797 (see below).

We have seen that a similar pragmatism framed Constant's stance on "popular opinion." Popular opinion should not be ignored, according to Constant. Indeed, if it were ignored the government would find itself more and more isolated and, eventually, identified with a particular interest at the expense of the general interests of society.[140] But, on the other hand, popular opinion—mercurial and fickle—should not always and immediately translate into political power. Here, one sees the residual anxiety of one who had observed revolutionary crowds claiming to be the transparent expression of the popular will, as well as Constant's anxiety as one who had observed temporary majorities opposing the ideals of the Revolution. Constant recognized that public opinion could be manipulated to damage the safety and health of individuals.[141] The government needed to be the expression of the will of the people, but it must have some autonomy from the daily fluctuations of popular opinion.

His pragmatism also translated into a complex relationship to tradition. On the one hand, Constant was a man of principle, as his commitment to the ideals of the Revolution illustrated. But tradition could not be ignored. If tradition failed to be respected, then a government would find itself imposing changes contrary to accepted mores and reigning ideas, a scenario that could lead in extreme cases (like the French Revolution when it attacked property rights) to unnecessary bloodshed and, in response, a vitriolic reaction.[142] To avoid these extremes, Constant advocated "intermediate principles," which would arbitrate between universal principles and existing circumstances.[143] The embrace of intermediate principles would avoid a rigid Burkean traditionalism, but equally would avoid the danger of acting for principles entirely divorced from social and political reality. Differently expressed, Constant embraced a traditionalism not wholly *identified with* the institutions of the past *à la* Edmund Burke; he advocated incorporating the ideals of the Revolution into extant tradition.

This meant that, for Constant, "ending the revolution" involved appreciating the power of historical continuity. He here parted ways from those who believed that the revolution of 1789 was a definitive break with the past; that it had created a "tabula rasa" on which a new order could be built. Constant believed there were inevitable continuities between past and present. Andrew Jainchill has argued that this is related to a "republican" intellectual heritage that insisted that all societies, including republics, exist in time and, therefore, experience degeneration.[144] I believe that this sensitivity to tradition came from recognition that it was the nature of politics to require constant negotiation and compromise, and that this entailed a rejection of the aspect of the revolutionary mentality that believed "regeneration" was a wholly rational and transparent process. One must begin, not with naive hopes of creating a wholly new world, but with full recognition of actual historical possibilities. Whatever the provenance, there is little questions that Constant, by 1795–97, had come to reject revolutionary utopianism. Revolutions do not miraculously transform individuals into something new; quite to the contrary, the tendency of revolutions is to encourage passions and furies. All people come to tumultuous historical events like revolutions with emotional baggage and, indeed, with tarnished pasts; and the experience of revolution inevitably inflames sentiments and inflicts immense new sufferings. For stability to be reestablished in a country like France, which had endured years of revolution, it was essential, Constant believed, that human nature with all its faults be carefully weighed. And for stability to be attained, it was necessary for violent emotions to be contained, and for the human impurities and differences that one perceived in others to be accepted.

> Fickle beings that we are, looking into ourselves, feeling ourselves totter at every step, by what absurdity do we judge so differently our fellow creatures? Let us profit from our own instability, from our own inconsistency, and from all the other defects of our feeble nature, in order not to ascribe a depth of guilt to others that ignores these weaknesses.[145]

One of the greatest dangers was that those who had been injured during the revolution would wish only for revenge. Constant worried about those who are "at the same time bitter and frivolous, insensitive but vindictive, consoled without being softened; who have forgotten their ailments without having forgiven their country; who, though distracted or satisfied while running after pleasure, renew their grief the moment they have an opportunity to gratify their revenge. Detested hypocrites, they profane the most sacred of all earthly things, tears and sorrow, and confound virtue with crimes, so that they may commit crimes with impunity."[146] Peace and political order demanded that compromises be made and wrongs be forgiven, or at least forgotten. Reconciliation must replace revenge.

# 3
# Liberal Dilemmas (1797–1802)

The years straddling the 1799 *coup d'état* of 18th Brumaire are finally receiving the serious scholarly attention they deserve. We are learning more about the dangers faced by the Republic, more about the difficulties the government had balancing justice and security, and more about the ferocious political debates that these problems stimulated.[1] Constant's political activities during these years led to a deepening of his commitment to liberal politics. He served as a local official (in his commune of Luzarches) and as a member of the *Tribunat* (1799–1802), experiences that led him to formulate his own intricate constitutional proposal. At the same time, he participated in theoretical disputes about politics and history that, he believed, were related to the security of the Republic: he worried that France might repeat an objectionable part of England's revolutionary history; he confronted the anarchist alternative outlined by William Godwin. Constant's pragmatic liberal agenda, formulated in 1795–97, was not significantly altered during these years. What did change were his evaluations of the political forces at play and his assessment of the relationship of these forces to the survival of a liberal representative regime. Constant's liberalism became more clearly articulated as he faced the political crises of the late-Directory and the Consulate.

## The Coup of 18 Fructidor, an V (4 September 1797)

The first of the crises was the reorganization of the government of the Directory in September 1797—the so-called coup of 18 Fructidor. This coup came on the heels of the legislative elections of spring 1797. In the first stage of these elections (21 March 21–4 April), royalists made a strong showing, with many of the republican holdovers from the Convention (kept in office by the Two-Thirds Law of 1795) failing to be reelected. This meant that the monarchists, uniting their new

81

electoral gains with their previous ones of 1795, now outnumbered legislators who supported the Republic, a political shift to the Right confirmed at the conclusion of the second stage of the elections on 18 April.[2] When the legislative session opened on 20 May, the new monarchist majority exerted its power. They elected two of their own as leaders of the Councils,[3] and quickly followed this with actions and legislation directed against the Left. On 27 May 1797, Gracchus Babeuf and his compatriot Darthé were executed for their leadership roles in the notorious "Conspiracy of Equals" of the previous year.[4] On 14 July 1797, the penal legislation of 1792 and 1793 against non-juring Catholic priests was abrogated. During the same summer, the controversial law that had excluded from public service *émigrés* and their relatives (the so-called Law of 3 Brumaire, mentioned above) was also repealed. The result of these developments was increased anxiety for all those, including Constant,[5] who wished to protect the liberal Republic from a monarchist takeover. What would happen to the constitutional order established by the Constitution of 1795 if royalists continued to pursue an anti-republican agenda?

The political situation in 1797 was complicated, which helps explain the maneuverings of the various parties. Most royalists, suspecting that they had the support of the majority of the electorate in the country, wanted to respect the republican constitution that would give them power, even though their objective was to dismantle the Republic and install the monarchy. Most republicans, on the other hand, knowing that they were in a minority, believed that the only way to protect the Republic was to prevent the royalists from taking power, even if this meant violating the strict letter of the constitution. Moderate constitutionalists in the center were split over whether scrupulous respect for the constitution or preservation of the Republic should take priority. Constant was a member of the second faction of this moderate group, which placed a high priority on protecting the Republic. His positions during the crisis of 1797, like the actions of the government, have always been controversial.

One of the central issues during the summer of 1797 was whether to restructure the executive to conform to the new majority in the legislative Councils following the spring elections. Royalists favored restructuring, as did moderates like Pierre-Louis Roederer. They argued that the ideological disposition of the ministers—that is, the executive branch of five Directors—should reflect the ideological orientation of the legislative majority. Members of the governing party, like Barras, argued against this, basing their claims on the need for a "separation of powers." Constant, now joined by Staël (who had supported a moderate constitutionalist position in 1795–96), sided with the governing party. As we have seen in the previous chapter, Constant published, in April, 1797, his second major essay, *Des réactions politiques*, which took a strong line in support of the government. It called for a respect for legality and attachment to the principles of the revolution, and it counseled all to be attentive to the great danger presented by reactionaries. He was especially eloquent in his support of constitutional regimes that were based on general principles and clearly critical of those individuals who violated legal norms and, thereby, favored some version of "arbitrary" rule.[6]

The journalistic response to Constant's essay was mixed. The Right wing, not surprisingly, was critical. One article, conflating the differences between moderates and left-wing radicals, characterized Constant's position as "the most pure Jacobinism" and suggested that "between this writing and those of Babeuf, there is no difference except style."[7] Constant decided he needed to respond. He, therefore, republished *Des réactions politiques* in June 1797 with some new pages that attacked the Jacobin Left. Entitled *Des effets de la Terreur*, these new pages were designed to defend his moderate position. Having clearly expressed his dislike of the royalist Right in *Des réactions politiques*, he wished to reemphasize his disapproval for the arbitrary and violent actions of the radical Left. There was no better way to do this, in his mind, than to remind people of the brutality and dire consequences of the Terror. All of this, in the political context of the spring and summer of 1797, buttressed his strong support of the government.

Another important forum for Constant, and for liberal political activity more generally, was the Cercle Constitutionnel, sometimes referred to as the Club de Salm. The Cercle Constitutionnel was organized during the spring of 1797 by Constant and others, including Pierre-Claude-François Daunou, Charles-Maurice de Talleyrand, Marie-Joseph Chénier, Pierre-Louis Ginguené, Pierre-Jean-Georges Cabanis, and Jean-Lambert Tallien. It met at 64, rue de Lille, at the former home of the German Prince Frederick III of Salm-Kyrbourg who had been guillotined during the Terror (today this building is the home of the Légion d'honneur); it subsequently moved to the hôtel de Montmorency, also on the rue de Lille. It was created to oppose the royalist Club de Clichy, and more specifically to support the government of the Directory during the 1797 crisis. It ceased meeting after 26 October 1797, then met again briefly in February 1798 in the Palais-Egalité (the Palais-Royal).[8] The executive branch of the government was modestly reorganized following the legislative elections. A new cabinet was installed on 16 July 1797.[9] It continued the ascendancy of the governing party, but with the addition of Talleyrand as Foreign Secretary, assumed to be close to the moderate constitutionalists. This did not satisfy royalists, however, and general anxiety continued to be high during the summer and fall. Constant's uneasiness is clearly expressed in his correspondence. In a letter to his uncle Samuel de Constant on 1 August, for example, he referred to the growing strength of the counter-revolutionaries in the press and in the Councils, and despaired about the survival of the Republic. "If in the next two months something does not happen that puts the Republic back on its feet [*remette la République à flot*], it is not possible to have any hope, and even this event is able to be a calamity by its consequences."[10] He does not elaborate concerning what sort of potential "*événement*" he had in mind (were there already rumors of the forthcoming coup?[11]), but he was obviously worried that the government had no good options. In another letter to his uncle eight days later, Constant referred to a forthcoming "counter-revolutionary attack" by the Council of 500 against the Directory, which he said would require "all friends of order and liberty" to come to the government's defense. "I do not know of anything more worrying [*ennuyeux*] than this foretaste of civil war."[12]

Constant and Staël attempted to convince moderate constitutionalists that they should support the government. We know, for example, that on 13 August, they arranged a dinner with Antoine-Clair Thibaudeau *chez* Staël to press their case. Thibaudeau responded that they were exaggerating the royalist danger, and argued that the Directors should respect the rules of the representative regime, meaning that the executive should reflect the majority in the Councils.[13]

It was not to be. Fearing that they were losing control of the situation, some of the governing party carried out a coup on 18 Fructidor, an V (4 September 1797). Three members of the Directory (Barras, La Révellière-Lépeaux, and Jean-François Reubell) called in the assistance of generals Lazare Hoche and Charles-Pierre-François Augereau to seize power and, they claimed, protect the Republic. Their version of protecting the Republic, however, required violating electoral procedures and legal norms. The remaining executive Directors—now a Triumvirate (but quickly expanded to five with the addition on 8 September of François de Neufchâteau and Merlin de Douai)—reimposed restrictive legislation, like the Law against non-juring priests and the Law of 3 Brumaire that disenfranchised the relatives of *émigrés* (both laws were adopted on 5 September, the day following the coup). They also placed new restrictions on the press and purged local administrations. The Directors also condemned sixty-five people to deportation, including the former Directors Lazare Carnot and François-Marie Barthélemy. One hundred and seventy-seven men were dismissed from the Councils, and the election results in over half of the departments were annulled.[14] The new regime of repression affected not just the royalist Right, but also the moderate constitutionalists who had refused to close ranks with the government.

The Second Directory (as the government established in September 1797 is called) insisted on the legal character of the new regime, but most analysts have viewed the coup and its aftermath as a catastrophe for constitutional government. Georges Lefebvre, for example, writes that the coup "consecrated the failure of the constitutional and liberal experiment attempted by the Thermidorians,"[15] and suggests that the resort to force was nothing less than a new manifestation of the Terror. M.J. Sydenham analyzes the coup and its aftermath in a chapter entitled "the abandonment of legality."

> [T]he initial political position of the regime was as reactionary as its methods and objectives were revolutionary. Not only was the *coup d'état* of 18 Fructidor a blow struck by a narrowly-based government which deliberately repudiated popular aid: it was also a successful repudiation of one possible way in which legitimate political evolution might have taken place within the framework of the Republic. Lépeaux, Barras and their associates constantly claimed that they had acted to uphold the Constitution of 1795 against organised royalist infiltration; in fact they violated that Constitution, manipulating the law by a mixture of force and chicanery.[16]

Howard Brown suggests that the Fructidor coup constituted the beginning of the "authoritarian republic."[17] Henri Grange, more strongly, writes that "the coup d'état of Fructidor was nothing other than a purge in the Robespierrist or Stalinist style, executed by republicans to liquidate other republicans."[18]

Constant and Staël disagreed. Staël lamented that the Constitution of 1795 had not provided sufficient means for the branches of government to resolve differences. She specifically pointed to the need for the executive to have a suspensive veto over legislation and, also, to have the authority to dissolve the legislature and call for new elections. Barring constitutional revision that would moderate the excessively rigid separation of power and/or provide for some balance of power,[19] the coup was justified.

What is 18 fructidor? All the parties respond: one saying that it is an atrocious thwarted conspiracy; another, that it is a tyrannical act of a barbarous faction. I would respond: it is the necessary effect of a bad constitution; it is the breaking of a machine that was not calculated for action. 18 fructidor is the right to dissolve the English Parliament, exercised violently because there did not exist a legal means for a dissolution when there was a positive necessity for dissolution, and because the instinct for individual and political conservation only ever respects the boundaries which protect and reign individuals at the same time.... In order to save the constitution, it was necessary to infringe it [*l'enfreindre*].[20]

Constant also supported the coup, arguing, in a speech delivered on 16 September 1797 to the Cercle Constitutionnel, that this patently unconstitutional action was necessary to stabilize the Republic against the threat of a monarchist takeover.[21] It was necessary, he argued, to "republicanize" France, which meant that it was necessary to centralize power in the hands of republicans, even if this required that "the banner of the Constitution" be "momentarily lowered for the general interest."[22] He commended the leaders of the coup for not resorting to the type of violence—executions—that had marked previous episodes of the revolution, ignoring the fact that deportations were often death sentences of another sort. He commended the government for protecting the institutions of the Republic and for avoiding "*l'arbitraire*," thereby attempting to diminish the constitutional and legal violation that the coup represented.

[N]othing is able to supplant *l'arbitraire* except the moral force of institutions. The power of conviction is indispensable to those who renounce violence; and in order to prevent forever the dangerous recourse to illegal jolts [*secousses*], it is necessary to assure a progressive and regular forward step.[23]

He did his best, in short, to present the coup as a moderate and pragmatic, if extraordinary, action that was required to protect the Republic. He pointed to the unfortunate residues of monarchical *moeurs* that continued to infect French politics, especially among advocates of a return to the monarchy who wished "to destroy piece by piece the edifice of republican institutions."[24] He argued that one could not save liberty and constitutionalism without first saving the Republic.[25]

Staël's and Constant's willingness to accept this coup demonstrates their high anxiety about the survival of the Republic. They chose the course that seemed to them the least menacing to the protection of liberty and constitutionalism.[26] Soon, however, they were uneasy about the position they had taken. Constant was shocked by the extent of the purges orchestrated by the government, and increasingly concerned about the stance that one must violate the constitution to save it (which is the way he characterized the Fructidor coup years later[27]). In the months following the coup, Constant expressed his deeper criticism in various ways. On 27 February 1798, he gave an address to the Cercle Constitutionnel in which he attacked the Jacobins and the royalists (a standard trope), but went out of his way to defend property and legality.[28] He emphasized, more than ever before, the need for legal forms and legal consistency.[29] He stressed that a free press was necessary against "arbitrariness," though he still admitted that "circumstances" could necessitate temporary restrictions.[30]

This was the period when Constant assumed the office of the President of the municipal administration of Luzarches, beginning in November 1797.[31] He took his duties seriously and was a strong supporter of the various republican festivals that were held to attempt to broaden popular support for the regime.[32] Like many others at the time, he placed considerable hope in public festivals and patriotic education.[33] His correspondence to members of the government indicates his ongoing concern. He claimed that, without proper vigilance, extremists—in his own words, "some royalists and some anarchists"[34]—would take control of the local administration.

Constant also ran for a seat in the legislature the following spring (March–April 1798), but did not succeed. Unlike the electoral campaign of the previous year, when moderates were worried about the strength of Right-wing monarchists, they now were concerned about the renewed power of Left-wing neo-Jacobins. Local Jacobin clubs had reorganized following the Fructidor coup, and they were now vigorously pressing their agenda of a wider franchise, universal public education, veterans' bonuses, and progressive taxation, while at the same time attacking the "aristocratic" politics of moderates. Constant was elected to the primary assembly of his own canton of Luzarches, but was defeated in the second stage departmental elections (Seine-et-Oise) that chose the members of the Assembly. During his campaign, he wrote of the need to oppose radicals on both extremes: those who wished to "cut the throats of all property owners," and those who, "regretting the loss of the monarchy, want to banish all republicans."[35] In the electoral assembly of the department, there was a split between the majority neo-Jacobins and a minority of moderates that formed a "secessionist" assembly, of which Constant was a leader. The "mother" assembly prevailed, however, with the decisions of the minority "secessionist" assembly declared null by the law of 22 Floréal, an VI [11 May 1798]. This electoral maneuvering led some of Constant's critics to depict him as a closet monarchist.[36]

The legislative elections of the spring of 1798 gave new strength to the neo-Jacobins. The response of the government was, as in 1797, to intervene to exclude some of those elected. On 22 Floréal [May 11, 1798], the Council of Ancients approved a law passed by the Council of Five Hundred on 8 May. This law invalidated the elections in forty-eight departments, and validated the elections in nineteen other departments. In fact, these were the "secessionist assemblies" that had been created by the government in opposition to the legal assemblies. [The "secessionist" assembly in the Seine-et-Oise was not one of these.] The excluded deputies of the sixty-seven departments were on the Left. The government claimed that they could not respect the election of individuals who would not take an oath of loyalty to the constitution. In fact, of course, it was again an illegal intervention into the electoral process.

The elections of 1798 indicated the instability of the republican framework, and it also demonstrated how unwilling were most political figures (government supporters and their opponents) to see political conflicts negotiated by electoral party politics.[37] Constant found the entire electoral experience searing, and he told his friends that he was determined to return to his scholarship. During the campaign, Constant unexpectedly had run into the opposition of some members of the government who leaned toward the Left, a group that had become suspicious of Constant's connections with Barras, Talleyrand, and (always under a cloud of suspicion) Staël. This is one reason, no doubt, that the "secessionist" assembly in the Seine-et-Oise was not favored by the Law of 22 Floréal; and it was also, no doubt, why there were rumors that Constant was a closet monarchist. Not surprisingly, Constant's willingness to criticize the government increased. His reservations concerning the dubious measures taken by the government were also growing. He, nonetheless, held his tongue publicly, believing that extremists did threaten the stability of the Republic.

One obvious issue that this raises is opportunism. Was Constant willing to support the government only when he was interested in gaining office and banking on the support of government officials? And was he, on the other hand, willing to criticize the government when this support was lacking?[38] Such questions are always difficult to answer definitively, especially given Constant's high hopes for playing a serious political role.[39] But, for all Constant's ambitions for a public role, it is difficult to accept that he sacrificed principle to expediency. He never deviated from his stated liberal political agenda; what changed was his evaluation of the political forces at play and his assessment of the relationship of these forces to the survival of the representative regime. Constant also did not hesitate to defend his honor when such charges were made. In mid-1798, following the unsuccessful campaign for the Assembly, and resulting from the nasty articles published in *L'Ami des Lois*, Constant had a duel with Georges Sibuet, one of the owners of the newspaper. Fortunately, the duel in the Bois de Boulogne concluded with no injuries, with reconciliation, and with a public apology from Sibuet.[40] If Constant's liberalism was a balance of competing principles—as I have argued above— his maneuverings in the summer of 1797 were not a betrayal of his position.

The fallout from all of this, in any event, was Constant's new criticism of the government for both its foreign and domestic policy. Constant expressed opposition to the government's policy objective of "liberating" Switzerland.[41] In France itself, he began to oppose the repressive measures of the government. He was now prepared to give up his *carte blanche* support for a new position, one not unlike that of members of the moderate constitutional opposition before the coup.[42] He now seemed ready to position himself not necessarily *with* the Directors, but *between* the Directors and the die-hard opponents of the regime, royalist or neo-Jacobins. This meant that he might need to defend the constitution *against* the government. Given Constant's growing unease with the repressions by the government, it is not surprising that he reconciled with Roederer (a prominent member of the moderate opposition) in a meeting at Coppet in the summer of 1798. For all of Constant's new criticism of the government, his political objectives and his pragmatic stance remained remarkably consistent. The goal, a liberal representative regime, was always the same. What changed in mid-1798 was the context for this agenda. Constant's assessments of the appropriate moves shifted accordingly. In 1795–97, he believed that the survival of the constitutional regime required curious legal initiatives (like the Two-Thirds Law) and, more radical, extra-legal interventions (like the coup of 1797). He did not wish to impose unrepresentative institutions, nor did he wish to elevate the suspension of legal norms into a principle. He wished to protect legality and constitutionalism, but judged that this occasionally required some extraordinary actions, namely the elevation into power of individuals and administrations that would protect liberty and prevent tyranny—in short, protect the constitutional regime. Basically, in this period Constant did not yet have sufficient faith in the political maturity of the French political class; hence, extraordinary actions were sometimes required to protect the constitutional regime. He feared that strong and destructive political passions, resulting from monarchical traditions and the torrent unleashed by the revolution, would combine with powerful anti-constitutional political groups to overwhelm the constitutional order. In the months following the Fructidor coup, and growing in intensity following the elections of spring 1798, his assessment of context and the reliability of government officials changed. The Republic still needed to be led by republicans. As he himself put it in his speech of 27 February 1798, it was important "to confide only to republicans the functions of the republic."[43] But he now worried that the government itself might threaten the constitutional order. It was pursuing a dangerous foreign policy, and it was introducing new repressive legislation. Hence, the protection of the constitutional order required a stricter adherence to legal regularity.

## The Consequences of Counter-Revolution

In early July 1799, Constant published *Des suites de la contre-révolution de 1660 en Angleterre*. Focusing, as the title suggests, on the English restoration of the monarchy in 1660, its message was directed to political actors in France in 1799, another difficult year for the Republic. Not only did French armies suffer some serious setbacks during the spring against the Second Coalition (French armies were forced to evacuate most of Italy), but domestically France continued to be unstable. The Left was strengthened by success in the legislative elections of Germinal, an VII (9–18 April 1799).[44] Now in control of the Councils, they began to flex their muscle. On 30 Prairial an VII (18 June 1799), they forced the resignation of three of the Directors— Jean-Baptiste Treilhard, Louis-Marie de La Révellière-Lépeaux, and Philippe-Antoine Merlin de Douai—replacing them with Louis-Jérôme Gohier, Pierre-Roger Ducos, and General Jean-François Moulin. In the aftermath of this reconfiguration of the Directory, they instituted laws reminiscent of the emergency measures of 1793. On 27 June, for example, the government passed a "Forced Loan" to be levied on the rich. On 10 and 12 July, it approved the "Law of Hostages," which gave departmental administrations the power to take as hostages the parents of *émigrés* and their allies and, further, to deport four of these persons for each patriot assassinated. On the other political extreme, the counter-revolutionaries were gaining strength in provincial centers such as Toulouse. Combined with the losses by the army, this gave royalists new hope that the Republic could be defeated. Finally, there was talk of a compromise between former republicans and monarchists to overturn the Republic and institute a constitutional monarchy.

In these lights, Constant, like other moderates, continued to worry about the stability of the Republic. His correspondence is filled with his concerns.[45] To his aunt, he lamented that "I believe that the revolution has exhausted its physical and moral ardor, and that we are at the point at which M. Buffon maintains that all ought to die."[46] To Sieyès, who was elected to the executive of the Directory on 18 May 1799, Constant wrote that he viewed him as "the last hope for the Republic, this poor Republic, which, for eighteen months has had to fight against immorality and foolishness."[47] Constant recounted years later that at this time he hoped that Sieyès, who he saw almost daily, would be "the principal mover of this modification" so needed by the Republic.[48]

Constant's book was a response to the political maneuverings of the various parties during this period, but it was directly precipitated by two recently published books: one by Boulay de la Meurthe entitled *Essai sur les causes qui, en 1649, amenèrent en Angleterre l'établissememt de la république;*[49] the second by Joseph de Maistre entitled *Considérations sur la France.*[50] The book by Boulay de la Meurthe focused on the excesses of the republican forces in England in 1649, excesses that he claimed had led to the restoration of the Stuart monarchy in 1660. Its message to the domestic French audience was this: a neo-Jacobin victory was dangerous because it could easily lead to political turmoil and a restoration of the monarchy. In terms of domestic political debate, therefore, the book had a clear anti-Jacobin agenda. Not surprisingly it was greeted with enthusiasm by French royalists. Constant's book responded by examining the same period of English history, but focusing not on the failures of the republicans, but rather on the excesses of the monarchical forces in England *after* the restoration of the Stuart monarchy in 1660. The "lesson" to be drawn from this history was, therefore, quite different from Boulay de la Meurthe's. The danger was allowing a restoration of the monarchy. The book had, therefore, an anti-royalist agenda. This does not mean that Constant disagreed with Boulay de la Meurthe's claim that neo-Jacobinism was dangerous, something that Constant also believed. What it demonstrates is how concerned Constant was about the strength of the royalists, and about their hopes for a monarchical restoration. Given what we know of the politics of both Boulay de la Meurthe and Constant, it seems clear that they both were wary of the growing power of the extremes. In fact, the message of the two works, considered jointly, was that either a neo-Jacobin revival *or* a royalist revival would be dangerous.

Constant's differences with Joseph de Maistre were more straightforward. Maistre had argued in the last chapter (chapter 11) of *Considérations sur la France*, published in April 1797 just before the Fructidor coup, that the French Revolution would inevitably follow the same course as the English Revolution, and that, therefore, the ultimate outcome (which for Maistre meant the providentially ordained outcome) would be a restoration of the monarchy. Maistre's chapter was entitled "Fragment d'une Histoire de la Révolution française, par David Hume," and it relied a good deal on citations from David Hume's *History of England*, used anachronistically (Hume, who died in 1776, obviously had never written about the French Revolution) to make his own point about the inevitability of a restoration. Moreover, the previous chapter of Maistre's work (chapter 10), was entitled "Des prétendus dangers d'une contre-révolution," and it was a pointed rejoinder to the argument Constant had made in 1797 in his *De la force du gouvernement actuel.*[51] Constant, as we have seen above, had argued that any counter-revolution was essentially a new revolution, one that was likely to be more bloody than its predecessor. Maistre never mentioned Constant by name in *Considérations sur la France,* but we know from his correspondence that he intended his work to respond to "this half-baked work of Constant" [*"ce petit drôle de Constant"*] and to "his vile pamphlet" [*"son vilain pamphlet"*].[52] In the chapter in *Considérations sur la France,* Maistre dismissed the dangers of a counter-revolution and recommended the restoration of the monarchy, which "far from producing the evils that you fear for the future, will end those that consume us today." He tried to assure those who worked for the counter-revolution that "all your efforts will be positive; you will destroy only destruction."[53] Constant, in his new work, argued that a counter-revolution was not inevitable, reemphasizing his earlier point that counter-revolution equaled a more brutal and destructive revolution. To make his arguments, he also turned to the works of famous English historians like Hume,[54] but reframed them to make his own polemical points against Maistre.

Constant referred to *De suites de la contre-révolution* in his correspondence as *"un ouvrage de circonstance,"* indicating that his principal intention was to intervene in the political dialogue taking place in France.[55] He was very unhappy with some of the new laws that the neo-Jacobin French government had passed following the elections of the spring of 1799, characterizing them in a public address as "violent, absurd, and prosecutorial."[56] In his correspondence, he mentioned "his aversion against most of the [recent] measures taken, under the pretext of consolidating the Republic,"[57] and specifically referred to the new laws passed by the government as "disgraceful and useless."[58] He also explicitly distanced himself from the government in *De suites de la contre-révolution,* stating that "Our misfortunes without doubt come from the dictatorship granted to the Directory."[59] Nonetheless, for all his distaste for the government and its new heavy-handed legislation, he remained convinced that an even greater danger was presented by the potential success of the counter-revolution in France. This would lead to the persecution of everyone associated with the Revolution and to the destruction of the constitutional order.

Constant made this argument, first indirectly but then directly, by examining the reaction that had taken place in England after the restoration of 1660. He is unrelenting in his criticism of Charles II and the government, which promised moderation at the outset, but subsequently institutionalized revenge. Constant singled out for criticism the duplicity of the government, the persecution of prominent republicans, the renewal of religious intolerance, and the seizure of property.[60] "The Parliament resuscitated the most tyrannical statutes of a forgotten jurisprudence. The spirit of servitude, distrusting even of itself, and troubled with the lights which surrounded it, evoked past centuries of widespread barbarism, searching them for laws, tortures, and irons."[61] The new regime destroyed not only legal regularity and religious toleration, it corrupted English mores. It carried out heavy-handed punishments that were cruel and inhumane: "to the excess of injustice was joined the refinements of cruelty."[62] The government even instituted a law that made having had a *conversation* with a republican rebel a treasonous act.[63]

The implication, of course, was that any victory of the counter-revolution in France would lead to similar persecutions and similar excesses; it would bring about, in his own words, "monarchical despotism."[64] Indeed, Constant argued that the reaction in France would be even worse than the reaction had been in England after 1660, partly because it would be influenced by the reactionary forces aligned in Europe against the French Republic. He, therefore, implored the French government to protect itself against the reaction, but also to avoid the sort of authoritarian actions that could only encourage radical opposition on both extremes. He was critical of the continuing tendency of the government to overstep its legal boundaries. Looking back *now* on the coup of 18 Fructidor (September 4, 1797), he saw it as the first of a series of executive coups that eroded confidence in the constitutional order.

> It is not possible to forget the departure from national representation on 18 fructidor, or the departure of the Directory on 28 prairial [the date of the reorganization of the government in 1799], and no supernatural power will descend from the sky to suddenly persuade us that that which has happened twice, without obstacles, will not repeat itself.[65]

It was necessary, in short, to respect the constitution. If changes needed to be introduced, he now suggested that the appropriate pathway was constitutional revision. This was, in fact (and as he hints in this work), the precise focus of his attention at this time, as we see below when we consider another of his writings of this period, *Fragments d'un ouvrage abandonné sur la possibilité d'une constitution républicaine dans un grand pays.*[66] Constant ends his article with a clarion call for adherence to the principles of the revolution—abolition of hereditary privilege; national sovereignty; representative government; the division of power. And he implores the divisive voices representing the various radical factions in France to pull together to help generate a public spirit that will encourage enthusiasm, respect morality, and stimulate virtue.[67]

## Liberalism Confronts Anarchism: William Godwin

In the late-1790s, Constant became intensely interested in William Godwin, the famous English political theorist and novelist: the author of (among other things) *Enquiry Concerning Political Justice* (1793) and *Caleb Williams* (1794). He read Godwin's *Caleb Williams* and worked on a translation of his *Enquiry Concerning Political Justice*. Why this fascination with Godwin, who notoriously called for the elimination of all government and attacked the institution of property? What does this tell us about Constant's evolving politics? What does it tell us about his stance concerning how intellectuals should engage in (or with) politics?

The answers to these questions have personal, political, and intellectual dimensions. Personally, Constant was frustrated by his electoral failures. Immediately following his unsuccessful attempt to gain national office in 1798, he commented in his correspondence that he was enjoying the natural beauties of the spring time, and that he was returning with enthusiasm to his work on religion, the intellectual enterprise that throughout his life he considered his most important.[68] But, as so often in his life when separated from active politics, he very quickly turned to writing about politics. Part of his purpose was, no doubt, to chart a path for the unstable Republic—the purpose, as we have just seen, of *Des suites de la contre-révolution*. He also, however, wished to salvage his political reputation against those who had accused him of being a closet monarchist. This double agenda is the context of Constant's decision to translate Godwin's *Enquiry Concerning Political Justice*.

We have, unfortunately, very little explicit information concerning Constant's initial reaction to Godwin and his ideas. In March 1796, he wrote to Isabelle de Charrière that Godwin's novel *Caleb Williams* was "a work in which there are passages which drag on, but which has a very great and very new merit."[69] In a letter to Comtesse Anne-Marie-Pauline-Andrienne de Naussau in October 1798, Constant was probably referring to Godwin when he mentioned "an English author" who stated "that property always belongs rightly to those who have the greatest need."[70] It is about the time of this second letter (autumn 1798) that Constant began the translation of Godwin's *Enquiry Concerning Political Justice*. The first explicit mention of this translation is in a letter to Ludwig Ferdinand Huber on 27 November 1798.[71] He refers to it in subsequent correspondence during 1798 and 1799.[72] Constant ceased working on the translation at the end of 1799 or beginning of 1800. The translation was not published during his lifetime.[73]

In an unpublished essay written in 1810, Constant emphasized the political purpose that led him to translate Godwin:

> In bringing myself to this work, I had a goal that I believed useful. At a time when some men…were throwing disfavor on the principles of liberty, exercising in the name of these principles many vexations of tyranny, I wanted to prove that it was not liberty that caused this tyranny, but its pretended defenders. I had, consequently, chosen a writer very exaggerated in his opinions, but an enemy nonetheless of all systems of violence and of all measures of persecution.[74]

If this, although entirely retrospective, is an accurate portrayal of his attitude a decade previously, the translation was directly related to his political goal of defending the principles of the Revolution and avoiding recourse to violence and persecution.

Etienne Hofmann has remarked that Constant's translation of Godwin must be seen as a "*machine de guerre contre les jacobins.*"[75] This is partly right, in that it was an attempt to stake out a position in support of the principles of the Revolution that, at the same time, was critical of the Jacobins who were gaining power in the Directory government in 1798–99. It was also, however, an attempt by Constant to defend his reputation from the charge of being a monarchist. To understand why Godwin was ideal for this careful balancing act, we need to say something about Godwin's ideas.

During the mid-1790s, Godwin was the most famous intellectual representative of British radicalism. This was based on the influence of his famous work *Enquiry Concerning Political Justice*, first published in 1793, and on his prominent public role during the 1794 Treason Trials. He was widely admired by fellow English radicals who celebrated the French Revolution and revered by many young romantic poets. This singular popularity did not last long. In 1795, he had a public argument with John Thelwall, a leader of the militant wing of the London Corresponding Society (LCS) who advocated unlimited popular agitation to compel the government to grant reform. Godwin's more moderate position, insisting on nonviolent persuasion, alienated many of his Left-wing admirers. In spite of this relatively moderate position on violence and revolution, however, conservative propagandists identified Godwin with the radical phase of the French Revolution. And, because he was opposed to private property and marriage, he offered an ideal target for all who wished to protect the status quo.

Given that Godwin was the English political theorist most identified with a defense of the principles of the French Revolution, one might expect to find Godwin advocating a political system that was republican or constitutional monarchist. He embraced neither, arguing in Book III of *Political Justice* for the wholesale elimination of government. There are passages in *Political Justice*, especially in the early part, where Godwin defended democracy, but his advocacy was essentially negative in the sense that he saw it as the least pernicious form of government given current levels of human intelligence and progress. Rejecting the idea that the state was the legitimate locus of sovereignty, he called for its gradual elimination, a progressive dismantling of all compulsory restraints, including laws and government. "[S]ince government, even in its best state, is an evil, the object principally to be aimed at is that we should have as little of it as the general peace of human society will permit."[76] Godwin criticized the theory of complex and balanced government; and he faulted any government interference in intellectual life. He argued that it is morally preferable for each person to govern him/herself without the imposition of any compulsory restraint. Even representative governments, therefore, are defective. And, elections are only shams that bring out the most questionable of human characteristics: inflated rhetoric and demagoguery on the part of the political figures; obsequiousness and timidity among the general populace. Godwin was so distrustful of group decisions that he even opposed political "associations," seeing them as encouraging "impetuosity and incontinence of temper" rather than the dictates of sober reason.[77] Constant was attracted to Godwin because he had unimpeachable revolutionary credentials. In 1798 and 1799, when Constant found himself attacking the Jacobins and being accused of being a closet monarchist, this was useful. On the other hand, there is no indication that Constant ever accepted Godwin's famous arguments against law, government, and property; indeed, everything we know about Constant's views suggests the opposite. In 1810, for example, Constant suggested that Godwin's stances on a number of issues were so bizarre that they required no disputation. But, one must wonder if Constant's stance was so rigid in 1798–99; perhaps the intellectual engagement with Godwin helped clarify his own stance on the importance of certain constitutional forms. The months devoted to the translation did overlap with Constant's work on another manuscript focusing on "the possibility of a republic in a large country."

But there was a fundamental divergence between Godwin and Constant: Constant supported government itself, political associations, and the give-and-take of social and political life, while Godwin insisted that intellectual liberty and private conversations would be sufficient to bridge the divisions among individuals about collective concerns. As Constant would put it in 1810, the "moral part" of Godwin's work, "where he develops the needs of individuals among themselves, is entirely defective. As the most scrupulous veracity is one of the distinctive traits of his character and his writings, I believe him [Godwin] of good faith in his paradoxes on pity, recognition, promises, etc. But his ideas denote such an ignorance of man in society, resulting, one says, with a life purely contemplative, that, as bizarre as they are, they scarcely merit the pain of being refuted."[78]

Moreover, Constant never retreated from accepting popular sovereignty. What Constant did recognize, at variance here with many of his contemporaries, was that popular sovereignty could be as dangerous for liberty as the monarchical authority of the Old Regime, especially when popular sovereignty was centralized in the state, and when there were no other powers to check the will and action of the sovereign state. Constant would later accuse Rousseau and Mably of having prepared the theoretical foundations for the dangerous revolutionary claim that there was no real difference between society and the state. For Rousseau, the general will of society was synonymous with the will of the state; society and the state were simply one another in different guises. According to Constant, this allowed an excessive concentration of power; and the worst manifestations of such a concentration of power were counter-revolution on the Right and Terror on the Left. Moreover, Rousseau's recommendation that ancient liberty, reliant on virtue, was appropriate for a modern regime overlooked the new dispensation of liberty in modernity, where citizens were looking above all for repose. Constant's most famous articulations of this theory were in *De l'esprit de conquête et de l'usurpation* (published in 1814) and in his 1819 lecture *De la liberté des Anciens et à celle des Modernes* but he was making similar points in his writings of the late-1790s (see below).

Constant believed that popular sovereignty required plural powers, and he argued that each locus of power must be constrained by some other power. This was true even if all bodies with power ultimately gained legitimacy from the same source—popular sovereignty. Plural powers were essential. The Old Regime had a number of powers exterior to society—namely, the King and the Church. The Revolution had destroyed these, and had thereby collapsed the state into society. The new regime required a constitution that legitimated and guaranteed competing sites of authority to challenge claims for one absolute sovereign.

This insight led Constant to reject Godwin's attack on the state. Godwin famously argued that the state was the single most dangerous institution to the liberty of individuals. When contemplating the power of the state during the Terror, Constant was inclined to agree—this, in part, may explain Constant's interest in translating Godwin into French. But, Constant rejected Godwin's stance because he understood that, in the modern world, it was naive to believe that the elimination of the state would create the conditions for the preservation of liberty. Instead, the state must be one institution in a larger polity. A proper political system placed power in many locations other than the state. Constant, like Godwin, favored the freedoms of society against the state. He did not, like Godwin, believe that one could sustain society *without* the state. To put it another way, Constant did not see the state, as Thomas Paine did, as a necessary evil. The state had a positive role to play; it must help guarantee liberty. There is a long passage in Constant's 1810 manuscript article on Godwin that states this clearly:

> The political part of Godwin is thus the only important part. It is not that this part of his thought is exempt from great errors. It begins with a principle fault. Government, he says, is a necessary evil. This idea...is...completely erroneous. Government has a sphere which is proper to it.... When it leaves its sphere, it becomes evil, an incalculable evil; but this is not in the nature of government, it is as usurpation that it is an evil....This is not a thing of indifference. When one declares government evil, one hopes to inspire in men a salutary defiance against government. But, as the need of government always makes itself felt, such is not the effect one produces. It happens only that governments adopt this doctrine: they resign themselves to being an evil. They represent as inevitable all the evil that they cause....[79]

The state, in short, could use the doctrine "government is always evil" to justify truly evil actions. States can and do perform evil acts (*viz.* the Terror), but this need not be the case. Indeed, it will not be the case if the state respects the appropriate limitations to its reach. Another way to state Constant's position *vis-à-vis* Godwin would be that Constant wanted to realize Godwin's anti-statist aspirations (the protection of individual freedoms within civil society) through the beneficent agency of the constitutional state. However attracted Constant was to a position like Godwin's that opposed the state, he consistently favored a constitutional state that recognized its primary role in the defense of liberty.

There were portions of Godwin's work that Constant found more attractive. First, there is Godwin's belief that historical progress is brought about only through human thought and innovation. Godwin wrote in *The New Annual Register* for 1788: "It was long a kind of problem in philosophy, whether or not the human species collectively, like the intellectual powers of the individual, were in a state of gradual progress.... This problem is hastening fast to a decision. Liberty, humanity, and science are daily extending, and bid fair to render despotism, cruelty, and ignorance subjects of historical memory."[80] He echoed these thoughts in *Enquiry Concerning Political Justice*, claiming that mankind is perfectible, which he defined as "the faculty of being continually made better and receiving perpetual improvement."[81] Constant did not believe in perfectibility, but he did believe in progress, in the continuing improvement of humanity.

Constant also liked Godwin's attack on monarchy, aristocracy, and the prejudices engendered by hereditary privileges. Godwin devoted many pages of *Enquiry Concerning Political Justice* to a critical analysis of the mores (such as dissimulation and self-love) and the social relations (defined by money and power) that were encouraged under monarchies. Such mores, according to Godwin, are corrosive of the positive sentiment of "sincerity."

As long as the practice of courts is cabal, as long as the unvarying tendency of cabal is to tear down talents, and discourage virtue, to recommend cunning in the room of sincerity, a servile and supple disposition in preference to firmness and inflexibility, a pliant and selfish morality as better than an ingenuous one, and the study of the red book of promotion rather than the study of the general welfare, so long will monarchy be the bitterest and most potent of all the adversaries of the true interests of mankind.[82]

Godwin's depiction of the nature of monarchy combined analyses of dispositions and traits that earlier eighteenth-century political theorists like Montesquieu had identified with both monarchy and despotism. Constant found this attentiveness to sentiment and *moeurs* very salutary.

For Godwin, political reform required "the discovery of political truth" through quiet contemplation, temperate interchange between two persons, and rational reflection.[83] He was, as this indicates, a rationalist, believing that we are obliged and motivated to act in accordance with truths perceived through discussion and private judgment, not in accordance with the passions stimulated by harangues and declamation. This faith that reason could direct behavior came largely from Godwin's Sandemanian religious background, reinforced by the powerful currents within English radical religious dissent.[84] From both, Godwin took his belief in an elevated ideal of moral right and reason; a belief that one can overcome selfishness and pity by practicing "benevolence." In 1791, when Godwin reflected about the project that would become *Enquiry Concerning Political Justice*, he wrote the following: "It was my first determination to tell all that I apprehended to be truth, which by its inherent energy and weight, should overbear and annihilate all opposition and place the principles of politics on an immoveable basis."[85]

Godwin's rationalist predisposition, however—his advocacy of the rule of reason over human nature and human affairs—does not mean that he denied all emotion, or held a narrow rationalist view of morality. For Godwin, as for most thinkers during the eighteenth century, such rigid oppositions were not assumed; indeed, they were explicitly rejected. He did not claim that feelings, affections, passions were not important. He only wished to claim that they were not sufficient to point to correct action. Godwin was a rationalist who believed that reason should not be a slave to passions and emotion, even if it was dependent on them. Both passions and emotions were thus recognized and embraced, but they need to be guided by reason, which was to be the final arbiter. Godwin did not share Hutcheson's belief that there was some innate moral sense that could point to correct action. Nor did he share Adam Smith's and David Hume's belief that humans were guided by social affection. Reason was essential. But, once reason determined the correctness of a principle or stance, it must be invigorated by emotion. "[W]ithout doubt," he wrote, "passion cannot be eradicated.... Virtue, sincerity, justice and all those principles which are begotten and cherished in us by a due exercise of reason will never be very strenuously espoused till they are ardently loved.... In this sense nothing is necessary but to show us that a thing is truly good and worthy to be desired, in order to excite in us a passion for its attainment."[86] Emotion was to provide a supportive, not a directive, role. "We must," as he puts it in *Political Justice*, "bring everything to the standard of reason."[87] But once recognized, we must be animated with a passion for its attainment and/or realization. As D.H. Monro has put it, "So far from wishing to sacrifice emotion to reason, Godwin wants reason to be charged with emotion."[88]

A comprehensive view of understanding and right action, therefore, had as much to do with feeling, emotion, and imagination, as it had to do with rigorous analytic cerebration. This is one reason why Godwin wrote novels that traced and dissected the conflicting motives of characters. His famous first novel, *Caleb Williams* (published in 1794), is a psychological novel. In 1832, Godwin wrote that during the writing of *Caleb Williams* he had been "engaged in exploring the entrails of mind and motive."[89] It was an analysis "of the private and internal operations of the mind" that had proceeded by employing a "metaphysical dissecting knife in tracing and laying bare the involutions of motive, and recording the gradually accumulating impulses, which led the personages I had to describe primarily to adopt the particular way of proceeding in which they afterwards embarked."[90] *Caleb Williams* is much as Godwin suggests. At its center is an analysis of the dangers of a "misguided love of fame." Concern for his reputation and "honor" leads one of the principle protagonists of the novel, Falkland, to commit horrible deeds, including murder, and to be forever burdened with what Godwin refers to as a "morbid sensibility."[91] Like his other novels, one of its main themes is the wretchedness of the individual who is cut off from sympathetic communion with others.

Constant, as we have seen, was also strongly supportive of "sensibility," believing that it had important personal, political, and social functions. And, like Godwin, Constant believed that reason and emotion must cooperate. But, again, there were important differences in Godwin's and Constant's stance. In the unpublished essay written in 1810 (from which I have already quoted), Constant stated his reservations clearly. He referred to Godwin's *Enquiry concerning Political Justice* as a book

> that reunites the most pure and just principles of liberty with the most bizarre paradoxes.... Its moral part, that where he develops the needs of individuals among themselves, is entirely defective.... [H]is ideas denote such an ignorance of man in society, resulting, one says, with a life purely contemplative, that, as bizarre as they are, they scarcely merit the pain of being refuted. It is not in stifling the most gentle affection that one will give happiness to the human species.... The most precious part of private existence over which society ought to have no authority, is to surround oneself with favored beings, with cherished beings, with close friends.[92]

In his writings of these years, Constant referred to sentiments such as self-respect, compassion, and enthusiasm as essential for a stable liberal society. He was especially worried that the "devastating torrent" of the Revolution in France had unleashed passions that would undermine a stable liberal politics. At one extreme was the impatience and intolerance characteristic of political fanaticism. At the other extreme he worried about self-absorption, passivity, and narrow self-interest, which he believed had been encouraged under the Old Regime monarchy and had resurfaced in the late-1790s.[93]

The most significant common ground between Constant and Godwin, however, was the commitment to radical reform that avoided radical violence. Godwin, like Constant, was a moderate. As early as 1793, Godwin attacked "the intemperate advocates of reform,"[94] and, in *Enquiry Concerning Political Justice*, Godwin attacked revolution in favor of "gradual, but uninterrupted change.... [I]f conviction of the understanding be the compass which is to direct our proceedings in the general affairs, we shall have many reforms, but no revolutions. As it is only in a gradual manner that the public can be instructed, a violent explosion in the community is by no means the most likely to happen as a result of instruction. Revolutions are the produce of passion, not of sober and tranquil reason."[95]

Godwin devoted a chapter of *Political Justice* to the subject of "revolutions," and the consistent message of these pages is to recommend reform and denounce revolution. Progress, he writes, "should take place in a mild and gradual, though incessant advance, not by violent leaps, not by concussions which may expose millions to risk, and sweep generations of men from the stage of existence.... Revolution is engendered by an indignation against tyranny, yet is itself ever more pregnant with tyranny."[96] There is, as he puts it in another passage, a danger when existing institutions are subverted too quickly.[97] Revolutions run the risk of "marring the salutary and uninterrupted progress which might be expected to attend upon political truth and social improvement.... The duty therefore of the true politician is to postpone revolution if he cannot entirely prevent it."[98]

Constant also despaired of the damage that revolutions brought in their wake, something that was especially on his mind in 1798–99, as he contemplated the instability of the French Republic. He was hoping desperately that the Revolution could be brought to a close. In 1817, Constant wrote that Godwin's 1793 edition of *Enquiry Concerning Political Justice* was published "in the moment when the French Revolution, filling Europe with astonishment and terror, engaged all friends of humanity to reflect on the bases of government in order to discover the means to prevent or to extirpate the abuses which had led this crisis to such violence and such disastrous ends."[99] Constant's translation, therefore, must be seen as part of his effort to conceptualize how to defend liberty against the Jacobins on the Left and monarchists on the Right. The dates on which Constant worked on the translation of Godwin's book are especially relevant because they frame the rapidly shifting political context. Constant ultimately decided against publishing his translation, and it is difficult not to conclude that this was because of the change from the Directory to the Consulate. With the rise to power of Napoleon, it was no longer necessary to demonstrate one's revolutionary credentials by staking out a position in support of the principles of the Revolution, but in opposition to the Jacobins.

But, if Constant's interest in Godwin was in part to design a moderate position in the specific political maneuverings of the late-1790s, it was also an attempt to clarify fundamental political issues. That is, it also was expressive of Constant's wider itinerary of conceptualizing a modern liberal politics. Constant's confrontation with the ideas of Godwin led to a maturation of Constant's political ideas. The confrontation led Constant to clarify his liberal political stance; as he put it in a letter to his uncle, it "had only confirmed me in my inclination for republican government."[100] It forced him to mark out the divide between anarchism and liberalism.

## The Possibility of a Republic in a Large Country

During these same years Constant began to consider more systematically the institutional framework entailed by his moderate republican position. The clearest articulation of this is in an unpublished manuscript, *Fragments d'un ouvrage abandonné sur la possibilité d'une constitution républicaine dans un grand pays*.[101] Mostly composed between 1798 and 1803, finished only in 1807 or 1808, and published only in 1991, it is a very revealing document. In the *Fragments*, Constant faced the problem of outlining the contours of a regime that would protect the reforms of the Revolution, but which would avoid the dangers of further upheaval and violence.[102] He confronted, in short, what he had called in his earlier brochure (and has been frequently referred to since) as the issue of *"terminer la Révolution"*—of how "to close the Revolution." Having rejected the anarchist alternative, he believed he needed to give serious attention to what political institutions he could support.

The influence of Germaine de Staël and of her father Jacques Necker is clearly in evidence in the *Fragments*, most notably in

Constant's positive orientation toward the English Constitution.
Necker had published in 1792 *Du pouvoir exécutif dans les grands Etats*,
which eulogized the English constitutional monarchy, and in 1796
*De la Révolution française*, which analyzed the constitutions of 1791
and 1795. Necker preferred an English style monarchy to a republic, but he devoted considerable attention to the separation and balance of authority among the various branches of government. He
also insisted that, when considering the appropriate constitutional
arrangements for a particular society, it was important to take into
consideration the extent of territory, the history of a country, and the
"general spirit" of the people. These Montesquieuian themes would
recur in Constant's thought.[103]

The communion with the ideas of Germaine de Staël was even
more pronounced. This was the period when Germaine and
Benjamin were lovers; and on 8 June 1797, Germaine gave birth to
a girl, Albertine de Staël, Constant's daughter. It seems highly prob-
able that the political writings of Staël and Constant during the
late-1790s were essentially joint projects, though they had minor
political disagreements. In 1795, Staël published *Réflexions sur la paix
intérieure*, which argued for support of the government by moderates of the Right and Left. In 1796, De Staël published *De l'influence
des passions sur le bonheur des individus et des nations*, which recommended sensibility and enthusiasm.[104] In both of these works there
are passages similar to passages in Constant's works of these same
years. Moreover, in *De l'influence des passions* Staël announced that
there would follow a treatise on politics that would indicate how to
unify the arts, sciences, and letters so vaunted in monarchies, with
the independence of Republics.[105] She announced, in short, that she
was writing a more explicitly republican work. She never, in fact,
published such a book, but we do know that during 1798 she worked
on a manuscript, published only in 1906, entitled *Des circonstances
actuelles qui peuvent terminer la Révolution et des principes qui doivent
fonder la République en France*.[106] Henri Grange has argued, convincingly, that Constant worked with Staël on *Des circonstances actuelles*.
Staël decided, however, that it was inopportune to publish this manuscript, and thereupon turned her attention to the composition of
the work that was later published as *De la littérature considérée dans
ses rapports avec les institutions sociales* (published in 1800). Constant
took over portions of *Des circonstances actuelles* as his own, continued to rework it, and transformed it into a work that more directly

reflected his own preoccupations. This manuscript is *Fragments d'un ouvrage abandonné*.[107]
Other influences are harder to weigh precisely, but were clearly important. There are frequent references in the manuscript to Montesquieu, a staple of any discussion of the composition of governments during this era. Most of these passages point to Constant's differences with his illustrious predecessor. We also know that, during this period, Constant read in manuscript Jean-Charles-Léonard Sismondi's *Recherche sur les constitutions des peuples libres*. And we know, as well, that during 1799 Constant frequently saw Sieyès, who, of course, had his own numerous constitutional plans. Constant and Sieyès shared a rejection of hereditary privilege and support of a representative system that included a complex executive structure (see below). But there were important differences: Constant supported the direct election of representatives, while Sieyès recommended indirect election, as did other contemporaries like Cabanis and Roederer. Sieyès at this time also advocated the governmental structure created by the constitution of an VIII (1799), which specified that the executive would introduce legislation, while the legislative assemblies would deliberate and vote on legislation. Constant rejected this separation, arguing that the executive should not have a monopoly on the introduction of legislation.

Analysis of Constant's work is complicated by the fact that it was written over many years, including those that followed Napoleon's *coup d'état* of 18 Brumaire (November 1799). At first, Constant's reaction to Napoleon's coup was mixed.[108] Very soon, however, Constant became a critic of the new regime, as his speeches in the *Tribunat* (he was a member from December 1799 to March 1802) and his actions and writings of the next years clearly reveal, and as analyzed below. Brumaire also affected the *Fragments d'un ouvrage abandonné*. In those sections composed before Napoleon's coup, Constant focused his analysis on the Constitution of Year III (1795); he was concerned with reforms that would provide political stability while at the same time assuring individual liberty. He hoped, in short, to reform this constitution. After Brumaire, when it obviously was too late to fix the Constitution of 1795, Constant's emphasis shifted to explaining the failure of this Constitution and to pondering the means for preventing such failures in the future.[109] Parallel and closely linked, Constant's pleadings in favor of a Republic were now joined by attacks on the regime that had killed it. These attacks included references to elements of the

Constitutions of 1799 and 1802. The tone of the work also changed, with more emphasis on the elaboration of a general political theory. This trenchant criticism of Napoleonic regime(s) goes a long way toward explaining why the work was not published. Some sections were so aggressive that they likely would have led, if made public or discovered by the police, to Constant's exile or imprisonment. Pages of this manuscript found echoes in his 1806 manuscript *Principes de politique applicables à tous les gouvernements* [published in 1980]. And, later, Constant reworked some of the passages for inclusion in his well-known works of the late-Empire, first Restoration and Hundred Days: *De l'esprit de conquête et de l'usurpation* (published in 1814); *Réflexions sur les constitutions, la distribution des pouvoirs et les garanties dans une monarchie constitutionnelle* (1814); *Principes de politiques applicables à tous les gouvernements représentatifs et particulière-ment à la Constitution actuelle de la France* (1815). It is clear from this text, however, that the essentials of Constant's constitutional thought did not wait for these works of 1814–1815; the details of his constitutionalism were formulated during the Directory and Consulate.

Constant, as the title of his manuscript indicates, believed that a republic was possible in a large country. This was a thesis at odds with that of most previous writers, who had argued that a republic was appropriate only for a small territory. Constant believed that a republic was particularly suited to France because of the specific historical situation in which it found itself.[110] Central here was the fact that a privileged nobility had been undermined by the Enlightenment and, more broadly, by the egalitarian ideal of civil equality. He found the Montesquieuian "principle" of *honor* "a confused, vain, uncertain sentiment, which finds its success in pleasing power,"[111] and clearly not suitable for a modern regime. Moreover, because the monarchy in France had been dismantled during the Revolution, any attempt to reestablish it would require a new revolution. But, the republic that France needed—and here the filiation with the ideas of Necker is evident—should parallel the constitutional and representative aspects of the monarchical regime in England.

The focus of *Fragments d'un ouvrage abandonné* is the elaboration of a constitution for a society based upon popular sovereignty in which the citizens would enjoy the most liberty possible. Two of the principal themes—popular sovereignty and liberty—were to become central tropes in all of Constant's future political writings. By liberty,

Constant meant the right for each individual to realize his or her aspirations and desires. This was not an absolute right, however, because human beings were social animals and must be cognizant of the potentially conflicting aspirations and liberties of others. One obvious implication of this was that political institutions were essential for mediating conflicting interests. However seductive Constant had found the libertarian vision of William Godwin, he was never convinced that rational interchange between individuals without government would, of itself, produce political stability and social justice. As we have seen, however, he was attracted to Godwin's faith in progress, so that the realization of a constitutional liberal regime would mark a new stage in humanity's positive development.

Constant also differed considerably from seventeenth-century predecessors who attempted imaginatively to reconstruct the pre-social, pre-political state. Constant rejected the notion that there was a "state of nature" to which one appealed for the theoretical defense of liberty. There was no contract—real or hypothetical—that defined the degree to which individuals alienated their liberty to the general will. But, even if individuals were not *de facto* prior to society, they were *logically* prior to society. That is, they possessed "rights independent of all association."[112] The protection of these liberties was one of the main purposes of laws and political institutions.

*Fragments d'un ouvrage abandonné* was Constant's defense of the institutions of the constitutional republic that he believed would best protect liberty in France. The work begins with a lengthy critical examination of "the hereditary system," which according to Constant must be contrasted with "the elective system." Constant had attacked "heredity" in *Des réactions politiques* (1797). In this earlier work, he had even gone out of his way to separate himself from the stance of Necker, who in 1791 had defended the principle of heredity with a utilitarian argument.[113] For Constant, the struggle between these two systems—hereditary versus elective—was "the principle question of the French Revolution, which is to say it is the question of the century."[114] Theoretical justifications of the hereditary system, he argued, were unconvincing. Rather than supporting a "natural inequality," as defenders of this system claimed, heredity in fact created an "artificial inequality" that subordinated "the superiority of talents and virtues" to "blind chance."[115] Constant favored "the elective system," which was a more "natural" mode of government, and which "conform[ed] more closely to the principle of equity, [and was] more acceptable to the favored inclinations of mankind."[116] While heredity emerged "from superstition or conquest" and maintained itself "by iniquity,"[117] the idea of equality was "never able to be eliminated from the heart of man."[118] It was human equality that provided the philosophical foundation of just government. Legitimate political authority must emanate from the people, but it must be articulated in a political structure that prevented excess. This double goal—to defend popular sovereignty and to protect individual liberty against excess—provided the unifying positive themes of the work.

Constant devoted a considerable number of pages to differentiating the various types of hereditary regimes, and clearly favored some over others. The most defensible, he argued, was a hereditary monarchy, because its authority rested on the "sanction that time has rendered independent of examination," thus rendering "submission easier and power less touchy [*ombrageuse*]."[119] Tradition, in short, had established long habits of acceptance by the people, and it also had the advantage of educating rulers for the role that they would be expected to perform. A hereditary monarchy was contrasted with the creation of a new monarchy, which would have none of the advantages of habit and tradition, and, therefore, would need to rely solely on force. After existing for a century, such a new monarchy might enjoy the advantages of tradition, but more likely it would fail and the country would endure continuous upheaval as new "usurpers" attempted to assert their control.

Constant also nodded to the argument that a hereditary monarchy benefited by having an established nobility. The nobility could counter the actions of a potentially despotic king; the king, in turn, could protect the people against the potential depredations carried out by the nobility.

> Without doubt, where there is a nobility, it is better that there is a king, because it is better that there is a man who had some interest in defending the people against the nobles. Where there is a king, it is good that there is a nobility, because where a sole individual governs, it is desirable that there are other powerful men to stand up to him.[120]

A *hereditary* monarchy also had the advantage of minimizing the instability that occurred when a new king took power. Constant's concern about the potential agitation and disorder attendant upon transfers of power led him to warn against systems where a monarch was allowed to nominate his successor, or was elected.[121] His references, here, were informed by his observation of the governmental transitions in France during the Revolution, not least that which framed the series of events in which Napoleon was "chosen" by the people. Some hierarchical governments, in sum, were more desirable than others. But, preferable to any such system was the institutional organization of a republic, based on the elective principle. "A republic is able to be excellent from the day of its establishment. A century is needed for a monarchy to be tolerable."[122]

Constant also addressed the cultural dimension. He noted that defenders of the hereditary system pointed to the importance of a financially independent nobility for the cultivation of refinement and elegance. Constant countered that these traits owed more to the progress of civilization and the spread of enlightenment than to hereditary honorifics. And, he pointed to the more unsavory behavior—for example, the harsh and vindictive vanity—that nobility frequently displayed.

Turning his attention specifically to France, he argued that the hereditary system of the late *ancien régime* had become "a singularly bizarre institution." Feudalism had declined, but its residues were apparent everywhere: nobles no longer possessed political power, but they enjoyed honorific privileges.

> Since heredity in France had ceased to be feudal it had become a brilliant decoration, but without precise goal; agreeable to its possessors, but humiliating to those who did not possess it; without real means, and above all without any power against authority. The advantages of the nobility became each day more negative, that is to say they composed themselves more around the exclusions of the lower class than around the positive privileges of the favored class. The nobility was not an intermediate corps which maintained the people in order, and which forced the government into the path of liberty; it was almost an imaginary corporation.[123]

The honorific privileges enjoyed by nobles were no longer as vicious as the feudal inheritances of earlier periods, but they served no positive function and were a constant social irritant. They encouraged a national culture based on habitual servitude to those with more privileges; it perpetuated *moeurs* of dependency and vanity. The order that bestowed such privileges on nobles "had not ceased being humiliating for the rest of the nation, and far from being a guarantee of stability, it contained a thousand seeds of resentments and disorders, without having any power to prevent them."[124]

Constant's criticism of the nobles in *Fragments d'un ouvrage abandonné* became even more strident after the coup of 1799. In passages written before this date, he defended nobles who claimed to be friends of liberty, even suggesting that some nobles represented "civilization." After 1799, he was less accommodating, arguing (in a passage written in 1800) that their actions justified "the accusations of their enemies. These pretended friends of moderation and of enlightenment had become persecutors.... The most irreconcilable enemies of liberty are the nobles."[125]

In the main body of the work, Constant discussed in considerable detail the governmental system that he favored. It should be, first of all, a republic. Though he had many good things to say about an English-style constitutional monarchy, Constant did not believe the English system appropriate for France. It provided a positive, specific reference for Constant, but it was a case apart, a historical and geographical exception that, for all its attractiveness, could not apply to France. He specifically mentioned the geographical insularity of the island nation, the stability of public opinion, the consolidation of the hereditary magistracy (more stable, in Constant's opinion than a hereditary nobility), the strength of legal protections (*habeas corpus*, free press, etc.), and the relatively peaceful change of dynasty in 1688.[126] What France required, because of its different geographic location and history, was a republic. But, it must be a republic that did not concentrate power in one place (as had been the case during the Convention).[127] The separation of powers was a central requirement for protecting liberty under a republic; its absence signaled a dangerous concentration of authority that threatened liberty.

From a slightly different angle, Constant had addressed the English case in his mid-1799 pamphlet *Des suites de la contre-révolution de 1660 en Angleterre*, which highlighted all of the unfortunate things, like confiscations and reprisals, which the English restoration of 1660 had brought in its train. Constant's message to his contemporaries obviously was that they should beware of a monarchical restoration in France: it would likely lead to similar reactions, with a similar concentration of power. There was little possibility, according to him, that France could replicate the extraordinarily unusual convergence of conditions and actions that had produced the constitutional monarchy in England in 1688. A stable hereditary monarchy no longer seemed a viable historical option for France.

Lamentably, what was possible and more likely was a dictatorship. France's cultural traditions and political instability made especially likely the emergence of an authoritarian system based on "warrior virtues."[128] Constant was clearly thinking here of the Convention during the Terror, and also of Napoleon. He argued that even the hereditary monarchy, however lamentable, was very much preferable to the usurpation of a dictator. The former at least ruled by appeal to the sacred rituals of tradition; the latter ruled by offering military glory and by instilling fear. Here, Constant rehearsed the arguments against "usurpation" that were to become a centerpiece of his famous political tracts of the late Empire.

How was the republic to be organized? The most important political body was the legislature, whose function was to make laws and, more generally, "to express the national will."[129] Constant insisted that this body be comprised of two assemblies, and that the members of both be chosen by property owners through direct elections. Here, Constant opposed political colleagues like Staël, Cabanis, Roederer, and Sieyès, who all favored indirect elections, the mode that had been established by the various constitutions of the Revolution. Constant wanted the legislators directly chosen by citizens, who, he hoped, would become closely tied to the republic through this electoral process.[130] The best mode of popular election, he argued, was to allow the electors of each arrondissement to choose a list of fifty candidates and a council of one hundred members. This council would narrow the list of candidates to five; the electors would then be asked to choose their representatives. This would prevent the executive having too much power over the choice of candidates; and it would keep representatives close to their constituents and to the local issues that were their concern. He argued that representatives should not receive a salary, again separating himself from previous authors like Necker.

The legislature was the institution in which the "national will" was most directly expressed, because this institution *made* the laws. One legislative assembly would propose and debate laws; the other would vote on them. The assemblies would be elected in different years to assure continuity from one legislature to the next. They were also responsible for electing the members of the executive. Constant, however, did have some anxieties concerning potential abuses of power by the legislature; no doubt, he was again thinking of the actions of the Convention during the Terror and/or of the powerful assemblies during the last years of the Directory. Legislative power, therefore, needed to be limited. He argued that the legislature should have no authority over foreign affairs or the conduct of wars, though it was to be kept informed about such developments. And, its authority was to be limited by three other institutions—the executive, the judiciary, and the *pouvoir préservateur*.

The most important of these other institutions was the executive, which was "to accomplish the national will."[131] The executive was to be made up of five to seven members, and was to be chosen by the legislature. Though chosen *by* the legislature, it was to operate as an independent and autonomous body. It had the power to propose legislation, to veto legislation that it opposed, and to dissolve the legislature and call for new elections. The executive also had the right to declare war, though such decisions could be overturned by a lifetime council that Constant termed the *"pouvoir préservateur"* (see below). Clearly central in important areas like foreign affairs, the actions of the executive were limited, and they could be overturned by the concerted action of the other branches of government. Most important, here, was the power of the judiciary, which could intervene to protect the life and liberty of citizens against executive actions.

The most unusual aspect of Constant's imagined executive power was that it was to be composed not of one person, but of five or seven persons who would form an executive council.[132] Election of these members of the executive would not take place at the same time; elections would be in a series, perhaps replacing one executive each year. The advantages of this organization, Constant argued, were numerous. It would provide continuity of personnel and, therefore, make transmissions of power less disruptive. It would allow for more internal debate and, therefore, encourage the expression of multiple points of view. It would make it difficult for one person to impose his will, and this would make the government less prone to cultivating popular support by pursuing military glory.[133]

The *strength* of the executive also received much attention, deriving from Constant's concern to keep the executive and legislative branches balanced, a view informed by his recent experiences during the Directory and Consulate. There are some especially interesting pages on the Directory. He still noted the exceedingly difficult context in which the Directory was born: it came on the heels of six years of revolution and eighteen months of the Terror; and it faced enemies who were "dispersed more than vanquished."[134] But, Constant now placed great emphasis on the flaws of the Constitution of 1795, in particular criticizing it for not containing any provisions that would have allowed the executive branch to dissolve the Councils or veto the legislation passed by the Councils.[135] This meant that there was no legal means for the executive to oppose the legislative power *"dans sa marche."* "If the Directory had been able legally to dissolve the Councils, it would not have broken them by force, it would not have proscribed its members."[136] Constant was implying that the coup of Fructidor and the subsequent authoritarian actions of the Directors could have been avoided if there had been a better constitutional structure. It would not have needed to follow the path of "severe justice" and "unjust wars." He now took the position that the Directory, when it had subverted legislative initiatives and had nullified elections, "had become an illegal power."[137] "This necessity [of protecting itself] and the vices of the constitution obliged it [the executive] to follow a severe internal course, a rigorous solidarity which, pushing it often to injustice, finished as injustice often finishes, by surrounding it with hate and causing its fall."[138]

The executive and the legislature were to balance each other to prevent the concentration of power that Constant viewed as detrimental to liberty. These two powers, he wrote, potentially present "some inconveniences, some dangers, some abuses on different fronts,"[139] and it was, therefore, necessary to give to each some prerogatives to allow it to control the activity of the other, while maintaining between them an equilibrium. Wishing to avoid the situation in which either body could claim it was the *sole* expression of the "national will," Constant searched for a "prudent association" between the two, what Necker had termed an "ingenious filiation" [*"ingénieux entrelacement"*].[140] Either power, according to Constant, should be able to initiate legislation; and he hoped that by the participation of ministers from the executive branch in the deliberations of the legislature, there would be an ongoing *entrelace-ment.* Equally, of course, as a consequence of the law-making primacy of the legislature and the veto power of the executive, either could prevent enactment of the initiatives of the other.

In addition to the executive power and the legislative power, Constant called for the creation of a third power, entirely independent of the other two: a lifetime council also elected by the people. This *pouvoir préservateur* was to protect citizens against any abuse of power by the others branches of government, and to prevent either the executive or the legislative branch from becoming tyrannical *vis-à-vis* the other. It was given the right to intervene when there was a political crisis; it could dismiss the executive; it could call for new legislative elections; and, it had the power, as indicated above, to intervene with the executive in directing the armed forces. It could even temporarily take control of the government in times of chaos, or if there was a seizure of power by one of the other branches of government. It could commute sentences and grant judicial pardons, and it could even sanction modification of the constitution, though this latter power required the agreement of the other branches of government. It was, therefore, powerful, but it was not to have any direct political authority. It was expressly prohibited from proposing legislation or influencing elections. Its members were prohibited from becoming members of the legislative or executive branches, though he expressly required political experience as a criterion of entry. There was an age requirement (forty years); and members would be given sufficient property by the state to assure their independence.

Constant imagined the *pouvoir préservateur* to be composed of mature independent men of political experience who would be able to resist, because of their financial independence and lifetime appointment, the threats and influence of the other branches of government. Its main purpose was to act judicially in times of need—to be "the supreme judge of the other powers."[141] In the long final section of the manuscript that deals with the *pouvoir préservateur*, there are numerous references to the Constitutions of an VIII (1799) and of an X (1802). The latter had named Napoleon "first consul for life," and Constant obviously was attempting to construct a constitutional order that could constrain the authority of a powerful executive.[142]

Constant's anxiety about the inappropriate use of the armed forces was expressed in a variety of ways. He was especially concerned that the army not become the instrument of a dictator like Napoleon or of a legislative body like the Convention. To prevent this, he insisted that the military be distinguished from the police, that the military be prohibited from use against civilians, that military commissions and tribunals be eliminated and prohibited, and that troops be stationed only on the frontier of the country. He also specified that while the executive had the power to declare war, the *pouvoir préservateur* could intervene to dismiss the executive and prevent war. Much of his discussion of the army focused on the type of military spirit that was essential for a successful army, but dangerous when introduced into domestic politics. He was especially concerned that military *moeurs* not infect social relations generally. When the military is used internally,

> The military spirit slips into all civil relations. One imagines that for liberty, as for victory, nothing is more appropriate than passive obedience and rapid developments. One considers principles as corps of soldiers that it is necessary to enroll or combat, representative assemblies as instruments of authority, opposition as acts of indiscipline, law courts as the weapons of a party, judges as warriors, the accused as enemies, judgments as battles.[143]

Again, Constant raised the themes that would become central to his writings of the late-Empire and First Restoration.

Finally, there was the judiciary. The judiciary was not, strictly speaking, a political power, but it did have a political function.[144] Most importantly, it had to have the authority to protect citizens against the actions of the legislative and executive branches of government. Citizens must have the right to criticize the government and organize politically. To assure these rights there needed to be judicial protections. Constant insisted that ordinary tribunals handle all of these legal issues, specifically criticizing the variety of extraordinary tribunals that had been created during the Directory and Consulate.[145] Judges were to be independent and permanent, which was more important than their manner of nomination. Constant indicated, however, that he favored the election of judges by the propertied class. Worried about the vulnerability of citizens, Constant also insisted that citizens have the right to petition the *pouvoir préservateur* about potential violations of liberties.

In all of these branches of government, political authority was to emanate from the people. In Constant's own words, the goal was "to establish the empire of opinion by the periodic and free renewal of its interpreters."[146] He was optimistic that such a political and judicial system would protect liberty and lead to the gradual emancipation of the lower classes. Constant wished to open access to politics to groups that had been excluded in the hierarchical and hereditary systems of the past. But he wished to open access incrementally. Initially, political office should be limited to property owners, who would defend the social order against *"les barbares,"* against "the ignorant and ferocious multitudes."[147] Property provided the leisure and the possibility of enlightenment that were essential for sound political judgment. Fortunately, in his mind, the access to property had been equalized by the legal changes introduced by the Revolution and was expanding because of social changes brought by economic development. These developments, he reasoned, would create more and more property owners and, therefore, a larger active citizenry and the eventual triumph of democracy.

Constant's optimism on these matters was closely tied to his belief that "interest" was the animating spirit of modern liberal societies. He did not believe that "virtue" or "honor" would work for modern societies like France. Honor had unfortunately degenerated into a "vain, confused, and uncertain" sentiment.[148] In the modern world, interest was the "principle" (to use Montesquieu's term) that operated between individuals and that defined the relationship between individuals and government. Constant was not sanguine about this, however, recognizing that "the calculation of interests is a very delicate thing." In his own words, "It is certain that it is necessary to give to all [political] authorities the interest to observe the Constitution and to remain within their limits."[149] Moreover, he believed that no constitution could protect itself against conspiracy and overturn if people were estranged and/or morally bankrupt. He was convinced that the institutions of a representative constitutional republic, such as he had outlined in the *Fragments,* would provide the best hope of channeling private interests—especially those within the government—into what was best for society.

Concerning the relationship of local administrations to national power, he was unusually sensitive to the dangers of centralization.[150] For many in France at the time, the local administration was viewed as an arm of the national government; it was responsible for applying national laws though not for making decisions. Constant, following

Necker, was more sensitive to the needs of local administrations, and believed that local administrations should be responsible for affairs of local interest. As he himself put it, "The decision of the affairs that concern everyone belongs to everyone, those which interest only a fraction ought to be decided by this fraction."[151]

Constant also came to the conclusion that governments should not be in the business of forming cultural ideals. He was critical of the propensity of new governments to extirpate old "principles" and "prejudices" and of their attempts to replace old principles with new ones.

> One has said that new governments, seeing old governments surrounded by a cortège of prejudices and errors, desired as an essential part of their dignity, to have a similar cortège. The French Directory pushed this weakness further than any other government; it persecuted existing prejudices with some puerile and disgusting harassments and, at the same time, attempted to reanimate the disposition to prejudices in its favor.[152]

Here, Constant was more critical of government efforts at "cultural education" than when he had been a local governing official. The government, he now argued, should restrict its conservation efforts to guaranteeing liberty, independence, and the physical security of individuals. It should restrict its efforts to protecting those general principles that would likely stimulate enlightenment and progress.

As this indicates, Constant was sensitive to the dangers of government intrusion into society. He began his ruminations about a constitution worrying that there was an inevitable division between those who govern and those who are governed. He suggested that this "primitive discordance" was a constituent element of any government, even a representative government.[153] Institutionally, Constant addressed this negative tendency of government by reaffirming his old belief that sovereignty was never to be concentrated in one place. In Constant's mind, however, this separation of institutions and balance of power did not entirely eliminate the potential danger of officials looking out for their own interests at the expense of the governed.

> It is necessary not to have any illusion on the efficacy of these means [the separation of legislative and executive power], nor

to flatter oneself that one succeeds in completely amalgamating these two interests [of those who govern and of those who are governed]. It is necessary always to be on guard against the effects of this primitive discordance, because its cause is sometimes so hidden that it is not able to be perceived.[154]

Constant thus articulated a strong political pluralism, but he remained anxious about the propensity of the powerful to impose their will on the powerless.

## Between Immanuel Kant and Edmund Burke

Constant's political and constitutional writings of these years indicate that he was carefully positioning himself philosophically between the positions of Immanuel Kant and Edmund Burke. Kant, of course, supported the categorical adherence to principles irrespective of experience. Burke supported adherence to traditions and "prejudices" in opposition to "metaphysical" principles. Constant found both positions unacceptable.

The first mention of Burke occurred in a letter to Isabelle de Charrière dated 10 December 1790: "I occupy myself at present with reading and refuting the book of Burke against the French levelers. There are as many absurdities as lines in this famous book....He defends the nobility, the exclusion of parties, the establishment of a dominant religion, and other things of this nature."[155] He never completed his refutation, but he did return to address Burke directly in *Des réactions politiques*, published in 1797. He identified Burke with those who rejected principles in favor of arbitrary rule. Burke, he writes, maintains, "that some axioms, metaphysical truths, are able to be politically false, [and prefers] to these axioms the consideration of prejudices, memories, weaknesses, all things vague, indefinable, fluctuating."[156] In the same work, Constant referred to "a German philosopher," obviously referring to Kant, who maintained that if an assassin came to your door demanding to know if your friend, who he is pursuing, is in your house, you would be obliged to tell the truth. "Lying would be a crime."[157]

Constant opposed both positions.[158] Against Burke, Constant makes clear that the total absence of general principles in politics is dangerous, especially for those without the power to defend themselves.

Without articulated and enforceable principles, there are no laws that apply equally to all; without general laws, there are no political institutions with fixed boundaries. Without principles and legality, in short, there is the likelihood of arbitrary action based on power. For the average person, this would entail "all of the shackles of *l'état social*, and all the hazards of *l'état sauvage*."[159]

On the other hand, the adherence to general principles, as Kant argued, is dangerous because it would lead, in the specific case mentioned, to a greater evil: the death of a friend. This is because principles are too abstract if they are divorced from "intermediate principles" that inform us about how they are to be applied in specific contexts. Principles are necessary, but they must not be too abstract. When they are abstract, and their method of application is not obvious, there is also the risk that they disguise someone's partisan interest. This is what he calls the "Machiavellian" use of principles.

> All that I want to prove, is that the exaggeration of principle, being the most infallible means of rendering them inapplicable, will always be one of the most dangerous arms that the partisans of prejudices are able to employ.[160]

Constant took pains to make clear that he was proposing a "balancing," finding an "equilibrium" between, on the one hand, the adherence to abstract principles regardless of situation, and, on the other, the justification of existing conditions regardless of their injustices and inequities.

Constant's opposition to abstraction dates from his first political pronouncements. In a 1793 letter to Isabelle de Charrière, for example, he clearly articulated his reservations. "Besides, I am not...the friend of abstractions. I regard them as the cause of the greatest part of our errors, religious as much as political. I am all the more confirmed in this opinion because pious people and aristocrats, both equally, have recourse to the abstractions they make to dazzle and mislead our sorry species. The sans-culotte return to them now."[161] As Etienne Hofmann has cogently pointed out, such statements indicate that Constant's political reflections were suspicious of vague speculations. "The definitions that he invokes do not have value in themselves, but only in their concrete consequences for the happiness of individuals."[162]

Constant was eloquent when he criticized legislation that looked just in principle, but was unjust in application. This was because laws, by their nature, do not take into consideration all the facts relevant in any given instance of applying the law. "The more a law is general, the more it is distant from the particular actions on which it is destined to pronounce. A law is not able to be perfectly just except in a single circumstance.... Facts nuance themselves infinitely; laws are not able to follow these nuances in their multiform modifications."[163] Constant devoted a chapter of his work on constitutions to argue that experience was ultimately the only standard by which one could determine whether a constitution, however abstractly perfect, was or was not good for a particular society.[164] For all of his attention to institutional constitutional arrangements, Constant was not willing to argue that one system was appropriate for all societies at all historical moments. This was to fall prey to the rationalist illusion.

Given Constant's pragmatic orientation, it is not surprising that he judged Kant's political ruminations of little value. Kant insisted that the construction of the state was to be based on reason, and wrote movingly about the importance of intellectual freedom (at least for philosophers) and of the relationship that should obtain between ethical freedom and abstract political right. But he gave no attention to pragmatic constitutional arrangements, never considered concrete issues like the separation and balance of power, and advised anyone who objected to a specific government and/or to violations of freedom by secular authorities to (as he put it in "What Is Enlightenment?" [1784]) "argue as much as you like and about whatever you like, but obey!"[165] In "The Consent of Faculties" [1798], Kant encouraged monarchs "to govern in a *republican* (not a democratic) manner," but immediately qualified this seemingly progressive assertion by adding that this was true "even although they may *rule autocratically*. In other words they should treat the people in accordance with principles akin in spirit to the laws of freedom which a people of mature rational powers would prescribe for itself, even if the people is not literally asked for its consent."[166] This was just the sort of rule from above by an elite attached to abstractions that Constant found unacceptable.[167]

This did not mean, however, that Constant rejected principles. These played an important role, not least because they qualified too fulsome an embrace of tradition. Constant strongly disagreed with those who recommended retaining traditional institutions and practices simply because they *were* traditions. He recognized that institutions that were based on tradition were often supported for no other reason; they were "sanctioned by time," as he put it in *Fragments*.[168] Questionable institutions that did exist, but had no hope of introduction in an age of reason, had a good chance of surviving if they had tradition on their side. "Consecrated by a long following of centuries, [an inherited institution] captivates or subjugates the imagination of men, and forces the passions to submit because of some imposing memories."[169] But, institutions based on reason were always to be preferred. It is their reasonableness that makes equality and liberty so commendable. "One is able to resign oneself to a [questionable institution or custom]," he wrote, "when at the time of birth one finds it established; but it is impossible... to resign oneself to it, when one does not know the advantageous course."[170]

Change in the right direction was salutary and necessary. He argued that the human species was progressive, and that any defense of extant institutions must take into account the stage of human development, which meant that institutions that were demonstrably beneficial in the past might not endure.

> By a common mistake, when an institution or a law no longer produces the good that it produced in the past, one believes that the means of best rendering it again useful is to reestablish it in its ancient purity. But when an institution is useful, it is because it is in accord with ideals and contemporary enlightenment. When its utility ceases, it is because this accord diminishes or is destroyed. The more you reestablish it in that which you call its primitive purity, the more you render it disproportionate with all of the rest of that which exists. The *vague des mots* ceaselessly misleads us.[171]

A Burkean defense of "prejudices" was obviously unacceptable to Constant. No government should favor "prejudices" over "reason." New ideas need to be openly considered; new proposals for change need to be carefully assessed. Goverments "should follow ideas, in order to put behind the people barriers that will prevent them from going backward, but it ought not to put any barriers before the people which would prevent them from going forward."[172] Germaine de Staël captured the intermediate position that Constant was recommending when she wrote that "theory without experience is only a phrase, experience without theory is only a prejudice."[173]

## Constant in the *Tribunat*

On the morning of the 19th Brumaire, an VIII [10 November 1799], Constant wrote to Sieyès that he had heard rumors that the legislative Councils of the Directory government were about to be adjourned. He warned that this would be disastrous because it would destroy "the only barrier opposed to a man [Napoleon]...menacing to the Republic. His [Napoleon's] proclamations, in which he speaks only of himself, and says that his return had led to hopes that he would put an end to the evils that afflict France, have convinced me more than ever that in everything he does he views only his own elevation."[174] In fact, of course, it was too late. The day before, the two Councils had moved to Saint-Cloud, had received the resignations of the two Directors (Roger Ducos and Sieyès) who were leading the coup, and had named Bonaparte the director of the Parisian garrison. The next day, the day of Constant's letter, Bonaparte confronted the Council of Five Hundred in Saint-Cloud, and when things did not move in the way he wished, his brother Lucien called in the troops to disperse the Councils. That evening, a rump of the legislators favorable to the coup voted to adjourn the legislative assemblies and to replace the Directory with a provisional Consulate made up of a Triumvirate composed of Bonaparte, Ducos, and Sieyès. The following day (20 Brumaire [11 November 1799]), Bonaparte was proclaimed the president of the Triumvirate.

Subsequent letters indicate that Constant still believed that Sieyès offered the best hope of protecting liberty,[175] though he still did not share all of Sieyès' views of the appropriate constitutional order. The constitution that was in fact adopted on 22 frimaire, an VIII (13 December 1799) gave more power to the executive branch than either Sieyès or Constant would have preferred. Drawn up by Napoleon, Daunou, and Roederer, real authority rested with the three consuls, of which the first consul (Napoleon) was the most powerful.[176] The two legislative bodies were relatively less important. The first was the *Tribunat*, composed of one hundred men of at least twenty-five years of age, which was to discuss laws drawn up by the executive branch, and to recommend either passage or rejection. It did not have the right to amend legislation, and its vote was only a recommendation. Moreover, its schedule was determined by the executive branch. The opinion of the *Tribunat* was carried by three members of this body to the *Corps législatif*, a body with 300 members aged 30 or more. The *Corps législatif* could not discuss or amend bills, but had the power to accept or reject them. In the words of one recent analyst, "The *Tribunat* was thus an assembly of chatterboxes who decided nothing, while the *Corps législatif* was an assembly of mutes who effectively voted the law."[177]

Constant was named to the *Tribunat* on 24 December 1799, presumably because of the support of Sieyès.[178] He served until he was purged by Napoleon, along with other critics of the administration, on 17 January 1802 (though he served until 22 March 1802, when the replacements took their seats). Younger than most of his colleagues, Constant was nonetheless very active during his brief tenure, intervening more than twenty times, and delivering fourteen discourses. His interventions were mostly about the proper role of a parliamentary assembly, which he judged to be too restricted at this time, and the larger issue of juridical norms, especially as these related to protecting individual rights and the dangers of creating special tribunals.

Constant's first intervention, on 5 January 1800, set the tone for many that followed. He argued that the *Tribunat* needed to remain independent, provide measured consideration of legislation, and defend liberty. It should not assume the role of always accepting or always rejecting bills presented to it by the executive, but rather should focus on the general interest. Though in subsequent sessions he frequently opposed government-proposed laws, he was careful to frame his rejections with an appeal to principle. "The opposition [to the government] is without force when it is without discernment, and men whose vocation would be to resist the establishment of useful laws, will soon be heard only with indifference, even when they combat dangerous laws."[179] He referred frequently to the proper role of the parliamentary assemblies, and was openly critical of the limited role that they had been given under the Constitution of 1799, lamenting that the legislature did not have the right to initiate legislation, that it did not have sufficient information (especially about financial issues) to make informed decisions, and that it did not have control of its own schedule. All of these criticisms drew from

Constant's convictions of appropriate constitutional organization, outlined in his unpublished *Fragments d'un ouvrage abandonné sur la possibilité d'une constitution républicaine dans un grand pays.* More broadly, Constant's discourses between 1799 and 1802 reflected his conviction that in the current context strict legality was essential. Constant insisted that there must be respect for the Constitution and for the strict letter of the law, which required, in addition, that laws be explicit and clear to prevent the government from exceeding its authority through skillful but devious interpretation. He retained his theme that legislation should protect individuals from the intervention of government. For example, he argued for the rejection of the revolutionary legislation on inheritance that prescribed the equal division of property, arguing that individuals should have the freedom to dispose of their property as they saw fit.[180] This was closely connected to his longstanding view that private property ownership was important for the stability of the political order.

His advocacy of strict legality was informed by his concern that the government was intervening too aggressively into the private lives of citizens, thereby trampling on their civil liberties. On 23 February 1800, he opposed all "formal and criminal violation of the liberty of citizens."[181] On 25 January 1801, in an extended discourse, he was especially eloquent concerning the dangers of establishing special criminal tribunals.[182] These tribunals suspended the right to trial by jury and often imposed laws retroactively. With such actions, Constant argued, tribunals essentially dispensed arbitrary justice. Constant rejected the argument that in certain circumstances it might be appropriate to respect the "spirit" of the law over the "letter" of the law.

> If to these written rules [of the Constitution], which one calls particular, one is able to oppose some rules that one will call general, and which, not being written, will always be what one wants in each circumstance; if for the letter of the Constitution, which is the only positive thing, one substitutes a spirit that one calls the protector of the law, must I tell you that there no longer exists a Constitution?[183]

Such protections against arbitrariness were especially needed in capital cases. The greater the chance of a trial leading to a death sentence, "the less one ought to permit any removal of the legal forms that are intended to protect the innocent."[184] Constant's position concerning legality had shifted from what it had been following the Fructidor coup of 1797. Given the current political administration, he now argued that scrupulous respect for laws was necessary to prevent arbitrariness and persecution. Constant's stance revealed the depth of his suspicion of the new government. He criticized the vague nature of the law; the imprecise length of existence of the tribunals; and the retroactive nature of the actions to be taken by the tribunal. He now argued that clear and explicit laws were necessary for the protection of individual liberties.[185]

Constant continued to argue that the protection of individual liberties entailed limiting the centralization of power. He noted the obvious advantages—efficiency, speed, and unity—of a centralized administration, but he still believed that local officials chosen by the people should retain authority over local issues. The power of the First Consul, through his authority over prefects, sub-prefects, municipal councils, and *conseils d'arrondissement*, was excessive. Another manifestations of centralization was, again, the appointment of special criminal tribunals, which not only eroded legal due process, but also largely eliminated the role of local magistrates chosen by the people. Rather than restricting the role of local magistrates, the government should multiply their number, according to Constant. This would create a corps of magistrates who had detailed knowledge of local communities and local conditions, which would enable them to make informed, and therefore better, decisions.[186]

\* \* \*

Constant's experience in the *Tribunat* was an apprenticeship for his later legislative role during the Restoration, when he became a leader of the Liberal Opposition.[187] He discovered that he was an effective political speaker and an accomplished political organizer. As his contemporaries attested, the legislative arena forced Constant to clarify political issues that he addressed theoretically in his writings. Isabelle de Charrière, for example, wrote of his discourses on the justices of the peace and special judicial tribunals: "They are admirable, as much for their substance as for their form. He has never reasoned with this power, nor written with this simplicity."[188] Isabelle de Charrière also recognized how beneficial such legislative activity was to Constant's state of mind.

> At twenty years you believed yourself to be indifferent towards all objects, at 25 years you came around to politics, a little later to love, to eloquence, to wit. Now you travel down your chosen path with a sense of duty, necessity, habit, without asking of objects and your heart, as previously, to provide you with some lively sensations. All this is good. So many men seem to me unhappy because they count on more happiness than life is able to give to them. You are not bored, that is worth a lot.[189]

In short, Constant had found his vocation, though unfortunately for him it was a vocation that he would be unable to pursue actively for many years.

Many scholars of Constant's political thought have argued that Constant's "liberalism" is clearly expressed only in the writings that followed his experience in the *Tribunat*; that is, only after 1802.[190] In fact, his "liberalism" was already present in his writings of the Directory, and matured because of his experiences during the Second Directory and the Consulate. It developed from principles clearly articulated in his earlier writings. His commitment to individual rights, always at the heart of his liberal stance, became more consistent as he faced the growing authoritarianism of government administrations. His critique of the unified concept of sovereignty became sharper as he contemplated the dangers of legislative or executive monopolies of power. His appreciation of the importance of historical change increased as he weighed the relative importance of general ideals and idiosyncratic local traditions. All of these refined his appreciation of the critical importance of pragmatic political action within the framework of a representative government based on popular sovereignty. All of these had become central components of his liberalism.

# 4
# Liberal Culture: *Sensibilité* and Sociability

Constant exited the *Tribunat* as a liberal politician who had found his vocation, but there was no public arena for active politics until the fall of the Empire in 1814. He turned to other areas of writing, especially his ongoing scholarship on religion, as well as literature. He also continued to think and write about politics, which is the focus of chapter 5. This chapter gives attention to the nonpolitical writings of these years, especially Constant's novel *Adolphe* and its relationship to the wider culture of *sensibilité*. It begins, however, with a brief discussion of Constant's stormy separation from Germaine de Staël and his marriage to Charlotte von Hardenberg.

## Constant, Staël, and Charlotte von Hardenberg

Staël and Constant were clearly attracted to each other's intellect, as we have seen in their shared outlook to liberal politics. Unfortunately, from the middle of 1798 there were severe emotional strains in their relationship. In a revealing letter to his aunt dated 15 May 1798, Constant complained that in the relationship with Staël he was "isolated without being independent, subjugated without being united with her. I see the last years of my youth passing by with neither the repose of solitude nor the gentle affections of a legitimate union. I have tried in vain to break it off."[1] Constant alternated between wanting a public career and longing for a quieter existence that would allow him to follow his intellectual pursuits. Staël, on the other hand, dreaded isolation, expected devotion and attention from those around her, and required a lively social scene. By all accounts, she was an enthralling conversationalist and an enthusiastic and generous supporter of her friends and acquaintances. Generally surrounded by a veritable court of admirers, she suffered when confined to a more restricted lifestyle.[2]

The first decade of the new century was filled with dramatic confrontations interspersed with temporary reconciliations. Though Staël and Constant did not definitively part ways until 10 May 1811, the emotional closeness of the first few years became more intermittent, and they were more and more apart. The strain is revealed most starkly in Constant's *Journaux intimes*, where he vacillates between his desire to rupture with Staël and his desire to "return to this tie because of memories or some momentary charm."[3] Psychological makeup and character—both were narcissistic and melancholic—had a lot to do with the breakup of this dynamic relationship.[4] By the time they parted in 1811, Staël and Constant had long ceased to be intimate. Staël had taken on a succession of lovers. Constant had a passionate affair with Anna Lindsay in 1800–1801, and in June 1808 married Charlotte von Hardenberg, regularizing what was arguably the most emotionally stable, and certainly the most enduring, relationship of his life. What is so impressive about the Constant-Staël relationship is the intellectual power and output of the participants, something that generated deep mutual respect and a closeness that survived all of the emotional storms of their years together. Even their breakup generated novelistic analyses of the fraught relationship of human nature and social context, as is discussed in detail below.[5]

Charlotte von Hardenberg (1769–1845) belonged to a Hanoverian family, though she herself was born in London. Cosmopolitan like Constant, she read and spoke French, German, and English. Constant first met Charlotte in Brunswick in January 1793. At the time, Constant was married to Minna von Cramm and Hardenberg was married to Baron von Marenholtz, a man sixteen years her senior. Though Constant and Hardenberg saw each other frequently for the next couple of months, there is no indication that there was a sexual liaison at this time.[6] They were infrequently in touch during the next decade.[7] In 1798, Hardenberg divorced Baron von Marenholtz and married the Vicomte Du Tertre, an impoverished French royalist. In 1802, they moved to a Paris, and in the late summer of 1803 she and Constant began again to correspond. They met in May 1805,[8] and became lovers in October 1806.[9]

There followed four years of extreme emotional turmoil, marked by confrontations, illnesses, and apparent suicide attempts by both Hardenberg and Staël. Constant spent time with both. Constant first told Staël of Hardenberg in early-November 1806; she predictably exploded with anger, an anger that would not abate in subsequent years. During the spring of 1807, Du Tertre agreed to a divorce from Hardenberg; on 11 April 1808, the Catholic Church declared the marriage null and void; on 5 June 1808, Constant and Hardenberg married in Basel. Constant was so worried about Staël's reactions to the news of his marriage that it was hidden from her until May 1809, when there was a stormy scene between Hardenberg and Staël. The emotional hurricane continued for another year and a half, during which time Constant was characteristically unable to make a decisive move to distance himself from Staël. When they saw each other briefly in Lausanne in early-May 1811, they both believed that they would likely never meet again: Staël was planning her trip east into exile; Constant and Hardenberg were headed to Göttingen, where they lived for the next few years. Staël and Constant did meet again in Paris after the defeat of Napoleon in 1814, but by this time the old affection had been replaced by a mutually critical regard.[10]

Following the stormy period between 1806 and 1810, Constant and Hardenberg's subsequent years were relatively calm. Constant recognized the positive and stabilizing force that Hardenberg played in his life; as he put it in his *Journaux intimes*, she provided "an unexpected port that the heavens have presented to me."[11] Though his diary also records periods of boredom and disaffection, he also respected, and was comforted by, her good sense, her tolerance, and her deep affection.[12]

## *Delphine, Corinne,* and *Adolphe*

Constant obsessively analyzed his own character and his relationships with women. He was impressed with the elusive quality of emotional attachments. "In the present state of society," he wrote in 1806, "personal relations are composed of fine nuances, undulating, impossible to grasp, which would be denatured in a thousand ways if one tried to give them greater precision."[13] He was cautious about predicting the consequences—intended and unintended—of intimacy. As he put it in the preface to the second edition of his novel *Adolphe*,

[T]here is in the simple habit of borrowing the language of love, and of fostering in oneself, or of exciting in others, transient emotions of the heart, a danger which has not been sufficiently appreciated hitherto. One heads down a road whose end one is unable to foresee; one knows neither what one will inspire, nor what one may experience. One makes light of the blows of which one can calculate neither the force, nor the reaction on oneself; and the wound that seems only to graze the skin may be incurable.[14]

Both Constant and Staël wrote novels during Napoleon's rule, turning their attention to intimate relations and the ways that society impinged on these relations. Staël's novels *Delphine* (1802) and *Corinne* (1806) were fictional portrayals of sensitive and generous women who struggled in a world where sympathy and enthusiasm were overwhelmed by hypocrisy and stifling social conventions.[15] Constant's novel *Adolphe* is principally concerned with the fragility of intimate relationships, even the tragedy of their failure. It tells us much more, however, than how difficult it is to find an ideal partner in a troubled world. It is bound up—in consonance with late-eighteenth and early-nineteenth century notions of *sensibilité*—with the issues of how emotions are to inform social comportment, and, even more, how "affections" such as sympathy and enthusiasm are to provide a foundation for conscience, morality, and politics. At the core of *Adolphe* is a critical analysis of modern character that is closely connected with Constant's portrayal of the new political culture and the altered contours of sociability created by the Revolution.

Stael's novels, as feminist scholars have pointed out, involve an implicit critique of Rousseau's well-known strictures concerning the education of women and the relegation of women to the private world of home and children. In spite of his praise of sensibility and enlightened domesticity, Rousseau *au fond* believed that anatomy was destiny—women's physiology determined their fate. This was especially the message of book V of *Emile*, where Rousseau argued that "emotional" and "fragile" women were inferior to men in intellect and creativity. Their education should be geared toward domestic matters; such training would best prepare women for the homemaking and family nurture for which they were biologically destined. Because of their natural inferiority in abstract thought, and because their natural place was in the home, women should not aspire to public life.[16]

Staël resisted this ancient theme in Rousseau, as did Constant and others. She was critical of Rousseau's attack on women's aptitudes as well as his insistence that women be confined to the private sphere. Women, according to Staël, should pursue all knowledge, because it would strengthen their morals. Moreover, women should have a chance for active participation in some parts of public life, especially as writers. Staël, in her own essentialist stereotype, argued that women were especially good at probing the human heart and that they were, therefore, especially competent to portray the passions that animated human actions. Related to this perception of women as especially sensitive was Staël's partial agreement with Rousseau concerning the constitutional differences between men and women. Women, she suggested at several times during her life, were naturally inferior to men physically; and men were thus more naturally oriented to public action. Although Staël thus embraced a traditional view of society and emphasized the importance of family, she had a distinctively romantic conception of the centrality of the passions and railed against any cultural or social impediments that might keep her from realizing her hopes for a more active life.

This was especially true in her mature years, as reflected in novels like *Delphine* and *Corinne*, both critical of social conventions that constrained natural expressiveness. In her first published novel *Delphine*, the principle character Delphine represents love and goodness; her lover Léonce, on the other hand, represents society and worldly opinion—that is, everything that forces the unspoiled Delphine to suffer. Writing about this novel, Staël suggested that "the power of love is the source of all men have done that is noble, pure, and disinterested on this earth. I believe that works that develop this power with nuance and sensibility will always do more good than harm: nearly all the human vices presuppose hardness of heart."[17] *Corinne*, similarly, is critical of the English social conventions that defined the world of Oswald and his family because they constrained Corinne's natural expressiveness and contributed to her disappointment and, ultimately, suicide. In both novels, the purity of unfettered feelings holds out hope for a transparent communion of souls. But in both novels, this purity runs against circumstances that make those most overcome with passion most likely to end up alone, in opposition to others, despairing. It is as though illness and loneliness are the last retreats of the morally pure. Much of the tension in these novels is between unfettered emotion leading, on the one hand, to transcendence and connection, and on the other, to melancholy and frailty. The fundamental emotional calculus of Staël's novels is about the goodness of natural spontaneous emotions and how these are constrained and spoiled by social conventions.

*Corinne* exemplifies a lament that hopes for transparent love, or for constant notoriety and adulation, are doomed to frustration. The failure of Corinne to find fulfillment in love with Oswald is, as suggested, related to the social constraints under which she finds herself. But the failure is equally related to Corinne's search for unconditional acceptance as a dramatist, poet, and genius. Corinne is, in the words of Naomi Schor, "perhaps the most exhibitionistic female protagonist in the history of women's writing. Actress, improvisationalist, conversationalist, Corinne is constantly engaged in spectacularizing her life."[18] It is difficult to imagine any workable society in which the "spectacularizing" Corinne would be able to find satisfaction. Staël, however, implies that it is primarily "society" that prevents Corinne from living a fulfilling life; in her eyes, Corinne is emotionally healthy, but she can scarcely imagine a European country in which her happiness is possible.

Constant's *Adolphe* is also about the play of passions such as pity in human relations, but there is a contrasting perspective. Like Staël's Corinne, *Adolphe* ends in disappointment, depression, and (probably) death. But, Constant focused on a male, not a female, as the sensitive individual confronting his emotions.[19] Moreover, the novel implies that much of the problem is embedded in the character of modern individuals.

*Adolphe* was written in 1806, rewritten in 1809–10, but published only in 1816.[20] Constant originally intended to write a novel to celebrate his love for Charlotte von Hardenberg. After a passionate week together in October 1806, Constant noted in his journal that he had written to Charlotte and "begun a novel which will be our history. All other work would be impossible."[21] This was also the period, however, when Constant was painfully separating from Germaine de Staël. An "episode" of the originally conceived novel about Constant's love for Charlotte—an episode more reflective of Constant's difficulties with breaking up with Staël—became the principal focus of the novel that we know as *Adolphe*.

Traditional critical appraisals of *Adolphe* have devoted considerable attention to identifying the real individuals represented by the novelistic characters, though different scholars have seen different women—Germaine de Staël and Anna Lindsay (another intimate of Constant) are frequently named—as the model for the principal female protagonist of the novel, Ellénore. Often explicit in these accounts, and always at least implicit, is the suggestion that Constant was trying not only to analyze his amorous failures, but also to justify his actions and to salvage or enhance his reputation. The dates of original conception, rewritings, and ultimate publication become significant here, for Constant's intentions likely changed at different moments of his life. We can surmise, for example, that the motives leading to the near-simultaneous publication of the novel in London and Paris in 1816—a time when Constant was in need of money and was attempting to launch a public political career—were different from the motives that led him to write the early draft of the novel in 1806.

Modern critics have preferred to emphasize the aesthetic and formalistic qualities of the novel, recognizing that, like most novels, it draws from personal experience and reflection, but that it transforms these into an artistic creation that must be considered on its own merits. Narrative structure and aesthetic coherence are at the center of such analyses, though the spillover into an assessment of the personality or character of Constant is by no means absent.[22] Here, we shall take a course between personal history and formalistic analysis, using *Adolphe* as a point of entry into Constant's discussion of the intersection of character, sentiment, sociability, morality, and politics. We seek to analyze the novel in terms of Constant's broader intellectual itinerary and in terms of the wider cultural discourses within which he operated.

*Adolphe* analyzes the character of an upperclass German man in his early twenties who, because of social convention, decides to acquire a mistress. He fixes his attention on Ellénore, a woman of Polish origin with two children, ten years his senior, who has become the female companion of Comte P***, an old friend of his father's. Ellénore is beautiful, engaging, and uncommonly attached to social proprieties because of her precarious position on the margins of upperclass society. Adolphe writes Ellénore a love letter; her negative response stimulates an intense love that he had previously only feigned. He presses his suit, and after some hesitation she yields and the pair become lovers.

The second part of the novel, the shortest, is about the brief period of ecstasy they both experience as a consequence of their love for each other. The third and longest part of the novel is about the disillusionment and restlessness of Adolphe in the aftermath of this period of glowing intimacy. Adolphe experiences increasing discomfort as Ellénore develops a tenacious passion for him and becomes, due to her own social position and temperament, more and more dependent; as Constant famously put it, "she was no longer a goal: she had become a tie."[23] Adolphe feels responsible for Ellénore's happiness and despair, but his lack of forthrightness about his waning love leads to actions that make her dependence even more acute. She leaves Comte P*** and her two children to establish a life with Adolphe; she follows Adolphe to another city; she insists that Adolphe accompany her to Warsaw to care for Ellénore's dying father. Adolphe acquiesces to each request because he feels pity and responsibility for Ellénore's situation, but he regrets that his affair has postponed a career commensurate with his class and background, and he longs for his independence. He is vacillating but caring, racked by a convulsive sense of loyalty and remorse. He lacks a clear vision of himself and his needs; he is unable to anticipate the consequences of his actions or to understand the power of the feelings that are imperceptibly taking hold of him.

The tragic end comes when a baron stationed in Warsaw, an associate of Adolphe's father, gets Adolphe to write a letter promising his father that he will separate from Ellénore in order to regain his independence. Unbeknownst to Adolphe, the baron sends the letter to Ellénore, who develops a fever and ultimately dies in Adolphe's arms. Adolphe is left grief-stricken and depressed; he disappears.

Alison Fairlie refers to *Adolphe* as "that most quietly disruptive of all French novels," suggesting that the appropriate framework for understanding the focus and tone of the novel is tragedy.[24] It is the nature of a tragedy, she points out, to place the protagonist in an insoluble situation that leads to destruction. This calamitous mix can be the result of an inherent character flaw or, alternately, of an impossible social situation, but in the most effective tragedies the character traits leading to the ultimate disaster are, ironically, the finest qualities of an individual, the very qualities that lead him/her to act in ways so lamentably unsuited for the society in which he/she lives. Tragedy results, in the words of Fairlie, from the "exact counterpoise between the outer pressures which crush the character (fate, society, heredity) and an ineradicable conviction of inner responsibility."[25]

Everything Constant said about *Adolphe* supports this characterization of the novel as a tragedy. And this suggests that the novel was, in addition to whatever else, a means for him to examine the tragic incompatibility of certain character traits with the mores of society. It was closely connected, in short, with his analysis of human nature and society. In the first chapter of the novel, Adolphe refers to his own character in the following manner:

> I was at ease only when entirely alone, and even today such is the effect of this disposition of soul, that, in the least important circumstances, when I must choose between two courses of action, the human face troubles me, and my natural inclination is to flee in order to deliberate in peace. I did not have, however, the depth of egoism that such characteristics would seem to suggest: although interested only in myself, this interest was weak. I carried deep in my heart a need for sensibility of which I was not aware, but which, finding no satisfaction, separated me from all the things which in succession aroused my curiosity.[26]

Adolphe is shy, awkward, and sensitive, but articulate. He thinks constantly about his fluctuating emotions, and has a vague but self-centered idea that a love affair will draw him out of himself. An affair will provide a release for his emotions and bring him a richer engagement with the rest of society. Instead, the relationship with Ellénore, given society's severe judgment, makes him even more detached from the world. In Chapter VII, Constant describes Adolphe's new state as a more intense form of egoism.

> I cast my gaze on the grayish horizon whose boundaries I could no longer see, and this gave me, in a way, the feeling of boundlessness. I had experienced nothing like it for a long time: having been entirely absorbed by personal reflections, with my eyes always fixed on my own situation, I had become a stranger to all general ideas. I concerned myself only with Ellénore and myself; with Ellénore, who inspired in me only pity mixed with fatigue; with myself, for whom I no longer had any respect. I had shrunk, as it were, into a new type of egoism, into an egoism devoid of courage, discontented, and humiliated.[27]

As Constant put it in an unpublished fragment, "only his vanity is permanent."[28]

*Adolphe* can easily be read to suggest that sensitive, self-critical individuals, in the context of modern society, will find life difficult. *Adolphe* is painted with such dark colors that there seems to be, given the narcissistic expectations of both of the principal characters and the social constraints placed on their actions, little hope for happiness. It can be argued, further, that *Adolphe* is about the unintended consequences of actions generally, and about how, even under relentless self-scrutiny, one performs acts that lead to tragedy. There is not only a pessimism that self-scrutiny is generally unable to provide a clear vision of how to act, but a more pervasive malaise that self-scrutiny *itself* may be one of the causes of dissatisfaction and catastrophe. For Constant, man is simply too emotionally flaccid, too spiritually dead, and too intellectually self-critical to find a path that will not lead either to ill-health or tragedy.

The nature of modern society had accentuated these qualities. Constant intentionally so constructed the novel that, once the relationship between Adolphe and Ellénore was established, their natures would inevitably lead, given current social arrangements, to tragedy. As he put it in the preface to the second edition, "His position and that of Ellénore were without resources, and that is precisely what I wanted." The central dilemma of the novel is that Ellénore's love and society's expectations give Adolphe little room for maneuver; there is no way for him to respond that would not culminate in disaster. "I have shown him tormented, because he loved Ellénore only feebly; but he would not have been less tormented if he had loved her more. He suffered because of her, for want of sentiment; with sentiment more ardent, he would have suffered for her."[29] The next sentence makes the weight of society's norms even more explicit. "Society, disapproving and disdainful, would have poured all its venom on the affection that its authority had not sanctioned."[30]

More deeply, the novel is about the failure of character in post-revolutionary society. Implicated in this charge are not only relations between intimates, but also human relations more broadly conceived. Constant laments that in his day character is not up to the demands imposed by society. In an unpublished passage for the preface to the second edition of *Adolphe*, he wrote the following:

> I wanted to portray in Adolphe one of the principal moral maladies of our century, this fatigue, this uncertainty, this absence of

force, this perpetual analysis, which places a mental reservation beside all sentiments, and because of that corrupts them from their birth.... And it is not only in the intimacies of the heart that this moral weakness extends, that this impotence of durable impressions is evident; all is tied together in nature. Fidelity in love is a force as in religion, as with liberty. But we no longer have any strength. We no longer know how to love, to believe, to want. Everyone doubts that which he says, smiles with vehemence on that which he affirms, and hastens the end of that which he tries."[31]

In this remarkable passage, Constant addressed the all-important issue of character, and how it resonated in personal relationships, in religion, and in politics. The passage suggests that just as successful love requires strength and consistency of character—qualities unfortunately not predominant in the fictional protagonist Adolphe—religion similarly requires belief, and liberty requires enthusiasm. What Constant laments, and what the novel *Adolphe* analyzes with such coruscating rigor, is the failure of modern man to measure up. Modern character is not equal to the moral requirements of the modern age; the paramount values of love, belief, and enthusiasm are being lost because men's emotions and energy are damaged, weak, vacillating.

Character was a central issue for Constant because he believed it to be essential for moral action and for emotional and spiritual fulfillment. It was also important for the survival of a liberal political regime. His anxiety revolved around his perception that modern character was deeply flawed, especially in France, "a nation weakened by the excess of civilization, a nation which has become vain and frivolous due to the education of the monarchy, and in which even the enlightened have become sterile, because they make clear only the route, but do not give men the power to move ahead."[32] In such a weakened nation, Constant suggests, love is tragically doomed to failure, religious belief is undermined by skepticism and institutional intolerance, and political freedom is precariously balanced between absolutism and usurpation. This modern condition of vertigo was, thus, simultaneously emotional, religious, and political.

Staël's *Corinne* and Constant's *Adolphe* are, thus, tragedies that portray societies as ruthlesslessly insensitive to the needs of *sensibilité*. But they differ. In the words of Adolphe, "The laws of society are stronger than the whims of men; the most urgent sentiments are crushed by the fatality of circumstances. In vain one pays heed only to one's heart."[33] Staël's *Corinne*, however, is informed by a hope that compassionate individuals may, in the appropriate setting, find fulfillment. *Adolphe*, on the other hand, offers a bleaker assessment of society and modern character: it suggests that the times are characterized by a negative play between social conventions and the sensitive temperaments of its most insightful souls.

## Sensibilité

One of the contexts within which Constant's analysis of character can be usefully situated is the concern with *sensibilité*. The ascendancy of *sensibilité* in French culture dates from the 1760s, though it built on an exploration of subjectivity and affection—what Joan DeJean has called a "rewriting of the language of the emotions"[34]— that reached back into the late-seventeenth century. In 1760, the verse of Ossian (purportedly the work of a third-century Gaelic bard but in fact forged by James Macpherson) appeared; in 1761 Rousseau's *La Nouvelle Héloïse* was published; in 1761 and 1765 salons featured the paintings of Jean-Baptiste Greuze. The rehabilitation of sensibility meant a new attentiveness to the passions and public demonstrations of deep feeling. It was associated with the widespread belief that there were moral sensations to which all individuals had access. This shift continued apace in the following decades. In 1774, Christoph Willibald von Gluck's *tragédie-lyrique Iphigénie en Aulide* took Paris by storm.[35] In 1776, Goethe's *Werther* was translated. By the end of the 1770s, to live simply and honestly was to shed tears, experience convulsions, and above all to open the soul to gentle sentiments.[36]

The author who had most spectacularly transformed the prudent empiricism of the early Enlightenment into sentimentalism was, of course, Rousseau. In novels like *La Nouvelle Héloïse* and in discursive writings like *Discours sur l'origine et les fondements de l'inégalité*, Rousseau rehabilitated sentiments and "principles prior to reason."[37] He was immensely influential. Germaine de Staël, for example, credited Rousseau with being "the first person who believed that one ought to express the burning agitations of one's heart." She congratulated him for the rediscovery of "natural sentiments" at a time when they were ignored. He valorized "sentiments that are at the same time ardent and tender, delicate and passionate."[38] Like many at this time, Staël identified with Rousseau and with the characters of his novels because they expressed some of her deepest aspirations and longings—for love, as well as for motherhood and domestic felicity. Constant, also, was deeply influenced by Rousseau and by other eighteenth-century writers who analyzed "sentiments."

If *Adolphe* is a moral tale that draws heavily from Rousseau, it does so in several respects. It can easily be read, for example, as an attack on the corruption of aristocratic society. Adolphe is presented as a young man with a "natural heart" who is driven to seduce Ellénore not because of the impulses of his own heart, but because of social pressures, and because of the conventions of aristocratic society, like the one that expected a young man to have a mistress. And, it is "society" that passes judgments on the appropriateness and inappropriateness of Adolphe's and Ellénore's relationship. As such, "society" imposes constraints that distort admirable human sentiments; it is the inauthentic aristocratic world of *amour-propre* that Rousseau so famously criticized. Adolphe continually struggles between his own authentic feelings of responsibility for the woman he has seduced and the misleading social expectations, deeply internalized, that he should pursue a successful career. This struggle leads to his vacillation between the desire to be free and the desire to be part of this increasingly unhappy relationship.[39]

But society also provides Adolphe the incentive for winning respect and, more importantly, fulfilling his justified desire for high social achievement. Though Adolphe fails to achieve anything in society, the latter is not presented as hideously falsifying and inherently negative. There is no sense in *Adolphe* that the individual, with his feelings and dreams, is inevitably positioned only against society. This is because corrupt society is only one side of the equation. The other is modern man's feeble character.

Before the late-eighteenth century, it had been common to identify passion with narrow self-interest and with socially destructive fantasy. Sociability was, therefore, problematic and required that passions be controlled or contained by some countervailing force. One obvious solution in politics was to follow Thomas Hobbes and imagine an all-powerful ruler who forbids all destructive passions. If one was to avoid such implicit authoritarianism, it was necessary to find another force—like religion or "republican" virtue—to contain passion; and indeed during the eighteenth century a good deal of intellectual labor was expended on thinking through such issues.

Late-eighteenth century proponents of *sensibilité* transformed this view of the passions and, hence, of sociability. Not all passions were destructive and driven by self-interest; some passions were beneficial. And these passions—eventually termed "feelings," "affections," or "sentiments"—were to be embraced so as to counter the more destructive passions of selfishness and cruelty. This entailed a sociability that transcended self-interest not through political repression or external control, but, rather, through cultivation of those sentiments and passions conducive to social concord and peace. In France, this general discussion was intensified by the violent upheavals of the Revolution and those dangerous passions evident especially during the Terror. There was a widening concern, therefore, with how to restrain or channel socially undesirable passions.[40]

One approach to this issue was suggested by Kantian idealism, a "solution" that was discussed seriously in France during the 1790s. Kant had proposed, in his moral writings, that one should, out of duty, follow those universal ethical rules in conformance with the categorical imperative, regardless of immediate costs and benefits. We know that Constant and Isabelle de Charrière discussed Kantian ideas with Louis-Ferdinand Huber in Neuchâtel, and that Constant was a friend of Charles de Villers, who was instrumental in introducing Kant into France.[41] Both Constant and Charrière rejected the Kantian alternative as too idealistic, too abstract to be useful in concrete situations. Morality was not a question of abstract appeals to principle that fail to take consequences into consideration. Morality was about acting in complex situations in ways that respect moral dignity and conform to justice. As early as 1797, Constant publicly defined a position in opposition to Kant's categorical imperative. He recommended "midrange principles" to mediate between universal principles and circumstances. Principles were clearly important for Constant (he rejected "utilitarianism"), but consideration of the consequences of actions in specific situations dictated that principles might need adjustment or qualification.[42]

A more popular strategy than Kant's absolute moral austerity was to emphasize and encourage the individual passions that supported socially beneficial actions. For Rousseau, the sentiments of "self-respect" (*amour-de-soi-même*) and "compassion" (*pitié*) were believed to be the two sentiments upon which a worthy society could be based. Staël and Constant, like so many others, shared Rousseau's high regard for "compassion" and its close associate "sympathy."

Constant, for example, wrote that "All that is generous and great has its principle in sympathy, that is to say in the impossibility of contemplating the suffering of another without emotion, and without wanting to help."[43] Germaine de Staël argued in *De l'influence des passions* (1796) that "only one sentiment is able to serve as guide to all situations, compassion."[44] Constant, writing in 1798, could even credit Danton with "being susceptible of compassion, of this virtue of generous hearts," even though he remained critical of his revolutionary role.[45]

One of the other passions that Constant viewed as positive was "enthusiasm." Enthusiasm was ardent and tender, delicate and tolerant. It implied a spontaneous outpouring of positive emotion, an intense and unfettered feeling that could raise one to sublime heights. Enthusiasm was a generous emotion that created ties between and among individuals. It was beneficial for both personal development and political stability because the health of both was seen as connected with escape from narrowness and egoism. To quote Germaine de Staël, "Enthusiasm is tolerant... because it makes us feel the interest and beauty of all things.... Enthusiasm finds in the reverie of the heart and in the vastness of thought that which fanaticism and passion lock up in a single idea or a single object."[46]

Constant was careful to distinguish "enthusiasm" from fanaticism, which he characterized as the misguided attempt to reduce everything to one idea, a misstep that often arose from the failure to recognize that, in reality, life was complex and that everything was conditioned by place, environment, and a plurality of ideas.[47] Both religious and political fanaticisms, fed either by passion or reason, were dangerous because they could narrow individual choice to one exclusive idea.

Constant's analysis of character, therefore, raised issues critically important for his view of all dimensions of human interaction—intimate, social, and political. And, his thinking was powerfully shaped by the sentimental views of Scottish thinkers and, especially, of Rousseau. Like many of his contemporaries, he saw character and sentiment as constituent elements of politics. There were good passions—like compassion and enthusiasm—that could be encouraged because they helped citizens avoid fanaticism and self-absorbed isolation. And there were social arrangements that promoted an enlightened sociability conducive to these beneficial passions—literature, conversation, and open political forums.[48] Critical as he was of modern character and of the potential authoritarianism and repressiveness of some governments, Constant was ultimately optimistic about the prospects of progress. There was, as he put it at the time, a "general impetus toward liberty."[49]

In *De la force du gouvernement actuel*, Constant addressed the issue of the psychological contours of political regimes by analyzing the lack of sociability that had characterized the French old regime monarchy.

> I have observed that this inactivity [under a monarchy] is the source of one of our greatest misfortunes, a misfortune which is not only political, but individual. It is the source of this arid and burning sentiment which consumes our existence, discolors all objects, and, similar to the burning winds of Africa, dries out and withers everything that it encounters. This sentiment, which is not able to be found in ancient languages or in the languages of free people,...was born principally of this privation of goal, of interests, of hopes other than those which are narrow and personal. It haunts not only the obscure subject of monarchies, but the Kings on their thrones, the ministers in their palaces, because the soul is always penned in [*resserrée*] when it is thrust into egoism: there is always something dull, withered in those who regard only themselves, in those who do not spring from nature and march toward liberty. Ambition, in monarchies, even when it wants to ascend to that which is good, is always driven back upon itself. One is not able to forget oneself, one is not able to be carried away with enthusiasm, one is not electrified by the recognition of equals, one bows down before the thanks of a master. One feels oneself made smaller by the surrounding narrowness. Disgraceful *ennui* marks with its seal all that which is not either degraded by servitude, distracted by ignoble pleasures, or preserved from contagion by study and isolation: and if the Republic, which emerged, still experiences so many obstacles, and above all encounters so much inertia, it is due to monarchical education. Characters are still too small for the spirits, they are worn down, as the body, by the habit of inaction or by the excess of pleasures.[50]

What is so interesting about this passage is not only that it shows the influence of Montesquieu's discussion of the principles that animate different political regimes—though it certainly shows this—but that it also extends this discussion to a general reflection about personal character and activity.

We know, from his earliest political ruminations, analyzed above, that Constant believed that the success of the Republic was being undermined by the *moeurs* that had characterized the old regime monarchy. He indicated that "enthusiasm" was the antidote. There are a number of ways that this cut across French traditions of political discourse. It was, first of all, a departure from previous theories of republicanism. For Montesquieu, Rousseau, and Robespierre—to name French republicanism's best-known theorists—a republic required that the population be animated by "virtue," by a renunciation of private personal gain for the good of society. Constant, as we have seen above, rejected this, arguing that modern societies must be animated by "interest." But what this long quotation indicates is that Constant recognized that "interest" alone could lead to narrowness, egoism, and privatized sterility; the "arid and burning sentiment" of egoism ran the risk of withering emotions and undermining enthusiasm. Already well developed in monarchies, which prided themselves on their principles of "honor," but which in fact (in Constant's judgment) had become degraded by servitude and distracted by ignoble pleasures, this egoism unfortunately was sapping the vitality of the republic. Constant, however, called not for the traditional republican antidote—"virtue"—rather, he called for "interest" stimulated by "enthusiasm."

It is significant that "enthusiasm" was the term that Constant chose to use, for "enthusiasm" was a much-used term that carried a number of important associations. Many in the eighteenth century, to go back no further, had viewed "enthusiasm" as a mark of unreasonable religious belief; Locke and Voltaire are only two of the best-known critics of what they viewed as the fanaticism and intolerance of "enthusiastic" religious sects. Rousseau remained critical of "enthusiasm," but in a broad fashion he rehabilitated sentiment; in his *Discours sur l'origine et les fondements de l'inégalité*, as we have seen, he appealed directly to self-respect and pity—"two principles prior to reason"—as the basis of social interaction.[51]

Many subsequent writers echoed Rousseau's sentimentalist themes, but it was Germaine de Staël who extended the sentimentalist embrace to "enthusiasm."[52] In *De l'influence des passions sur le bonheur des individus et des nations* (1796) and in *De la littérature considérée dans ses rapports avec les institutions sociales* (1800), as well in mature works like *De l'Allemagne* (1813), Staël argued that the most exalted sentiment was enthusiasm, which she insisted must be distinguished from superstition and dangerous passions. "Many people," she wrote in *De l'Allemagne*, "are biased against enthusiasm; they confuse it with fanaticism, and this is an error."[53]

> Enthusiasm does not at all resemble fanaticism.... Enthusiasm is tolerant, not by indifference, but because it makes us feel the interest and the beauty of all things.... Enthusiasm finds in the reverie of the heart and in the vastness of thought that which fanaticism and passion lock up in a single idea or a single object.[54]

Years earlier, in 1788, she had claimed that "the soul has all its force only in throwing off all restraint [*s'abandonnant*]."[55] As these quotes indicate, Staël favored romantic lack of constraint, what in 1788 she termed "a profound passion," "*ce abandon sublime*."[56]

Staël was critical of enthusiasm only when it became melded with military glory, only when it became associated with patriotic passions central to republican "virtue." "The enthusiasm of a revolution," she wrote in 1798,

> no doubt adds greatly to the bravery of soldiers.... [But,] the military spirit is conquering, [while the spirit of] liberty is conservative. The military spirit accounts for everything, marches everywhere with force; liberty exists only with the support of enlightenment. The military spirit sacrifices men, liberty multiplies their mutual ties; the military spirit hates reason as the beginnings of indiscipline, liberty establishes authority on conviction.[57]

Summarizing her stance in 1800, Staël wrote that "the enthusiasm that inspires the glory of arms is the only enthusiasm that becomes dangerous to liberty."[58] The rehabilitation of "enthusiasm" was, therefore, a central theme in Germaine de Staël's writings, but this rehabilitation was to stop short of an embrace of patriotic "virtue."

At no place does the influence of Staël on Constant show itself more clearly.[59] Though in general less attracted to sentimental flights than Staël, Constant also favored enthusiasm, especially after the mid-1790s. At this time, he shed his youthful skepticism and cynicism and wrote approvingly of the sentiment of enthusiasm. "The greatest resource for mankind," Constant wrote in *De la force du gouvernement actuel*, "is conviction. The enthusiasm which promises victory, assures it. . . . Resignation by its nature diminishes strength by half."[60] Enthusiasm allowed one to escape the "burning winds of Africa," it allowed one "to forget oneself," to be "electrified by the recognition of equals." Constant seemed especially willing to countenance enthusiasm when it was connected with political attachment to the Republic.

Constant's appeal to the sentiments was a constant of his writings. In *Principes de politiques* [1815], he discussed the power of aesthetic experience and how this was connected with emotions, and ultimately with morality.

> [T]here is in the contemplation of beauty of any kind, something which detaches us from ourselves, making us feel that perfection is worth more than we are, and that, through this conviction, by inspiring us with a momentary disinterestedness, awakens in us the power of sacrifice, which is the source of all virtues. There is in emotion, whatever its cause, something which makes our blood circulate more quickly, which communicates to us a kind of well-being, which doubles the sense of our existence and our power, and which, by doing so, renders us capable of a generosity, courage, and sympathy, greater than we normally feel.[61]

## Religion

Reference to enthusiasm resonates with religious echoes. Constant's attentiveness to religion has traditionally been viewed as a curious anomaly that does not cohere comfortably with his political liberalism. This is now being reconsidered.[62] Central to these scholarly reconsiderations is weighing the motivations and importance of Constant's lifelong labor on the book that he considered his most important, *De la religion considérée dans sa source, ses formes et ses développements*.[63] Some scholars have come to stress Constant's religiosity as deeper than previously appreciated. Others, like Kurt Kloocke and Helena Rosenblatt, have argued that Constant's religious analysis was inextricably connected with his political liberalism, and that both dimensions (political and religious) were deeply imbedded in a Protestant tradition.[64] Others, finally, have claimed more categorically that "Constant certainly was religious" and that "his liberalism can be shown to have deep roots in theism and late eighteenth-century Protestant…religious thinking"[65] The interpretation advanced here will emphasize the relationship of Constant's religious thought to his abiding interest in *sensibilité*, the European cultural movement discussed above. Constant was convinced that religious sentiment was an elemental aspect of human nature, and he believed that any analysis of sociopolitical affairs must take this into account. But to fold his liberalism into this religious dimension is overly reductive. Religion, though important to Constant, was never as central to his *liberalism* as were his concerns for the protection of rights (including toleration of religious belief and practice), constitutionalism, the division of sovereignty, and his wider concern with fostering positive social *moeurs*.

But, first, a few words about Constant's own religious beliefs. Constant never participated in the rituals of an organized religion; he was never aligned with any confessional group; he was, as Pierre Deguise argued many years ago, essentially an agnostic.[66] He recounted in his *mémoirs* that he grew up a skeptic. "Having been nurtured on the principles of eighteenth-century philosophy and above all on the work of Helvétius, I had no other thought than to contribute my share toward the destruction of what I called prejudices."[67] This corresponds with the testimony of John Wilde, who remembered Constant as being an "atheist" at the time of his university studies in Edinburgh (1783–85).[68] It was shortly after leaving Edinburgh that he first conceived of writing a book about religion, one that likely would have recommended paganism over Christianity. While in Brunswick (1788–94), probably because of the influence of Jacob Mauvillon, Constant became familiar with German Protestant theology, and was impressed with the degree to which they "discard[ed] the whole dogmatic and miraculous part of Christianity."[69] Liberal Protestant theology, with its rejection of religious orthodoxy and its embrace of a spiritual and radically personal religiosity, made a deep impact on Constant, and probably changed the orientation of the manuscript on which he was working. Clearly, he preferred the liberal Protestant stance of these Enlightenment scholars to the sacerdotal and sacramental stance of Catholicism. In early-1794, he informed Isabelle de Charrière that he was hard at work on a "big book" about religion, though, of course, nothing appeared for many years.[70]

Constant was fascinated with the spirituality valorized by liberal Protestant theologians, and for a brief period during the late-1790s he was drawn to Theophilanthropy, a non-sacerdotal religion supported by the Directory at the end of the 1790s. Directors like Louis-Marie de La Revellière-Lépaux and intellectuals like Bernardin de Saint-Pierre and Pierre-Samuel Dupont de Nemours hoped that Theophilanthropy would replace Catholicism, and in so doing provide the French people with a belief system that would support republican stability.[71] Constant, we know, also favored at this time government-sponsored national festivals and civil ceremonies, informed by Theophilanthropic ideas; he promoted these while head of administration of the commune of Luzarches in the late-1790s. But, whatever his brief attraction to the social function of religiosity (he soon opposed all government support of civic festivals), he did not become religious. He did not recommend any formalized religious rituals, nor did he support any established church.[72] Even more tellingly, he did not articulate any belief in a supreme being, in revelation, or in Jesus as a prophetic personage. These latter, seemingly, would be minimal elements for any attribution of "Protestant" or "Christian." Before the 1820s, there is no evidence that Constant was attached to any specific theology—that is, to any belief beyond a conviction that individuals experienced an elemental drive toward spirituality.

Constant preferred Protestantism to Catholicism. He argued that there was a progression of religious forms, and he believed that Protestantism (deprived of some of its dogmas) represented the religious form that best corresponded to the enlightened thought of his historical period. As Deguise concisely puts it, for Constant Protestantism "is not a revealed, absolute truth, where one finds refuge in order to clarify all obscurity; rather it is simply a transitory form."[73] To prefer Protestantism to Catholicism does not add up to belief in Protestantism. As Constant put it in his journal in 1804, "That which upsets me is that this furor against Protestantism situates the question on the wrong terrain. One would believe that it is a question of knowing whether we should choose Protestantism or Catholicism, while there is every reason to believe that we were relieved [*nous étions débarassés*] of the one and the other."[74] The only rapprochement between Protestants and Catholics that Constant could support would be based on a "Christian tolerance that is born of the spirit of charity that the author of Christianity preaches to all his children." "This rapprochement is one of the heart."[75] Constant's religiosity, then, if one insists on using the term, is related to his belief that all individuals experience a deeply felt aspiration to connect with a higher force. He felt it himself. As he put it in 1805, "I have my religious corner. But it is entirely in the form of sentiment, in vague emotions: it cannot be reduced to system."[76] During the 1810s and 1820s, Constant became more respectful of religion, but continued to hold established religions at arms length. In *De l'ésprit de conquête et de l'usurpation*, published in 1814, he made a reference to how the human race had "fallen from the rank which Providence has assigned to mankind," indirectly suggesting that there was some Providential order to the universe.[77] In *Principes de politiques* [1815], he insisted that the basis of religion remained sentiment. It was "that vague and profound part of our moral sense, which by its very nature defies all the efforts of language."

> How would you define the impression of a dark night, of an antique forest, of the wind that moans across the ruins, or over the tombs, of the ocean that stretches beyond our sight? How would you define the emotions caused by the songs of Ossian, the Church of St. Peter, meditation upon death, the harmony of sounds or forms? How would you define reverie, that interior quivering of the soul, where all the powers of the senses and of thought come together and lose themselves in a mysterious confusion? There is religion at the bottom of all these things. All that is beautiful, all that it intimate, all that is noble, has something of the nature of religion.[78]

Similar statements are present in later works, suggesting that Constant came to embrace a belief closer to theism in the 1820s (he also became an active member of the Society for Christian Morals[79]). He wrote some passages that pointed to a belief in a supreme being. For example, in a long note in the first volume of *De la Religion*, published in 1824, he wrote that "to affirm that the germ of religion finds itself in the human heart is assuredly not to assign this gift from heaven a purely human origin. The infinite being deposited this germ in our body, in order to prepare us for the truths which will become known to us."[80] What sort of nonhuman "infinite being" is this? Constant never elaborated. It is certainly not the God of the Old Testament, who wants to be respected and to reign supreme through the distribution of justice. Nor, is it the God of the New Testament, who wants to be loved and who himself loves the rebellious creatures on earth. Nor is it the watchmaker God of the eighteenth-century Deism.

Again, Pierre Deguise is a reliable guide: Constant's God, he writes, "is an abstract phantom, guardian of the ideal of justice and liberty, whose existence is more often desired than certified.... This vague God, impersonal, abstract, and above all without power, would no longer have any consistency in a religion without beliefs. In contrast to the 'stationary forms [of religion],' religious sentiment signifies becoming and liberty."[81] Constant often wrote as though any notion of a supreme being was a compensatory human invention. In *Principes de politiques* [1815], he wrote the following:

> Against so many sorrows, we search everywhere for consolation, and all our lasting consolations are religious. When men persecute us, we create for ourselves I do not know what sort of refuge beyond human reach. When we see our dearest hopes, justice, liberty, our country vanish, we have the illusion [*nous nous flattons*] that somewhere a being exists who will reward us for having been faithful, in spite of the age we live in, to justice, to liberty, to our country. When we mourn a beloved being, we throw a bridge across the abyss, and traverse it with our thought. Finally when life deserts us, we launch ourselves towards another life. Religion is by its very essence the faithful companion, the ingenious and indefatigable friend of those in misfortune.
>
> This is not all. Consoler of our misery, religion is at the same time the most natural of our emotions.[82]

It is telling that in this discussion of religious belief, Constant employed reflexive verbs-forms—"*nous nous créons*," "*nous nous flattons.*"[83] This is echoed in *De la Religion*: "When we see our most precious illusions—justice, liberty, *patrie*—vanish, we flatter ourselves that there exists somewhere a being who knows how to be loyal to justice, liberty, and *patrie* in spite of our century."[84] Constant frequently suggested that we should resist giving in to such self-flattery and grandiosity, but he was sensitive to the depth and consoling power of religious belief. In sum, one should be careful not to conflate Constant's firm conviction that everyone knows the experience of seeking spiritual consolation with acceptance of a robust form of "religion."[85]

*De la Religion* was conceived in 1785, when Constant was eighteen years old, but the five-volume work was published only in the years surrounding Constant's death in 1830.[86] Neither an apology of nor attack on religion, it focused on a historical analysis of ancient polytheistic religions. Its underlying orientation was informed by Constant's firm lifelong conviction, already mentioned, that religious sentiment is a permanent and distinguishing aspect of human nature. He believed that this had important implications for the ultimate source of religious belief and for the nature of religious institutions. According to Constant, religious belief is not the result of some intervention by a transcendent being, as many religious individuals claim. On the other hand, religious belief cannot be dismissed as a manifestation of some underlying economic dislocation or social need, as suggested by various secular thinkers during the nineteenth century, though (as we shall see) these factors can influence the *form* organized religions take. At base, religion is an outgrowth of an innate aspiration to give meaning to life and the world; to make contact with the infinite. "Religious sentiment," he wrote in 1824, "is this faculty, this need of the soul, which leads or compels it to seek beyond the visible world beings with which it can establish communication." It is "the intimate sentiment which comforts and ennobles us."[87]

Religious sentiment, for Constant, is very much like other positive sentiments, like compassion and enthusiasm, which are also conducive of what is best in mankind. Like compassion, religious sentiment is clearly at odds with negative sentiments like fanaticism and selfishness that are conducive of strife and evil actions. Religious sentiment is basic and enduring. As he wrote in *Principes de politique* [1806], it is "the most natural of all our emotions." "All that is beautiful, deep, and profound is religious."[88] He speaks of it as the element of human nature that is capable of elevating man from the level of nature to that of superior values. It is the thirst for immortality; the thirst for liberty without limits; the thirst for harmony with the rest of nature; the consciousness of imperfection; the presentiment of a tie with something (a force or being) that is superior. Religious sentiment is fundamentally different, therefore, from science, which yields specialized knowledge. And, it is fundamentally different from morality, which strives to provide insight into proper behavior. The source of religion, Constant wrote in 1818, was to be found "not in reasoning, fear or hope, but rather in a need of the soul inherent to the nature of man, indestructible, which seeks always to satisfy itself according to the state of enlightenment and the stage of civilization."[89]

As this quotation indicates, Constant assumed that this universal underlying religious sentiment took different forms in different historical eras.[90] "Religion considered as a positive institution is a very different thing from religion considered as an individual sentiment."[91] Religions had taken many forms historically. It was this observation of the variety of religious forms that led to the *historical* method of analysis that is at the heart of *De la religion*, which focused on religious forms in the ancient world. Tzvetan Todorov has observed that the contextual and structural approach of this work was a truly "revolutionary method" in Constant's era, though it has become more common since. It is an approach similar to the one taken later by Max Weber in his positing of "ideal types." "Constant searched for a middle way," wrote Todorov, "between history and system: a discipline interested in abstract principles yet solidly based on fact."[92]

Constant divided religious forms into two "ideal types," or what Constant himself termed "combinations." The first were "sacerdotal religions" or "dependent religions" that were dominated by a priestly caste that imposed order, claimed authority, determined rituals, and therefore, according to Constant, generally resisted change. Sacerdotal religions also tended to foster ties with political authorities and confuse any neat separation of theological and secular power. Constant was critical of this religious form. While "religious sentiment" was universal, it frequently had been subjugated and manipulated by unscrupulous priests and political authorities; that is, it had been contained within sacerdotal religions. The second of the "ideal types" were "free religions" or "independent religions," which were not static and controlled by a priesthood, but rather were based on individual inspiration, open to change and improvement, and not compromised by ties to secular authorities. Constant clearly favored this form of religion, which fostered a privatized, sentimental, antidoctrinal, anticlerical religiosity. Free religions were inherently superior to sacerdotal religions because they rejected dogma and embraced change. The organization of *De la religion* is an alternation of chapters about sacerdotal religions with chapters about free religions.

Religion, according to Constant, was not synonymous with morality, because many religious forms were moral failures, and some were used to justify repressive politics. And, Constant could easily imagine individuals acting morally without religious belief. Nonetheless, as George Armstrong Kelly has pointed out, morality and religion were not viewed as indifferent to each other. Religion was useful in its opposition to a morality based on utilitarian calculation, which Constant believed was deficient. Religion, therefore, could be the vehicle for this higher morality. While there was no necessary connection between morality and religion, for many individuals they were tied; as a consequence, society would suffer if there were a total lack of religious sentiment. "I would not form a bad opinion of an enlightened man if he was presented to me as having no religious feeling. But a people incapable of this sentiment seems to me deprived of a precious faculty and disinherited by nature."[93] Therefore, if religion could be kept out of the hands of a sacerdotal priesthood, it could have an important and useful social role. It could stimulate wonder and enthusiasm, and it could encourage generous and expansive sentiments. Religious *sentiment* supported liberty; its absence favored tyranny. As he put it in *Du polythéisme romain, considéré dans ses rapports avec la philosophie grecque et la religion chrétienne*, "Religious peoples can be slaves, but no irreligious people has ever been free."[94]

Constant's uneasiness, therefore, was directed at two extremes—at the "prejudices" of established religions, and at the "vulgarity" of irreligion. He was always suspicious of state religions, or of state support of religions, because he believed that this inevitably gave power to a group interested in consolidating power. He believed the best way to prevent this was for there to be complete denominational neutrality on the part of the state. As we shall see in detail below, Constant consistently favored religious toleration. This would benefit both politics and religion. "So long as [political] authority leaves religion perfectly independent, no one will have any interest in attacking it. The question won't even arise. But if authority claims its defense, if it wants especially to make it an ally, then the independent thinker will waste no time attacking it."[95]

Constant's embrace of religious sentiment was closely tied to the sentimental orientation that we have noted above. And, similar to his care to distinguish good and bad sentiments, Constant also distinguished three "religious passions": enthusiasm, superstition, and fanaticism. Similar to Staël, Constant wished to castigate fanaticism and to warn against the dangers of superstition. But he recommended enthusiasm, though unlike Staël Constant wished to introduce some qualifications. Both contrasted enthusiasm with the cold, egoistic, materialistic modern world that stifled creativity and promoted mediocrity. "All that which inspires hope," Constant wrote in an unpublished manuscript, "excites enthusiasm."[96] Constant differed from Staël, however, in suggesting that enthusiasm could have a negative side. It could, he believed, stifle natural affections; he maintained that it must, as a consequence, always be susceptible to qualification by rational intervention.

## Sociability

Constant was aware of the obvious difference between recounting the fictional history of a personal relationship, with all its idiosyncratic components and insinuations of indefinability, on the one hand, and on the other, theoretical writings about morals or politics that purported to provide formulas for general application. But he was equally clear that his novel about a melancholic young man was related to his sociopolitical stance. As he himself put it, "I have painted [in *Adolphe*] a small part of the scene, the only part which, if not without sadness, was without danger for the painter."[97] And, as indicated above, he was quite specific about the more general issue he wished to analyze: the egoism hidden behind the mask of vanity that he called "one of the principle moral maladies of our century." Symptoms of this malady were "inconstancy or fatigue in love, a thousand forms of disbelief in religion, dull or dreadful, servility in politics."[98]

The political implications of "character" were widely recognized at the time. Since at least Montesquieu, analysis of political systems involved analysis of not just institutions, but the "spirit"—the mores—that animated a society's population. Discussion of politics, therefore, generally included reflections about personal character, moral comportment, and their implications for stability or change. Such concerns were especially pronounced during the late-eighteenth and early-nineteenth centuries, when almost everyone in France who advocated political change framed their diagnoses of society in terms of the corruption inherent in luxury and despotism, and the need to teach morals and encourage industriousness. Constant's concern for character and morals—for what we would term "political culture"[99]—was a common trope.

During the 1790s, as we have seen above, Constant was worried that continuing revolutionary activity had rewarded fanaticism and had created a political culture seething with resentments and memories of past injustices. This had led to a culture of ridicule that undermined orderly government.[100] Constant also lamented the quite different penchant among his French contemporaries for self-absorption and passivity. This trait had been encouraged under the Old Regime monarchy, when ambition "was always driven back upon itself...[and] one feels oneself made smaller by the surrounding narrowness."[101] This propensity toward inactivity had resurfaced in the late-1790s, encouraging a narrow self-interest: "this arid and burning sentiment which consumes our existence, discolors all objects, and, similar to the burning winds of Africa, dries out and withers everything that it encounters."[102] Constant expressed ambivalence about the expansion of the sense of privacy characteristic of the times: it was an advance for individual liberty, but it had the unfortunate potential of reinforcing narrowness, egoism, and privatized sterility.[103] Constant's recurring fear, in sum, was that the Revolution had reinforced French character traits—fanaticism and self-interest—that would undermine a stable liberal politics.

These concerns became more pronounced during the years of Napoleon's rule. Constant believed that the Napoleonic Empire fostered nationalistic fanaticism and systematic selfishness. In this era when politics was monopolized by the Emperor and his minions, individuals were left to focus on the careful calculation of their own self-interest. Constant's criticism was explicitly articulated in the theoretical political works he wrote (but did not publish) during these years.[104] The message, however, corresponded philosophically with the contemporaneous analysis of character central to *Adolphe*.

Constant did have considerable hope, however. Critical as he was of modern character and of the repressiveness of Napoleonic "usurpation," Constant believed that history demonstrated progress. There was, as he put it at the time, a "general impetus toward liberty."[105] There were good passions that could be encouraged because they permitted one to avoid fanaticism and self-absorbed isolation. The positive passions, public as well as private, were enthusiasm and sympathy. Important for personal relations, they were also the critical sentiments that would support a reasonable politics. Enthusiasm and sympathy provided the *via media* between opposing political dangers—the danger of the intolerant fanaticism of mob rule and Jacobin excess, on the one hand, the danger of monarchical fanaticism and excess, on the other. Equally important, enthusiasm and sympathy protected individuals against isolation, introversion, and political indifference—against the egoism hidden behind the mask of vanity that characterized Adolphe.

According to Constant, certain contexts were more likely than others to encourage positive emotions like sympathy and enthusiasm, and thereby to promote independence and liberty. Some social arrangements were more likely to promote an enlightened sociability conducive to these beneficial passions. One should avoid, first of all, the isolation that characterized the world of Adolphe and Ellénore.[106] *Adolphe* is a trenchant analysis of the potentially destructive consequences of sensitive, lucid, devoted lovers (with all their faults, Adolphe and Ellénore shared these traits[107]) attempting to find their way without the support of family, friends, and society. The implication is that sociability is important for emotional health.

In other works of Constant we find positive indications of what this means. In *Fragmens d'un essai sur la perfectibilité de l'espèce humaine*, there is an interesting suggestion that progress is related to intelligence and sociability, and that savage nations are characterized by their absence: "No intellectual progress, no increase of sociability is about to be seen in them."[108] And there is a closely related suggestion that "literature"—in the extremely broad sense of verbal and written communication—is central to this. Communication takes many forms, such as eloquence, poetry, and literature. All of these promote progress because they increase the curiosity and awareness of human beings. Human beings are able to sacrifice immediate desires for future benefits, and they are able to calculate the overall benefits of such sacrifices; these demonstrate the ability of ideas to dominate merely passing sensations. Morality and progress, he suggested, had resulted from the advance of facts and reason over the passions. In stating that passions needed to be directed by the will, Constant was closer to Godwin and even the Idéologues than to Staël, who focused more on rhetorical and sentimental progress than the march of reason.[109] Constant thus introduced a second logic concerning the emotions. Not only should positive feelings, affections, and sentiments be encouraged, but reason and will were also needed to control and guide the passions.

The context of sociability is closely related to both of these logics. It addressed the issue of where beneficial passions were most likely to be encouraged; where reason and civility were most likely to be found; where public issues would be judiciously discussed and weighed. Staël and Constant differed slightly in their views of where to find the "sociable communication" essential for refinement and progress, but they shared a belief that enlightened, sensitive persons would move toward truth if they were in honest dialogue in the appropriate settings.[110] Staël, as we have seen above, was a great advocate of the sociability that had defined the salons of late Old Regime France.[111] In her mother's salon, she had become familiar with a form of conversation and type of social interchange that would remain, in the words of Albert Sorel, "the ideal home of her spirit" and "the ambition of her existence."[112] It remained a touchstone for the form of sociability that would encourage and sustain emotional security, practical knowledge, and political insight. Salons had provided absolutist France with social centers for the moderation of passions, for the teaching of civility, and for the cultivation of political skills. And salons remained one of the most hopeful places for the emergence of an aristocracy of talent that would introduce and lead liberal political reform in France. Salons, Staël hoped, could once again be a place of enlightened sociability. In her posthumously published *Considérations sur la Révolution française*, she represented the revolutionary descendants of the old regime salon as the privileged participants in a dialogue in which public opinion would be shaped with maximum potential satisfaction for hostile parties. "Talk was still an acceptable mediator between the two parties.... It is the last time and in many ways also the first, that Parisian society could give the idea of this communication of superior minds among themselves, the noblest pleasure of which human nature is capable."[113] As Linda Orr has suggested, Staël returned at regular intervals to this utopian idea of the communion of great minds together, in talk or, at the very least, in books.[114]

Constant was also an advocate of "salon sociability," but he was more cautious in his appraisal. Potentially centers of intellectual curiosity and humanitarian enthusiasm, they could also degenerate into places where selfish interests and personal ambitions were pursued at the expense of what was needed for the general welfare.[115] This was especially true in times of political crisis, when even in salons passions and factionalism could overwhelm reason, or in times of oppression, when fear might increase such that the discussion of serious matters would lead to censure or worse.[116]

Staël also became less optimistic concerning the efficacy of salons during the late Directory and the Empire, as we have seen above. After the advent of Napoleon, independent salons were progressively choked off. Many salons were no longer allowed to exist; those that continued to meet had degenerated into a miserable spectacle in which "a labyrinth of interests and ambitions" prevailed.[117] She retained some residual hopes that French conversation and sociability would temper the arbitrary ire of French politics, but she lamented that France did not have English parliamentary institutions, which also seemed critical. There is a famous passage in Staël's *Corinne* in which English upper-class sociability is depicted as stifling and boring. This corresponds chronologically, but contrasts analytically, with her characterization in *De l'Allemagne* of the lively sociability of France. During the period in which she wrote these two works—roughly 1804–1810—Staël was struggling to analyze the very different paths taken by England and France, and what lessons one should draw concerning politics, sociability, and personal fulfillment. She was impressed by the nature of parliamentary representative government in England, with its protection of civil liberties and its long history of internal political stability. But she thought it was unfortunate that there was no counterpart of the French salon, where the sexes mixed in an amiable setting for intellectual discussion about serious issues. Instead, political action in England took place in Parliament and in party meetings—that is, outside salons—and, as a consequence, the polish of society and the conversational skills of the salon were less important than in France. Staël lamented that France did not have English civil and political institutions to protect liberty and the rule of law, but she equally lamented that England did not have the elite sociability characteristic of France. Both were important ingredients of a liberal society.

Constant shared Staël's concerns and her general political orientation. He, too, favored English parliamentary institutions and civil guarantees; he, too, was concerned with an energetic sociability to enliven and animate society. The general issue for both was the relationship between limited forms of "society" like salons, and the wider world of competing interests and prejudices. This, in turn, reflected the widespread concern of the age for how the reason, passions, and unfettered feelings of a few sensitive and intelligent souls were to be related to wider society. The problem, stated differently, was to tie the sympathetic alignment of feeling that seemed possible within the salon or some other small association with the mutuality of affections that could bring people together in a more inclusive social model. How were the positive judgments and sensibility of the few to be related to the sociability, morality, and politics of the many?

Constant wrote three laudatory reviews of Staël's *Corinne* in May 1807. In the first, he stated that "The morality of a work of imagination is made up of the impression that its whole leaves on the soul:

if, when one finishes the book, one is more filled with mild, noble, and generous sentiments than when one began the book, then the work is moral and of a high level of morality."[118] He drew a parallel between the potential moral impact of a novel and that of music and sculpture.[119] One of the issues that Constant was addressing here was the argument, widespread during this time, that novels were incapable of being moralizing agents at all; instead, they inflamed the passions and thereby contributed to a loosening of morals and a weakening of the body politic. On this front, Constant, in clear agreement with his famous female companions Isabelle de Charrière and Germaine de Staël, believed to the contrary that novels should lead to moral reflection. If novels raise significant issues, and readers do the right interpretive work, then novels, by stimulating the emotions, can inspire virtue and encourage the moral life.

Constant and Staël were concerned about the ways that not only novels, but also conversation, the salon, and political institutions encouraged moral reflection and promoted, or undermined, a stable liberal politics. They believed that while some passions should be denied, others, like sympathy and enthusiasm, should be cultivated and encouraged in order to have a liberal society and a healthy citizenry. This emerged from their analyses of human character and how it had responded to the social and political changes of the Revolution and Empire.

Constant was always careful to emphasize that the ideas and mores of society were as important for the cultivation of political liberty as were institutional protections. "I should say that by the phrase 'ideas or sentiments of liberty', I do not mean that which one calls political liberty, but the instinct, more or less developed, of individual independence, of the rights of all men in society, of equality, in a word of human dignity."[120] Literature had an important role to play in this larger world of ideals and politics because it could cultivate liberty and the "instinct of individual independence." Constant's *Adolphe* provided an analysis of modern character that depicted the tragic unintended consequences of unthinking behavior on the part of a self-preoccupied and indolent young man, who found society problematic and escape from isolation fitful and unfulfilling. Though the novel focuses on the character of Adolphe and his relationship with Ellénore, it was inextricably intertwined with Constant's more general analyses of *sensibilité*, sociability, and the difficulties of establishing and sustaining a liberal politics.

Constant praised Voltaire for the practical intent of his fictional works and for defending liberty at a time when *"le pouvoir arbitraire"* of the monarchy created a situation when "germs of liberty were hidden in the works of great French writers."

> Voltaire always endeavored to achieve a result applicable to the circumstances in which he wrote....He had to upset a power, to undermine the authority of the time and of some men, and to make prevail some principles everywhere threatened.[121]

Constant no doubt hoped *Adolphe*, written when France was enduring another period of arbitrary power, would perform a similarly edifying role.

\* \* \*

Let me conclude this chapter with a few comparative points that relate Constant's thought to the broader history of political thought. Constant's liberal stance, because of his view of temperament and his insistence on the importance of sentiment and character, was distinctive. It was different, first of all, from all those "republicans" who argued that the antidote to the narrowness of the Old Regime and to the selfishness of individuals was "virtue," the renunciation of private personal gain and the embrace of a patriotic devotion to society. Constant rejected this disposition, seeing it as characteristic of revolutionary Jacobins, who he referred to in 1796 as "a new species." They were, "at the same time mobile and ferocious, irritable and hard-hearted, merciless and passionate, [and] join that which until the present seemed contradictory, courage and cruelty, love of liberty and thirst for despotism."[122] Constant argued that modern societies must be more willing to take individuals as they are, which meant to take individuals as unheroic, self-regarding individuals looking, at least in peaceful times, for repose. The dispositions to be encouraged—those that would most likely contribute to legal and constitutional security—were the less-heroic "domestic virtues" like compassion and enthusiasm.

Constant's attentiveness to the importance of *sensibilité* also distinguished his liberal stance from some of his best-known liberal contemporaries. One such group—including many medical writers and intellectuals like the Idéologues—believed that there were firm natural laws upon which the analysis and improvement of temperament could be placed. Medical writers like Cabanis, for example, believed that a physician could modify temperament by carefully regulating the environment. Idéologues like Destutt de Tracy believed that scientific experts would uncover natural laws of temperament, self-interest, and sociability and, through education and linguistic reform, could improve individual character and reform society. The unity of this group should not be exaggerated, but they did dominate the philosophical discourse in the Institute and in central schools.[123] Constant did not share this faith in "social science"; he was, in many respects, closer to enlightened Rousseauist critics of the Idéologues like Bernardin de Saint-Pierre, who challenged the idea that science and reason were sufficient guides for political society. This was because, for Constant, the analysis of abstract forms so important for scientific understanding, and which had done so much for the advancement of understanding of the physical world, was fundamentally different from the analysis of the passions and sentiments that provided the bases of our understanding of character, *moeurs*, and political culture. Constant's liberalism was different because he did not believe science would provide sufficient insight into the motivations and sentiments that were integral to modern political understanding.

Constant's liberalism is also different from garden varieties of "liberalism" of the late-twentieth century, which generally focused on economic issues like free trade and narrowly conceived institutional protections. Constant favored a reduction of government regulation of the economy, but his analysis of the market and the broader economy, unlike most recent liberals, was always inextricably intertwined with his assessment of sentiment, imagination, and political culture. Constant's liberalism balanced a concern for institutional reform and for the constitutional protection of "rights" with an equally prominent concern for expressive individualism, for providing elbow-room for the enthusiasm of intersubjective emotional connection. The perennial problem for Constant was to bring people to awareness of their ethical obligations, an awareness that acknowledged the restlessness of modern individuals, recognized the dangers of fanaticism and isolation, and encouraged positive sentiments like compassion and enthusiasm. He believed that moral judgments and political decisions relied on sentiments. He was attentive, in short, to how the problem of character shaped politics as well as individual destinies.

# 5

# Liberal Pluralism and the Napoleonic Empire (1802–15)

Constant's most famous political writings, the focus of this chapter, were composed during the years following his expulsion from the *Tribunat* in 1802. Special attention is given to the 1806 manuscript *Principes de politique applicables à tous les gouvernements* [published only in 1980];[1] *De l'esprit de conquête et de l'usurpation* [published in 1814];[2] *Réflexions sur les constitutions, la distribution des pouvoirs, et les garanties, dans une monarchie constitutionnelle* [1814];[3] *De la responsabilité des ministres* [1815];[4] and *Principes de politique applicables à tous les gouvernements représentatives et particulièrement à la Constitution actuelle de la France* [1815].[5] These works drew from his writings of the 1790s and especially from the unpublished manuscript *Fragments d'un ouvrage abandonné sur la possibilité d'une constitution républicaine dans un grand pays*, discussed earlier. They present a more systematic liberalism than contained in these earlier writings, but nothing substantially new.[6] This consistency was also demonstrated in the speeches and writings of his later years—his addresses to the Chamber of Deputies and, most famously, his 1819 address "De la liberté des Anciens comparée à celle des Modernes"—which also drew from the earlier manuscripts.

The historical context of these works is the Empire, the First Restoration of the Bourbons, and the Hundred Days. There have been criticisms of Constant's political maneuverings during this period: he frequently has been presented as an opportunist rallying to each new regime, and, therefore, guilty of embracing inconsistent political ideals. The evidence, however, suggests a quite different conclusion. Constant desired to see established in France a constitutional and parliamentary regime that protected individual liberties and separated and balanced power.[7] What changed was the environment, especially the institutional context, within which his goals were pursued. French politics were, to say the least, in continuous flux during these years, and Constant's strategy to advance his political agenda was always being adjusted in consideration of these changes. As we have discussed in other chapters, Constant's politics (as opposed to his personal affairs) generally incorporated an element of pragmatism. This does not entirely allay the charge of political opportunism; Constant obviously desired to be an effective political actor. But, such a framework does correctly align the relationship of these actions to the consistency of his political philosophy.

The quick pace of events was especially evident in the period 1812–15. Constant interpreted the defeat of the Grand Army in Russia as a hopeful sign that European peace could be regained and that France could be constitutionally rehabilitated. He worked for a few months in late-1813 and early-1814 to advance the candidacy of Charles-Jean-Baptiste Bernadotte, the Swedish Crown Prince who was viewed as a possible future occupant of the French throne. When this hope evaporated (Bernadotte returned to Sweden on 29–30 March 1814), Constant turned his attentions to other ways to influence events. He returned to Paris on 15 April 1814, four days after the abdication of Napoleon, and threw himself into preparing texts for publication. On 21 April, his short article "Des Révolutions de 1640 et 1688 en Angleterre, et de celle de 1814 en France" appeared in the *Journal des Débats*.[8] This article encouraged the French to see the opening of 1814 as the chance to initiate an époque of constitutional liberty similar to that instituted in England in 1688 (when the monarchy "was happily and skillfully reorganized") and to avoid the reactionary potential of a restoration like that of 1660 (when the English monarchy unfortunately had left "a clear field for vengeful and arbitrary actions").[9] The article drew heavily from his *Des suites de la contre-révolution de 1660 en Angleterre*, published in 1799 (analyzed in chapter 3). The next day, on 22 April, the third edition (but first Paris edition) of *De l'esprit de conquête et de l'usurpation* appeared. A month later, on 24 May, Constant published *Réflexions sur les constitutions, la distribution des pouvoirs, et les garanties, dans une monarchie constitutionnelle*, his first extensive *published* manuscript on constitutional issues. With this work, Constant obviously hoped to influence the form that the Charter, being formulated by Louis XVIII and his advisors, would take.[10] As Béatrice Fink has cogently observed, Constant was conducting "a preventative war" against the centralizing tendencies of the proposed Charter, arguing that the separation and balance of power were essential.[11]

A central argument of all of these works was that it was important to avoid a return to the absolutism and reactionary culture of the Old Regime and to reconcile the return to monarchy with the revolutionary spirit of individual liberty. Constant also reasoned, especially in *Réflexions sur les constitutions* and in *De la responsabilité des ministres* (published after the promulgation of the Charter), that there should be a separation of the power of the monarch from the power of the executive branch of government. This was a refashioning of the proposal for a "neutral power" that had been central to *Fragments d'un ouvrage abandonné*, and which would remain an integral part of his subsequent constitutional proposals, as the one in the 1815 version of *Principes de politique*. This neutral power, however, was no longer identified with a council of lifetime elected officials, as had been the case in the earlier manuscript, but rather with the hereditary monarch. Constant obviously was making adjustments to accommodate the new political realities, though the overall institutional structure of government remained consistent.[12] We have more to say about Constant's constitutional proposals in the subsequent pages.

Constant's most notorious and controversial political maneuverings occurred following the return of Napoleon from Elba in March 1815. In 1814, Constant had reemerged, because of the publications mentioned above, as a strong political voice in support of the constitutional monarchy and critical of Napoleon. *De l'esprit de conquête et de l'usurpation*, especially, was vehement in its attacks on Napoleon, on the Empire, and on the military culture that the Napoleonic wars had fostered in France domestically. *Réflexions sur les constitutions* also criticized Napoleon, for violating "the independence of courts of justice," stifling the liberty of the press, and for "surrounding this beautiful country with intellectual deserts."[13] *De la responsabilité des ministres* lamented that Napoleon had created a large number of "henchmen and spies" who, like himself, were "imposed on the nation by force; he [Napoleon] brought pressure on the nation, like them, with lies and despotic force."[14] Constant penned more criticisms of Napoleon in articles that appeared in the *Journal des Débats* on 11 March and 19 March 1815. In the latter, he wrote that Napoleon "is Attila, is Genghis Khan, more terrible and more odious because of the resources of civilization which he has at his disposal."[15] Napoleon arrived at the Tuileries the following day (20 March); and Constant prudently took refuge in the American Embassy and subsequently fled the city.

To everyone's surprise, however, Constant returned to Paris on 27 March and subsequently agreed to work in Napoleon's new administration. On 14 April he had a personal meeting with Napoleon, and concluded that "he is an astonishing man." At this meeting, Constant agreed to compose amendments to the constitution (these became *l'Acte additionnel aux Constitutions de l'Empire*, frequently referred to as "*la Benjamine*"[16]). Subsequently, he met frequently with the Emperor to work out the details, and agreed a few weeks later (on 20 April) to be a *conseiller d'État*. This was quickly followed by the publication, in May 1815, of a new political work, *Principes de politique applicables à tous les gouvernements représentatives et particulièrement à la Constitution actuelle de la France*, which supported *l'Acte additionnel* and, obviously, assumed the continued existence of the Empire.

Constant was criticized at the time, not least by Germaine de Staël and her friends, for his willingness to work with Napoleon and to accept a position in his administration.[17] And, his seeming opportunism during the Hundred Days has been noted frequently ever since. In 1819–20, Constant himself publicly addressed the issue.[18] He justified his actions by arguing that the royalists in 1815 had not taken sufficient measures to protect the constitutional monarchy and, foolishly, they had refused reforms and alienated and betrayed liberals like himself who were willing to compromise with the regime. Pushed away from the monarchy by these reactionary policies, liberals had turned to the Emperor as the more likely defender of the liberties they valued. Knowing today what we do of Ultra policies at this time, it is not difficult to understand why Napoleon could appear more attractive to liberals in early-1815 than the Bourbons. A central issue, obviously, was Constant's assessment of what Napoleon would do. Constant's actions in 1815 suggest, and his subsequent discussions of his actions claim, that he believed the reestablishment of the Empire would not necessarily return France to tyranny. He permitted himself to hope that, with proper guidance, a new Napoleonic regime—one that respected liberty—could be institutionalized. And, he viewed his own actions to be a contribution to just such a progressive development.

However naive this looks in retrospect, it is not inconsistent with the stance *vis-à-vis* regimes that Constant adopted throughout his life. He always emphasized his pragmatism: how it was necessary to constantly assess and reassess the actions one should take to bring about a reasonable government; how it was necessary to assess and reassess the actions one should take to advance the goals of political and civil liberties. "I have always believed," he wrote in 1820,

> and this belief has been the rule of my conduct, that in matters of government it is necessary to start from the point where one is; that liberty is possible under all forms [of government]; that liberty is the goal, and forms [of government] are only the means; that there are some individual rights, some sacred rights, some indispensable guarantees that one ought to introduce under the republic as under the monarchy....As a consequence, it is never against a form [of government] that I have argued; there is not any that I proscribe, none that I demand exclusively. That which exists has the advantage of being, and in order to substitute that which does not exist for that which does requires sacrifices that are always good to avoid.[19]

Not only was Constant's strategy in 1815 consistent with his strategy at other times, so were his political principles. This chapter demonstrates this doctrinal consistency by examining the political writings of the Empire, First Restoration, and Hundred Days.

The chapter begins, however, with a brief look at French pluralism, a tradition that influenced Constant, and to which scholarship on French liberalism has given insufficient attention.

## Pluralism

Modern French pluralism crystallized out of an enormously complex historical inheritance, with elements extending back through early modern political thought to the ancients. Plato, Aristotle, and Polybius, for example, referred to the importance of separate branches of government. Medieval thinkers not infrequently argued that royal power should be subjected to feudal and popular restraints. British political writers during the stormy seventeenth century argued over the differences among a "mixed government," the "separation of powers," and a "balanced constitution." Finally, American constitutionalists and revolutionaries stressed the importance of federalism and "checks and balances."[20] All of these influenced French thinkers of the early-nineteenth century, though in ways difficult to trace with any precision.

By the late-eighteenth century, there were three dimensions of what legitimately can be referred to as French pluralism, though the term was not in use.[21] There was a political dimension that rejected the idea of unitary sovereignty; an administrative dimension that argued for local power *vis-à-vis* the central power; and, a religious dimension that insisted on religious toleration. Each of these appealed to various political actors and thinkers during and after the Revolution. The call for administrative decentralization during the early-nineteenth century, for example, was made by individuals from across the political spectrum: ultraroyalists, liberals, socialists, and anarchists. All criticized excessive administrative centralization and called for the rehabilitation of local powers, of "intermediary" institutions, and/or of "associations"—though there were strong disagreements concerning *which* local/intermediate/associative institutions were to be rehabilitated. The call for political pluralism, to offer a second example, was made by ultraroyalists of the *chambre introuvable* of 1815–16, who found themselves out of step with Louis XVIII's policy of accommodating changes introduced by the Revolution, as well as by liberals of the same era who wished to emphasize the importance of legislative power *vis-à-vis* the monarch. What both groups shared was a deep suspicion of the calls for national unity that characterized all "factions" and "parties"—that is, all opposition political groups—as detrimental to the public good.

A comprehensive history of early-nineteenth century French pluralism remains to be written.[22] It will need to consider the strong contrary forces that supported religious, administrative, and political unity: the legacy of the absolutist and patrimonial state; the pervasive cultural and institutional influence of Catholicism; the residues of Cartesian rationalism and Enlightenment radicalism. And, it will need to take into account how these traditions were reinforced during the Revolution with critiques of the privileged order of the Old Regime, with fears of military defeat, and with anxieties about plots and conspiracies (of counter-revolutionaries, of monarchists, and of other revolutionaries). These traditions and forces created a political culture during the French Revolution that emphasized national unity and characterized political disagreement as unpatriotic, even treasonous.[23] What was distinctive about the post-revolutionary thought of Benjamin Constant and Germaine de Staël was the manner in which the three dimensions of French pluralism noted above—religious, political, and administrative—were combined to oppose what Lucien Jaume has termed the *unanimisme mystique* of Revolutionary culture.[24] Before turning to their thought, however, a few words about each of these three dimensions are in order.

*Religious pluralism* in modern France emerged as a result of the devastation of the religious wars, though again there was obviously a deeper historical heritage. The spread of Calvinism in France during the sixteenth century produced confessional contestation and, ultimately, religious warfare. This led to the articulation of the principle of religious toleration in the moral writings of French humanists like Guillaume Postel, Sebastian Castellio, and Jean Bodin, and to the support of a pragmatic policy of coexistence by Michel de l'Hôpital and members of the French *politique* tradition who argued that the cost of enforcing religious uniformity would likely be the destruction of the commonwealth.[25] These led, as well, to the first attempts by the government to institute a policy of religious coexistence and conciliation. The early notable example on this front was the Edict of Saint Germaine recommended by l'Hôpital and issued by Catherine de Medici in 1562. This Edict granted Huguenots freedom of conscience and freedom of organized worship outside of walled cities and in the private homes of noblemen everywhere. It was the first time a modern European state had formally recognized the coexistence of two churches on its territory. Even the German Peace of Augsburg of 1555 had not gone this far; it had partitioned the German territories into Catholic and Protestant regions, neither of which would tolerate the religion of the other. The Peace of Augburg, in short, recognized religious differences, but it did not indicate acceptance of religious coexistence on the same territory. Catherine's "January edict" of 1562, on the other hand, did just that, even if it viewed coexistence as a pragmatic temporary measure that was intended to facilitate future religious unity, and even if it was limited to only one other Christian group, that is, French Calvinists.[26]

This bold step was not accepted by the religious factions, however, or by Catherine after 1572, and there ensued a serial civil war that lasted thirty years—a war between the Huguenots who viewed themselves as "warriors of God" fighting against papist "idolatry" and in defense of a new divine covenant, on the one hand, and the Catholic "warriors of God" fighting to defend the Church and a sacred land against an assault of heretics, on the other. Thirty years of war did not lead to a decisive victory for either side, at least until Henry IV converted to Catholicism; that is, until he famously decided (even if he did not say) "Paris is worth a Mass." Four years later, in 1598, Henry issued another edict of toleration, the Edict of Nantes, which in form was very similar to the earlier edict of Catherine. Unfortunately, even this progressive policy of toleration was revocable, as Louis XIV demonstrated in 1685.[27]

These two edicts—that of Catherine in 1562 and that of Henry in 1598—were critical steps for pluralism, but they did not introduce acceptance of widespread religious diversity or tolerance of individual religious beliefs. These notions, articulated by John Locke and Pierre Bayle in the late-seventeenth century, only gained significant ground in France during the eighteenth century, when prominent *philosophes* like Voltaire, Montesquieu, and Diderot made fun of religious rituals and campaigned against religious intolerance. Their calls for religious tolerance overlapped with the quite different arguments of Jansenists, who sought (especially after the 1713 papal bull *Unigenitus* condemning Jansenism) to construct a Christian rationale for tolerance, and who emphasized the privatization of religious sentiment.[28] Moreover, both of these were reinforced after 1750 by royal administrators who found the persecution of the *nouveaux convertis* (as French Protestants were euphemistically but inaccurately referred to) administratively inconvenient, socially divisive, and contrary to the new jurisprudential discourse of natural law. The coalescence of Enlightenment, Jansenist, and administrative forces led to the Edict of 1787, which formally acknowledged the civil existence of Protestants, allowing them to hold property and enjoy civil marriage; but it still prohibited public worship. It was only with the Revolution that full toleration of religious belief and practice was implemented, and even then there were hesitations. The Declaration of the Rights of Man and Citizen of 1789, for example, included the potentially incommodious qualification that people's religious opinions were free "provided their expression does not trouble the public order established by law."[29] And, there was some opposition to granting *political* rights to individuals who, it was claimed, owned primary allegiance to their religious group rather than *la nation*.[30] Religious toleration remained a staple commitment of liberal and Left-wing figures after 1789, but it frequently was conjoined with anxiety about the social instability that might result from moral and cultural divisions.

*Political pluralism* is harder to trace, but got its *modern* form later than religious pluralism. This is because early-modern French theories of political sovereignty focused on the monarchy, even when widely accepted metaphysical assumptions placed *ultimate* power elsewhere.

There was widespread agreement that all secular authority was limited by divine and/or natural law, as well as by customs and legal procedures, and by some vague understanding of the "constitution" of the realm. The contentious issue was the *exercise* of power, and the relationship of this to stability and prosperity. What was the appropriate relationship among those persons and bodies claiming to have partial or exclusive rights over the exercise of sovereignty?

The Wars of Religion raised these latter issues in the most acute way. Jean Bodin's famous response, *Les six livres de la république* (1576), was to insist on the monarch's right to exercise sovereignty absolutely. To avoid chaos, to preserve social order, Bodin argued, the sovereign authority of the monarch must be indivisible and inalienable. Whatever divine, natural, and customary limits there may be to the authority of the monarch—these Bodin never denied—there was no secular power that was to be allowed to contest the decisions of the monarch, of the "prince elevated above all his subjects, whose majesty henceforth suffers no division."[31] In short, the propensity of political writers in France to discuss the importance of checks on the king's power (i.e., Claude de Seyssel's discussion of the "bridles" on the king's authority in his *The Monarchy of France* [1515]) gave way to a defense of the king as standing above and apart from his subjects.

Bodin's assumption that unitary sovereign power was identified with the King was contested by a few writers, but largely held sway. One of those who argued for a more pluralistic view of sovereignty was François Hotman, whose *Francogallia* (1573) famously provided a modern defense of deposing a tyrannical ruler and advanced a "constitutional" political theory that justified resistance.[32] Hotman argued that the King of France was a customary leader who, like any other magistrate, was subject to removal by the people for violation of the duties of his office. He theorized that the public council of the realm—made up of the King, the aristocracy, and the people—had power over legislation and the ordinary conduct of government; that is, it had political sovereignty. But Hotman was exceptional. Most "monarchomach" writers of this period did not propose seriously dividing the *exercise* of secular sovereignty, which they assumed to be unified in the person and office of the king (though theoretically "checked" by law and customary institutions). During the religious wars of the late-sixteenth century, it is notable that most radical militants devoted their energies to attempts to capture the King, thereby hoping to seize the location of the exercise of sovereign power.

The monarch's sovereign unity became even more pronounced in the political thought of subsequent theorists like Jacques-Bénigne Bossuet, who argued in *La politique tirée des propres paroles de l'Ecriture Sainte* [1679–1709] that the monarch reflected a deeper spiritual union. Bodin and Hotman, for all of their differences, believed that French society was made up of a pluralistic universe of competing and overlapping orders, estates, corporate bodies, communities, provinces, and *pays*. Bodin's point had been that all of these were held together through their common subjection to a unitary sovereign power, the King. Bossuet claimed more for the King; namely, that he was a Divine representative on earth, the vehicle through which Divine will was manifested in the secular realm. He rejected the idea that society was a separate entity of orders, estates, communities, and corporations; rather, society existed as a unit only through the will and actions of the King. Contemporaneously with this new theoretical justification of the monarchy in France, new court ceremonies were devised that emphasized the personal majesty of the King.[33]

French national consciousness emerged contemporaneously.[33] An important component of this national consciousness was the mystique, power, and prestige of the monarchy, which acquired dominion over a large and compact territory, though the unifying force of the French language was also significant.[34] There was, however, early evidence of tensions between attachment to the monarchy and attachment to the growing "imagined community" of France. During the religious wars of the sixteenth century, for example, both Protestants and Catholics found themselves at times justifying their positions by claiming to be fighting for the nation against the King. And while this tension seems to have diminished following Henri IV's accession to power in 1594, it reemerged during the final decades of Louis XIV's reign (1661–1715), when a considerable number of observers again began to question royal policies by arguing that the interests of the Bourbon dynasty were not identical with those of the nation.[35] Conceptions of a "national will" rooted in the people, not the monarch, would emerge from such tensions.[36]

During the eighteenth century, the idea that the King was invested with sacred and secular power progressively weakened. There was, in the words of Roger Chartier, an "affective rupture" between the

King and the people.[37] This was likely caused by several trends: the diminished presence of the Church in everyday life (as measured by the decline of religious observance and of the importance of Church associations, confraternities, and institutions); the thinning of the sense of connection between the people and their King (partly the consequence of the decline of state ceremonies); and the growth of critical thinking associated with the Enlightenment, especially among the urban classes. The result was that religion was giving way to politics as the preferred frame of reference within French "public opinion," while, simultaneously, there was a new level of disenchantment with the King and the royal family.

Theoretically, the monarch's loss of prestige and sacred authority was closely associated with rethinking of the issue of sovereignty. These reconsiderations drew, as Keith Michael Baker, Dale Van Kley, and others have shown, from various strains of French religious and political discourse—constitutional, juridical, economic, religious.[38] The historical-juridical tradition of customary law was joined (and sometimes combined) with philosophical definitions of "natural" rights, with new economic theories that based authority on property and the "division of labor," and with various redefinitions of the importance of "representation."

By the late-eighteenth century, these various strains had coalesced around two opposing conceptions of French history and the nation. The *thèse nobiliaire*, updated during the Maupeou crisis of 1771, had developed into a "patriot" defense of the "nation" against the rise of monarchical and ministerial "despotism." Anchored in a socially conservative tradition that had defended noble privilege, and even hearkening back to Boulainvilliers' historical thesis that the true "nation" was composed of the descendants of Frankish warriors, it developed during the crisis of the "pre-revolution" (1787–89) into a radical call for national legislative sovereignty (against the "despotic" king and ministers), the separation of constitutional powers (to contain the monarch), and the protection of individual rights. The *thèse royal*, on the other hand, provided a social and institutional history of France that celebrated the power of the centralized monarchy against aristocratic "feudalism." Anchored in an administrative vision that stressed utility, reason, and the general good, and embedded in a historical view that celebrated the rise of royal power and its ability to liberate the common people from aristocratic pretensions and feudal anarchy, it developed during the "pre-revolution" into a "ministerial" defense of the central state (to fight back against aristocratic pretensions and power) and an attack, more generally, on corporate privilege. The "patriot" position was fundamentally anti-despotic; the "ministerial" position fundamentally anti-feudal.

What momentously happened in 1788, during the crisis over the calling of the Estates-General and the debate about its composition, was the "revolutionary conflation" (to use Dale Van Kley's phrase) of these hitherto opposed views.[39] Rejecting both "despotism" and "feudalism," new revolutionary pamphlets combined a frontal assault on the absolute monarchy with a rejection of the aristocratic order of privilege. These new "national" pamphlets condemned both the "patriotic" and the "ministerial" versions of French history; indeed, they rejected historical tradition entirely in favor of a more abstract conception of the nation, viewed as an association of equal citizens whose civil and political rights must be respected and protected. The positive side of this "fusion of anti-despotic and anti-aristocratic agendas" (again the phrase is Van Kley's[40]) was a radical expansion of the patriotic agenda that focused on political rights and constitutionalism combined with a radical expansion of the ministerial agenda of equal access to all professions and positions and, more broadly, equality under the law. These found expression in the "Declaration of the Rights of Man and of the Citizen" of 1789.

Where is "political pluralism" in all of this? To parse this out, it is necessary to say a few words about the influence of Montesquieu and Rousseau. One of Montesquieu's great achievements in the *Lettres persanes* (1721) and in *De l'esprit des loix* (1748) was to focus on the danger of arbitrary power. In the former work he excoriated the injustices and instability of despotic organizations, depicted in his account of "the myth of the troglodytes" and in the letters about Usbek's seraglio. In the latter work, he described two political models that provided some containment of dangerous arbitrary power. The first model was a moderate monarchy governed by law, with checks on royal authority provided by "intermediate, subordinate, and dependent powers." In French society such "powers" could be identified with the independent judiciary (as represented by the *parlements*), the privileged nobility animated by "honor," and the Church. Montesquieu's second model was an English-style "republic, disguised under the form of a monarchy"[41] in which there was a functional separation of power among three branches of government (King, Lords, and Commons) and in which there existed a variety of ways in which the power of any one branch was contained by a system of "checks and balances." Both models, therefore, provided institutional and procedural checks to the exercise of power. Both were "pluralistic" in the sense that they rejected the placement of unqualified political sovereignty in one location.

Montesquieu's thought had an immense influence on French (and American) political thinkers throughout the political spectrum. Many of these, of course, did not share Montesquieu's concern for the dangers of arbitrary power. But many did, advancing versions of his political thought that included the pluralistic aspects that concern us here. During the constitutional debates in the National Assembly, for example, Jean-Joseph Mounier, the comte de Lally-Tollendal, and other *monarchiens* called for the division of powers and for checks and balances. And Constant, as we have already seen, frequently referred to Montequieu when he was considering constitutional issues.

Equally powerful was the influence of Rousseau, but in a manner that pushed hard in the opposite direction. In his numerous political writings, Rousseau famously distinguished between the sovereign legislative will of the people, which was not to be delegated or "represented," and the executive power of government, which was to put laws into effect. Furthermore, Rousseau insisted that legislative will and executive power be strictly separated. This division meant that there was to be no representative body for the deliberation and passage of legislation, which was to emerge phoenix-like from the "general will." And, it reduced questions of "government" to putting into effect the laws that had thus emerged; that is, it confined "government" to functions we generally associate with the activities of the executive and judicial branches. The result of this dimension of Rousseau's thought (putting aside the influence of his rehabilitation of sentiment, of his critique of "the arts and sciences," of his utopian vision of asocial "natural man," and of his proto-socialist critique of property and inequity) was to encourage constitutional thinkers to insist on the unity of the "general will" and on extreme versions of the separation of powers with no "checks and balances." Effectively, Rousseau adopted a notion of political sovereignty remarkably parallel to Bossuet's, with the important difference that absolute sovereignty was transferred from the king to the nation. Like Bossuet, Rousseau insisted that there must be absolute and irrevocable submission of every individual to a single unitary entity. Like Bossuet, therefore, Rousseau believed that sovereignty was indivisible and inalienable. Unlike Bossuet, however, the single unitary entity that, for Rousseau, was the seat of this sovereignty was no longer the person of the Divine monarch; rather, it was the "general will" of citizens as a whole.

The debates surrounding the composition of the Constitutions of 1791 and 1795 demonstrated Rousseau's influence, especially when deliberations turned to how "the general will" was to be institutionally organized. There were, of course, voices looking for ways to provide for cooperation between the various branches of government, especially among those who had been influenced by English notions of a "mixed constitution" or by Montesquieu's ideas about "intermediate powers" and/or "checks and balances." The majority, however, deeply influenced by Rousseau, believed that unity would naturally emerge. They insisted on the separation of powers (as codified in Article 16 of the Declaration of the Rights of Man and of the Citizen), but with insufficient attention to how potential conflicts between the branches would be negotiated. The pious hope was that there would be "equilibrium" (or cooperation and coordination) between the branches of government. The reality, of course, turned out to be quite other, with each regime unfolding in a manner where one branch of government came to largely monopolize power.

Constant developed his political "pluralism" in opposition to Rousseau's theory of political sovereignty, and with this unfortunate history strongly in mind. He would insist on the importance of checks and balances among the separate institutions of government, and he would insist that it was a mistake to view the people's will as unified. Liberal constitutionalists like Benjamin Constant defended the principle of popular sovereignty, but insisted that it was not a unified entity that could miraculously express an unambiguous doctrine; rather, "popular sovereignty" was composed of a plurality of entities that gained a political voice through an ongoing debate among the representatives of the people.

*Administrative Pluralism* was closely connected with political pluralism. Contemporaneous with the emergence of new theoretical justifications of absolutist royal sovereignty during the seventeenth century, and with the new symbolic trappings of the court and the monarchy, there was *de facto* administrative centralization of the nation of France. This was reflected in the institutionalization of *intendants* and subdelegates who were dispatched to rule the provinces; in the new mechanisms of taxation; and in the new special courts created to try cases in which the administration had an interest. What is significant here is that theoretical justifications of the monarchy in France not only focused on the unity of the nation and the centralization of political decision making, it also insisted on a centralization of the administration. This, again, reflected a belief in the superiority of the state over civil society.

Critics of the centralization of the administration questioned the absorption of civil society into the state, and they attacked the new intrusions of the state administration into local affairs. They argued that corporate bodies, regional assemblies, and local governments were more appropriate overseers of administrative policy. As Tocqueville famously argued in his *L'Ancien Régime et la Révolution*, many aspects of the centralization associated with the Revolution and Napoleon were in fact new outgrowths of structures deeply rooted in the Old Regime. Much that appeared new was in fact continuous. Nonetheless, political and administrative centralization attained a new level of visibility during and after the Revolution and, not surprisingly, it elicited new levels of concern. Even the term "centralization" was new to the revolutionary era.[42] Constant insisted that there must be a separation of the state from civil society. Individuals, he argued, did not transfer all of their rights to the community; they retained rights that were immune from the intervention of government.

Liberals like Constant and Staël were consistent champions of pluralism during the early-nineteenth century, insisting that it should be pursued on political, religious, and administrative fronts. This needs emphasis because recent scholarship has often downplayed the importance of this ideological dimension of French liberal thought. Pierre Rosanvallon, for example, has viewed François Guizot as representative of early-nineteenth century French liberal thought, implying that we should take as normative Guizot's rejection of the revolutionary principle of popular sovereignty and his embrace of the principles of reason, truth, and justice.[43] More recently, he defined French-style liberalism as "yoking the cult of law to the praise of the rationalizing state, [and] the notion of the rule of law with that of administrative power."[44] Rosanvallon's view of French liberalism stresses its rationalistic roots and its centralizing impulse.[45] While this was an important component of one strain of French liberalism in the early-nineteenth century, there was also a competing pluralist strain.[46] Constant and Stael developed a political pluralism that insisted on administrative decentralization, on the protection of rights, on the institutional separation of different branches of government, and on ongoing political contestation.

## Political Sovereignty

The best-known aspects of Constant's liberal stance are his defense of individual liberties and his criticism of Rousseau's theory of political sovereignty. The defense of rights has many dimensions, but central to them all, according to Constant, was the assurance of free expression, both oral and written, and the protection of all the means of communicating the ideas generated by free expression.[47] Closely connected with the protection of these liberties, as we see in detail below, was Constant's concern to provide individuals access to the process of political representation. And both of these were intimately tied to Constant's views concerning political sovereignty.

The question of sovereignty is the focus of the opening section of Constant's 1806 manuscript *Principes de politiques*, of a central chapter of *De l'esprit de conquête et de l'usurpation*, and of the first sections of the published 1815 version of *Principes de politiques*. Constant agreed with Rousseau that all political authority must come from the general will, marking his distance from those who had argued that authority should be vested in a hereditary ruler and his distance from those who believed that authority descended from some transcendent force or being. But if Constant agreed with Rousseau's argument of the ultimate *source* of political sovereignty, he strongly dissented from Rousseau's argument that the authority of the general will over the individual was unlimited. As he wrote in 1806,

> In my view, this is the theory we must hold responsible for most of the difficulties the establishment of freedom has encountered among various nations, for most of the abuses which worm their way into all governments of whatever type, and indeed for most of the crimes which civil strife and political upheaval drag in their wake. It was just this theory which inspired our Revolution and those horrors for which liberty for all was at once the pretext and the victim.[48]

Unlimited political power concentrated anywhere was dangerous.

> The omnipotent nation is as dangerous as a tyrant, indeed more dangerous.... The mistake of Rousseau and of writers who are the greatest friends of freedom, when they grant society a boundless power, comes from the way their ideas on politics were formed. They have seen in history a small number of men, or even one alone, in possession of immense power, which did a lot of harm. But their wrath has been directed against the wielders of power and not the power itself. Instead of destroying it, they have dreamed only of relocating it.[49]

In the version of *Principes de politiques* published in 1815, Constant wrote in the same vein:

> No authority upon earth is unlimited, neither that of the people, nor that of the men who declare themselves their representatives, nor that of the kings, by whatever title they reign, nor, finally, that of the law, which, being merely the expression of the will of the people or of the prince, according to the form of government, must be circumscribed within the same limits as the authority from which it emanates.[50]

Political sovereignty must be limited to leave as great a space as possible for the liberties of individuals, which must be protected. "[T]here is a part of human existence which necessarily remains individual and independent and by right beyond all political jurisdiction. Sovereignty exists only in a limited and relative way."[51] Constant quoted with approval a passage of a speech Siéyès had made in the Convention in 1795: "In political life one communalizes, in the name of public power, as little as possible and only what is necessary for maintaining each person in his rights and duties. Power on this scale is far short of the exaggerated ideas with which people have blithely invested what they call sovereignty."[52]

Governments have legitimate roles to play, to maintain internal order and repulse foreign invasion, and these justify the levying of taxes. But, individual rights must be respected, and political authority legally restricted. What individual liberties should be protected? "Citizens possess individual rights independently of all social and political authority, and any authority which violates these rights becomes illegitimate. The rights of the citizens are individual freedom, religious freedom, freedom of opinion, which includes the freedom to express oneself openly, the enjoyment of property, a guarantee against all arbitrary power."[53] The final six chapters of the 1815 version of *Principes de politique* are devoted to discussions of the liberties that must be protected.[54]

Constant explicitly attacked Hobbes as "the man who most cleverly reduced despotism to a theoretical system." He was mistaken to argue that the sovereign could always act or speak in the name of the people; mistaken to claim that the unified body of the people existed only when represented by the sovereign.[55] Hobbes had attempted to justify *absolute* sovereignty and, further, had argued that sovereignty should be located in one place. Rather, according to Constant, "Democracy is power in the hands of all, but power only in such measure as is needed for the security of society."[56]

Constant also rejected a strictly utilitarian argument, refusing to reduce the protection of liberty to a matter of calculation.[57] Strictly quantitative consideration of the consequences of actions was important, but it was insufficient because it could lead to self-interested action masquerading for what was best for all. This was, in part, because such calculations relied on an unreliable sentiment.

> The principle of utility...awakens in the human heart the hope of advantage rather than the feeling of duty. Now, the evaluation of an advantage is arbitrary: it is the imagination that settles it. But neither its errors nor its whims can change the idea of duty.[58]

Constant was sensitive to how utilitarian justifications could be given to actions that violated individual freedoms, as had happened during the radical phase of the Revolution. The principle of utility needed to be buttressed by the protection of rights.

> You can find utilitarian reasons for all orders and prohibitions. Forbidding citizens to leave their houses would prevent all the crimes which are committed on the highways. To have them appear every morning in front of their town hall would stop vagabonds, thieves, and dangerous men from hiding in the big cities on the lookout for criminal opportunities. This is the kind of thinking which in our day turned France into one vast

prison.... Set [authority] up without limits and you fall once again into the bottomless abyss of arbitrary rule.... Law alone provides a guarantee."[59]

This did not imply that all laws should always be respected. There were clearly times when laws encroached upon freedoms, and other times when laws violated morality. Constant argued that if individual freedoms were transgressed or if unjust laws were implemented, individuals should passively resist.[60] His counsel was to act morally and to avoid fanaticism. This meant that laws should generally be followed, but there were times when it was appropriate, indeed a moral duty, to rebel against them. In his own words, "Obedience to the law is without doubt a duty; but this duty is not absolute, but relative."[61]

Constant also warned against precipitous revolutionary action, however, echoing reservations he had expressed in the 1790s when he observed with concern the viciousness of revolutionary actors on the political extremes. His recommendation, as before, was for moderation and forgiveness.

> Two movements are natural to any nation overthrowing institutions it finds oppressive or vicious. The first is to wish to see everything destroyed and constructed anew, the second to display implacable severity to those who profited from the vices of the former institutions. These two movements are precisely what make revolutions dire, what takes them beyond the people's needs, prolongs their duration, and jeopardizes their success.[62]

He suggested that there were two stages to revolutions, the first when the old order is overthrown, and the second "when by means of an artificial prolongation of a movement no longer nationwide, there is an attempt to destroy everything contrary to the viewpoint of a few." Thinking comparatively, he commended those revolutions, like the English and the American, which stopped at the moderate first stage, and condemned those revolutions that moved to the second stage. "[I]n the case of nations which reject all their memories and think everything must be changed, reformed, and built from scratch, revolutions never end. Interminable divisions tear these people apart."[63]

The actors in radical revolutions are also dangerous. They have the illusion, according to Constant, that their violent coercive measures in the present will be legitimated by the future perfect system that the revolution will create. They fail to recognize, however, that no system attains perfection, and that it is likely that the coercive measures to bring about the promised future will in fact not be justified by the result. "Thus you are not as you imagine doing uncertain and temporary harm to achieve positive and lasting good; you are doing certain and positive harm in exchange for uncertain, relative, and temporary advantage."[64] The consequence of such coercive actions was all too often the unfortunate creation of a new tyrannical order, albeit one constructed in the name of freedom. It could be even more oppressive than a traditional tyranny.

> Tyrannical government being denounced, the most tyrannical of governments is constructed. . . . The war against public attitudes is less evil when the despotism is blatant, since it is not of the essence of despotism to depend on [these public attitudes]. . . . Institutions claiming to be free ones, when they employ despotic means, bring together all the ills of a monarchy under an oppressive tyrant with all those of a republic rent by factions. Quiet men are persecuted for being apathetic, ardent men because they are dangerous. Servitude guarantees no rest; human activity lacks all purpose and joy. Freedom is adjourned. . . . [65]

Constant's experiences during the various phases of the Revolution led him to be suspicious of impatient leaders, factions, and institutions that employed coercive methods to hasten change. They foolishly ignored the state of public opinion, and they dangerously pushed aside, in their haste to realize reform, political dialogue and negotiation. This was precisely what Napoleon had done. In some stunningly modern-sounding pages in *De l'esprit de conquête et de l'usurpation*, Constant specified that unlike previous forms of despotism, modern [Napoleonic] usurpation was a new form of tyranny because it demanded assent while "counterfeiting liberty."

> Despotism stifles freedom of the press; usurpation parodies it. . . . Despotism, in a word, rules by means of silence; usurpation condemns him to speak, it pursues him into the most intimate sanctuary of his thoughts, and, by forcing him to lie to his own conscience, deprives the oppressed of his last remaining consolation.

When a people is but enslaved without being abased, there is still the possibility of an improvement in its situation.... [U]surpation abases a people at the same time as oppressing it. It makes it accustomed to trample under foot what it used to respect, to court what it despised.... [66]

A healthy polity avoided despotism and usurpation. It allowed discussion, unlike the silence of despotism; and it encouraged free discussion, unlike the forced conformity of usurpation.

Constant valorized political interchange, but he insisted that it was a mistake to believe that political contestation naturally led to an agreement about appropriate policy, to some uniform political agenda. It was to be expected that individual interests were not synonymous with the general interests; it was to be expected that the local interests of one region would not be identical with the local interests of another region. Politics, properly constituted, was the arena where negotiation and compromise occurred. There should be no expectation that differences would be subsumed into some fatuous unity.

A hundred deputies elected by a hundred different parts of the country bring individual interests and the local preferences of their constituents inside the assembly. This base is useful to them. Forced to debate together, they soon notice respective sacrifices which are indispensable. They strive to keep these at a minimum, and this is one of the great advantages of this type of appointment. Necessity always ends by uniting them in common negotiation, and the more sectional the choices have been, the more representation achieves its general purpose. [67]

This, as we have argued above, is the pluralist dimension of Constant's liberalism.

Constant worried that if elected representatives forgot their attachments to the interests of their local constituents, they would create an imagined uniformity at the expense of real differences. As in *Fragments d'un ouvrage abandonné*, Constant believed there was a natural tendency for a gulf to open up between the represented and their elected representatives.

Assemblies, however sectional their composition, tend all too often to contract an *esprit de corps* which isolates them from the nation. Placed in the capital, far from the section of the nation which elected them, representatives lose sight of the usages, needs, and way of life of their constituents. They lend themselves to general ideas of leveling, symmetry, uniformity, mass changes, and universal recasting, bringing upset, disorder, and confusion to distant regions. It is this disposition we must combat, because it is on particular memories, habits, and regional laws that the happiness and peace of a province rest.[68]

Constant's conception of the importance of representatives remaining close to the particular interests of their constituents contrasted with the view of contemporaneous theorists who claimed that representatives should transcend the narrow and parochial interests of their locality. Sieyès, for example, was suspicious of particular interests and argued that politicians should focus on abstract, general questions. Representatives, therefore, should focus on issues that transcended local concerns. Here, of course, Sieyès echoed Rousseau's misgivings about confusing the interests of particular individuals or associations with the interests of the whole political community. Sieyès, in effect, transported Rousseau's political agenda of realizing a unified national will into the institutional context of a representative system. Constant was suspicious of the underlying assumption of both, believing that differences were natural and healthy. "Unanimity always suggests an unfavorable campaign, and with good reason; because there never has been, on important and complicated questions, unanimity without bondage [*sans servitude*]."[69]

This was closely connected with Constant's conviction that the natural tendency of power was to corrupt, and that the natural tendency of representatives who distanced themselves from their constituents was not to pursue the general interest but rather *their own* interest. Given that this was the case, he argued that representatives would make better decisions if they remained accountable to their constituents and kept their interests clearly in view.[70] He advocated what we would term transparency.

This goal also underlay Constant's concern for the responsibility of ministers. He maintained that they were not above the law and, like every other citizen, could be prosecuted for breaking laws.[71] On the other hand, ministers making decisions in the performance of their official duties were to be assessed by political, not legal procedures, meaning that they could be removed from office but not prosecuted for crimes. "The subtle spirit of jurisprudence is opposed to the nature of those great questions which must be considered from the public, national, sometimes even European perspective."[72] More dangerous, however, was the impulse of governments to override legality and expect their ministers and agents obediently to execute orders without reflection.

[T]he possessors of power, convinced, in spite of examples, of the eternal tenure of their authority, search only for pliant instruments who will obey them blindly; they see nothing in human intelligence but an importunate motive to resistance.[73]

Given his suspicion of power, it is not surprising that Constant dreaded any governmental system that favored one branch over another. His proposal for a "neutral power"—which after 1814 was to be the monarch—with power to dissolve the legislature and/or dismiss the ministers, was expressly to prevent either the ministry or legislature from becoming too dominant.[74]

The desire to keep vigilant oversight of government personnel also explains Constant's advocacy of the direct election of representatives, in opposition to the indirect election proposals of contemporaries like Sieyès, Roederer, or Necker. The latter method of election distanced representatives from their constituents, according to Constant, and as a consequence gave them too much autonomy *vis-à-vis* the electorate. Constant favored a closer association, advocating what we would term accountability. Again, he viewed the essential element of politics to be the open negotiation of different interests and regional needs. He believed that this would be best carried out by the transparent interaction among representatives who were accountable to their constituents.

As this indicates, Constant valorized the exchange of views in legislative assemblies. It was in popularly elected assemblies that national political discussion could take place and that the honest negotiation of differences could be achieved. He favored frank discussion over formal written speeches.

It is only when orators are forced to speak extensively that a proper discussion is set in train. Everyone, struck by the arguments he has just heard, is naturally led to examine them. Those arguments impress his mind even if he does not realize it. He cannot banish them from his memory. The views he has encountered combine with and modify those he already holds, suggesting to him answers which present the same issue from different points of view. When orators confine themselves to reading out what they have written in the silence of their study, they no longer discuss, they amplify. They do not listen.... They do not examine the opinion [of others].... In this way there is no discussion.[75]

The contrast with Rousseau, again, is intriguing. Rousseau was so concerned about the power of *amour propre* to distort political deliberations that he wished to eliminate all public interchange; that is, he wished to confine people to "the silence of their study" where he imagined they would better recognize the general will. Constant agreed with Rousseau that political speeches that were well-prepared in advance were tailor-made for flights of eloquence that would allow individuals to indulge their lamentable "desire to impress."[76] But, Constant disagreed with Rousseau's argument that political deliberations necessarily degenerated to such a level. Indeed, frank and honest exchanges of views, and the ongoing negotiation of differences, were exemplary political activities, central to the health of a representative constitutional system.

The tyranny of the majority, translated into government policy, also must be avoided. "The assent of the majority is not enough in all circumstances to render its actions lawful.... When a government of any sort puts a threatening hand on that part of individual life beyond its proper scope, it matters little on what such authority is based, whether it calls itself individual or nation."[77] Constant recognized that individuals, like governments, could make bad decisions, but he worried more about the consequences of the heavy-handed actions of majorities or of government than he did about the actions of individuals. This was because governments and majorities have powers that individuals do not possess; and power often brings recklessness and coercion. "There is something about power which more or less warps judgment. Force is far more liable to error than weakness is. Force finds resources in itself. Weakness needs thought. All things equal, it is always likely that the government will have views which are less just, less sound, and less impartial than those of the governed."[78]

When...a mistaken majority oppresses the minority or, which happens far more often, when a ferocious and noisy minority seizes the name of the majority to tyrannize society, to what does it lay claim in justification of its outrages? The sovereignty of the people, the power of society over its members, the abnegation of individual rights in favor of the society, that is to say, always principles of government, never principles of freedom.[79]

Constant obviously had anxieties about the ability of any political system to protect the interests of individuals. Nonetheless, he was optimistic that a truly representative system, even one based on a limited franchise, was the best hope for modern societies. He also believed that this system would promote the easing of tensions between the classes, because the elected representatives, in order to be elected, would need to consider the interests of all.

Constant was also optimistic that representative elections would keep citizens involved in politics rather than allowing them to focus on their narrow personal interests. Making an argument that Tocqueville would later make famous, Constant feared that looking exclusively to one's own concerns at the expense of public involvement naturally conformed with populations resigning themselves to rule by political elites. "Citizens are interested in their institutions only when they are called to participate in them with their votes. Now, this interest is indispensable in the formation of public spirit, that power without which no freedom lasts, that guarantee against all the perils, always invoked in certain countries without it ever being created."[80]

These were not new positions. Constant and Staël had written similar passages before. As early as 1798, Staël had written that one of the main causes of the *malheurs* that had plagued the Revolution in France was "the false application of the principle of the sovereignty of the people in the representative government."[81] The correct application of this principle, according the Staël, was the creation of a constitutional order that would divide executive power into several parts and destroy the privileges of class.[82] The correct application, in short, would be the division of political sovereignty.[83] Twenty years later, reflecting on the Revolution and Napoleon, Staël described without regret the passing of monarchical "despotism" in which there was a union of executive and legislative powers in the hands of one individual,[84] but she lamented that the revolutionaries had failed to see the importance of separating political power among various institutions. "Checks are necessary to all forms of authority."[85] Unfortunately, in Staël's estimation, during the early phase of the Revolution a number of factors had converged to frustrate the triumph of liberty. The King had moved too slowly to make concessions; abstract ideas had become the norm among the people and their leaders; economic and financial matters were neglected; flaws were introduced into the new constitution of 1791 (placing of all power in the Assembly); and, the populace had descended into a state of insurrection, inaccessible to reason. Staël argued that these factors led to the political actors on the extremes uniting against the moderates, which in turn led to the overturn of the monarchy, the outbreak of war, and the growth of fanaticism. The result was the Terror and fifteen months of "anarchy" with the Jacobins in control—"arbitrary will, without limits, was their doctrine."[86]

After the Terror, according to Staël, and after a brief respite during the early years of the Directory, France stumbled into a political stew (following the Fructidor "coup" of 1797) where personal interest replaced patriotism, constitutionalism died, and Bonaparte maneuvered himself into power. Attached to no principles except his own egotism and personal ambition, Bonaparte established and organized a despotic regime, sacrificing others and the nation to his own ends. "It is almost always after periods of civil troubles," Staël lamented, "that tyranny establishes itself."[87] Nonetheless, Napoleon would ultimately fail, she reasoned, because it is not possible "to stop the progress of human reason."[88]

Constant was also consistent. He wished to see instituted in France a constitutional system that protected liberty and that avoided the concentration of sovereignty in any single body, however representative that body might be. This could be the executive branch of government, as under Napoleon, or the legislative branch, as during the Terror and Directory. Especially important was an independent judiciary, to protect civil liberties like free press and religious toleration.[89] In his earlier political writings, such as *Fragments d'un ouvrage abandonné*, Constant had favored a republican form of government for France. In the manuscripts and publications of 1806, 1814, and 1815, he was more agnostic concerning the system he preferred, but he devoted many pages to outlining the institutional checks required for the protection of liberty. What all of his proposals shared was an insistence on the separation and balance of power. In the manuscript of 1806, to offer one example, Constant referred to the Terror and the Constitution of 1795 as suffering from this refusal to balance the power of the legislative branch.

> [D]uring the ascendancy of our assemblies [that is, during the Terror] no constitution placed real limits on legislative power.

Now, when legislative power is quite limitless, when the nation's representatives think themselves invested with boundless sovereignty, when no counterweight exists to their decrees either in executive or judiciary power, the tyranny of those elected by the people is as disastrous as any other, whatever name it bears. The absolute, unlimited sovereignty of the people was transferred by the nation, or as is usual, at least in its name, by those who dominated it, to representative assemblies. These exercised an unparalleled despotism. . . . The constitution [of 1795] which first put an end to this period of despotism and madness still did not sufficiently limit the legislative power. It established no counterweight to its excesses. It did not enshrine either the indispensable veto of the executive power or the equally indispensable possibility of the dissolution of the representative assemblies. It did not even guarantee, as do some American constitutions, the most sacred rights of individuals against the encroachments of legislators.[90]

Institutionally, Constant insisted that there must be a separation of power among the various branches of government—what he referred to, echoing a common formula, as "the distribution and balance of powers."[91]

While Montesquieu and the American founding fathers distinguished three governmental loci of power, Constant distinguished five: the "neutral power" (the monarch or the emperor); the executive power of the ministers; the hereditary assembly (*"le pouvoir répresentatif de la durée"*); the elected assembly (*"le pouvoir répresentatif de l'opinion"*); and, the judicial power of the courts. Each had the ability to check the authority of the others. Constant devoted many pages to the details of government organization, always concerned with defining the functions of the various public powers in a manner that prevented any single body from endangering liberty. He discussed the issues of defense and diplomacy, the responsibility of ministers, the power of local authorities, the procedures for the introduction of legislation, the framework for discussion and acceptance or rejection of this legislation. He did not want to paralyze the functioning of government, but he was especially concerned with protecting liberty. He believed that the balance of power, and the "checks" that this inevitably entailed, was the most efficacious governmental structure for achieving this.

Benjamin Constant and Germaine de Staël were committed to a liberal constitutionalism based on a pluralistic conception of political sovereignty. It was essential to separate the power of the state from the absolutist inclinations of the old regime monarchy, from the tyrannical inclinations of the Jacobins, and from the despotic inclinations of Napoleon. This required the firm protection of individual rights, public access to and involvement with the process of representation, and the separation and balance of political power.

## Religious Toleration

Equally important, according to Staël and Constant, was religious toleration in the form of protection of religious practice and belief. As we have seen above, they were far from being irreligious, with Constant at times suggesting that religion was connected with the deepest and most sublime sentiments of humanity, and arguing that religion often performed the important function of reinforcing moral behavior. But, both insisted on freedom of religion and suggested that the Gallican Church was inferior to other, especially Protestant, sects.

The most positive comments concerning a particular *form* of religion are contained in Staël's 1798 manuscript *Des circonstances actuelles qui peuvent terminer la Révolution et des principes qui doivent fonder la République en France.* Concerned that modern societies were populated by individuals with strong wills, Staël suggested that organized religion was one of the most effective means of instilling morality. "Morality, and morality tied by religious opinions, alone gives a complete code for all the actions of life, a code that reunites humans by a sort of pact of souls, [which is] a preliminary indispensable for all social contact."[92] Staël went on to claim that it was necessary to have religious ceremonies that moved the people. "That which strikes its imagination is the splendor of the ceremony, and this splendor is not...a means of misleading reason; it unites some lively sensations to some simple truths."[93] Even in this manuscript, however, there is an insistence on religious toleration. Staël was horrified by religious persecution and especially was worried about the influence of an intolerant Catholic Church in France. She hoped that the Church in France could be replaced with a liberal form of religion, Protestant or Theophilanthopic. By 1818, she believed that it was necessary to more rigorously separate religion and politics,[94] though she still advocated a sentimental, tolerant religion, arguing that this was connected with "individual judgment."[95]

Constant was, if anything, a more strident critic of religious intolerance and the intervention of government into the arenas of religious belief or religious practice. He had a long history of distrusting organized religion and favoring religious toleration. In April 1796, writing about the importance of ideas, and in particular the force of the idea of equality, he wrote about the ill effects of religious organizations. "[T]here is no religion which has not, in its origin, given sanction to it [equality]; and one of the great sacerdotal frauds has been to pervert the spirit of the institution, in order to eliminate this idea."[96] One of the essential threads of continuity in Constant's thought, as we have seen above, was to distinguish positive religious sentiment, which all individuals experience, from the unfortunate forms that organized religions have taken historically. He disliked sacerdotal religions, and recommended wide tolerance of a multiplicity of religious organizations as a means of countering powerful religious superstition. In August 1796, he echoed Voltaire in arguing that religious intolerance was diminished by having a large number of sects. "One paralyzes superstition in dividing it. In order to assure the liberty of religion, it is necessary to multiply the number of religious groups.... It is necessary to make a republic of religious groups, in which the interest of the majority is toleration."[97]

In this article of August 1796, Constant focused specifically on the utility for French society of allowing Protestants to return to France. Compared to Catholicism, Protestantism was preferable. He noted the riches, the hard work, and the enlightened culture of liberty that Protestant exiles from France had brought to the regions they inhabited. And, he argued that these Protestants would bring a disposition of toleration back to France. Looking back historically, with a reference to the years of the religious wars in the late-sixteenth century, he argued that Protestantism was associated with toleration. Protestants, he wrote,

> will bring into France all the ideas of liberty. Protestantism has always been attracted to these ideas. I have on this point the authority of Montesequieu and of history. The first Frenchmen who conceived the project of constituting France into a republic were Protestants, and this bold plan was one of the principle causes of the persecutions that they suffered.[98]

In his reflections about Switzerland that he sent to Nicolas-Louis François de Neufchâteau on 17 May 1799, Constant again clearly stated his conviction that "Protestantism is much more republican than Catholicism."[99]

Though he consistently held that Protestantism was preferable to Catholicism, Constant insisted on rigorous governmental neutrality. In 1815, he stated categorically "Any government intervention in the domain of religion causes harm."[100] In the writings of the Empire and Restoration, his attacks of religious intolerance, like his attack on sovereign unity, frequently focused on Rousseau's theory of civil religion, which allowed the sovereign to banish anyone who did not subscribe to the "civil profession of faith." In both versions of *Principes de politique* [1806 and 1815], he attacked Rousseau, "who cherished all theories of liberty, while offering pretexts for every claim that tyranny makes....I know of no system of servitude, which has sanctioned more nefarious errors than the eternal metaphysics of the *Social Contract*."[101] He quoted with approval the statements of Stanislas-Marie de Clermont-Tonnerre, a moderate royalist, who served briefly as president of the National Assembly before being killed in the uprising of 10 August 1792.

> Religion and the state...are two quite distinct and separate things, whose bringing together can only distort both one and the other....Each person's religion is therefore his opinion of his relationship to God. Each man's opinion being free, he may take up or not take up such religion. The opinion of the minority cannot be subordinated to that of the majority. No opinion can therefore be commanded by social consensus. What is true of religion is also true of cults....The political body must not have dominion over any religion. It must not reject any of them unless the cult in question is a threat to social order.[102]

Constant, as we have seen, insisted that civil rights be protected by laws and by an independent judicial order. This applied especially to religious liberty, which was part of the "private" domain into which the state should not intrude.

### The Danger of Fanaticism

The mental and emotional disposition that would most commonly undermine legal rights, religious toleration, and the division of sovereignty—that is, liberal pluralism—was *fanaticism*. This was the term that Constant and Staël frequently used to refer to the stance of those who wished to impose tyranny. Fanatics wished to reduce the complexity of reality to one simple truth, regardless of the circumstances of time and place, and they wished to impose this simple truth on the complex and differentiated world of human reality. In 1798, Staël wrote the following: "Some want to derive everything from rights, others everything from interest, others everything from force, others everything from reason, and drawing some consequences from each of these principles which, having no counterweights, lead all to absurdity. What is necessary is to recognize and to amalgamate rights, interest, force and reason, in order to organize society as wisely as the physical world is organized.... Fanaticism, the most disastrous of passions, is nothing but the despotism of a single idea over the spirit of man."[103] Constant echoed this in *Principes de politique* [1806]:

Fanaticism is nothing save the rule of a single idea which wishes to triumph at any price. It is probably more absurd still when the question is freedom than it is when the question is religion. Fanaticism and freedom are incompatible. One is based on examination; the other forbids research and punishes doubt. The one thinks through and evaluates all views; the other sees the most timid objection as an assault. The one seeks to persuade, the other issues orders. The one, in a word, considers the need for victory a misfortune and treats the vanquished as equals whose rights it is keen to recognize, the other hurls itself on all questions as if on enemy redoubts and sees in its adversaries only still-dangerous captives it must immolate, so as no longer to have to fear them.[104]

There existed a political and psychological parallelism: tyranny is brought about by fanatics; a rigid political system is the result of a rigid mindset; a non-pluralistic political order is fostered by individuals with anxious and intolerant personalities.[105]

Severity, injustice, and slights of all kinds on the part of its leaders seem to [fanatics] meritorious acts, as it were gauges of sincerity. It finds the educated bothersome because they find it hard to embrace an opinion without certain restrictions and nuances. It is suspicious of the person of proud spirit, because proud spirits experience some kind of antipathy to the strongest peoples and serve the powerful only with distaste. The only qualities [fanaticism] demands are belief and will. It sees in morality obstacles, weakness, and chicanery.[106]

The danger of fanaticism was best countered by a stable constitutional order with the institutional framework outlined above, with the protection of rights, the rule of law, and the division and balance of political sovereignty. And, it was best controlled by a tolerant political culture that encouraged debate and political participation.

## Ancient versus Modern Liberty

Constant's most famous writing is an address that he gave in 1819 comparing liberty in the ancient world with liberty in the modern world.[107] He argued that the imposition of "ancient" political liberty was inappropriate in the modern age, because historical conditions had changed (e.g., the rise of commerce and the emergence of larger political entities) and because the "dispositions of mankind" had changed. Modern individuals best developed their capacities and found their greatest satisfactions, Constant argued, in everyday private activities. They, therefore, quite appropriately, demanded greater independence and protection against tyranny. "Modern" liberty, accordingly, required a legal and institutional framework. Civil and political liberties must be protected.[108]

The theme of ancient versus modern liberty was present in a number of Constant's writings after 1806.[109] Ancient liberty, according to Constant, was modeled on the small city-states of antiquity where slaves did essential work to sustain the economy. This permitted citizens to be intimately involved in day-to-day political deliberations. Modern liberty, by contrast, was characteristic of larger modern states in which the majority of citizens were directly involved in the production of material wealth, agrarian and commercial. As a consequence, modern citizens were less directly involved in politics, but wished to be protected from the intrusion of the actions of the community and of the state. In the ancient world, "the individual was entirely sacrificed to the collectivity. The ancients...had no notion of individual rights."[110] In the modern world, the opposite is true: the individual is protected from the collectivity, and the focus is on "his own work, efforts, and individual resources."[111] Much of the difference, Constant reasoned, was due to the different historical conditions that existed and, closely related, the different traits of character that obtained. In the ancient world, there were frequent battles over limited territory, and, therefore, warfare was the favored methods of gaining riches and power. In the modern world, commerce and trade replaced warfare as the mode for the acquisition of riches and power, and this had led to "a vast softening in manners, more indulgence toward women, more hospitality to strangers, and an exceeding love of individual freedom."[112]

> Formerly public interest went before safety and individual freedom. Today safety and individual freedom come before the public interest.
>
> Peace, calm, and domestic contentment being the natural and invincible tendency of modern peoples, more sacrifices have to be made for that calm than the ancients made. Disorder is not always incompatible with political freedom, but it always is with civil and individual freedom.[113]

Constant was always careful to point out, however, that the attainment of modern civil liberty would be secure only if some dimensions of ancient political liberty were retained.

> The inference I draw from the differences which mark us off from antiquity is absolutely not that we should abolish public safeguards but that we should extend satisfactions. It is not political freedom that I want to renounce, but civil freedom that I am demanding along with other forms of political freedom.
>
> Governments have no more right than before to arrogate to themselves illegitimate power; but legitimate governments have less right than in former times to fetter individual freedom.[114]

Summarizing the message of *Principes de politique* [1806 version], Constant articulated clearly the point he would publicly make in his famous 1819 address comparing ancient and modern liberty.

> That this book has dealt exclusively with issues connected to civil freedom does not mean to insinuate that political freedom is something superfluous. Those who would sacrifice political freedom in order to enjoy civil freedom the more peacefully are no less absurd than those who would sacrifice civil freedom in the hope of further extending political freedom.... If political freedom is not one of the individual possessions nature has given man, it is what guarantees them.[115]

There was a danger, Constant claimed, that those who govern, however chosen, would find it in their interest to prevent the governed from participating in government. Even a representative system runs this risk. Echoing his earlier writings, he pointed out that the way to contain this danger was three pronged. First, it was necessary to protect individual liberties against the arbitrary actions of government officials. "Wisely established limits [on authority] are the good fortune of [modern] nations because they circumscribe power, in such a way that no one can abuse it."[116] In his 1819 speech on liberty, Constant emphasized how important protecting civil liberties was for providing individual security.

> [I]t is the right to be subjected only to the laws, and to be neither arrested, detained, put to death or maltreated in any way by the arbitrary will of one or more individuals. The rights of everyone to express their opinion, choose a profession and practice it, to dispose of property, and even to abuse it; to come and go without permission, and without having to account for their motives or undertakings. It is everyone's right to associate with other individuals, either to discuss their interests, or to profess the religion which they and their associates prefer.[117]

Second, to protect modern liberty, it was necessary to provide individuals access to the process of representation, and to assure that there was no single person or institution that monopolized political power. In Constant's words, imperative was "the creation of various sorts of positions in government invested with different kinds of powers."[118] Third, there must be public involvement in political affairs. It was important to keep "alive in the nation—through watchfulness of her representatives, the openness of their debates and the exercise of freedom of the press applied to the analysis of all ministerial actions—a spirit of inquiry, a habitual interest in the maintenance of the constitution of the state, a constant participation in public affairs, in a word a vivid sense of political life."[119] The end of his famous 1819 lecture strikes the familiar chord that a culture of public involvement in politics is essential for the protection of liberty and for personal development.

# Conclusion
## Une Philosophie Engagée

Liberalism emerged in France during the late-1790s to deal with the difficult problems faced by the first French Republic. I call it "liberalism" because people like Benjamin Constant and Germaine de Staël began to refer to "liberal" principles in politics, and because they articulated concerns that have remained central to "liberalism" ever since. The specific spurs to their ruminations about modern politics were the voracious nature of revolutionary politics and, especially, the corrosive effects of the Terror on both institutions and culture. They appreciated how difficult it was going to be in the modern post-revolutionary age to protect personal liberty while restoring political stability. They appreciated the complexity of the cultural, juridical, and political world the Revolution had created. And, they were sensitive to the impact of this complex world on the individual.

This liberalism was refined during the Empire and, as we have seen above, advanced by Constant as an appropriate model for French political organization in 1814–15. Constant's greatest fame, however, came during the Second Restoration (1815–30), when he became a member of the Chamber of Deputies. Here, the rhetorical skills that he had honed in his subtle and lucid repartee with Isabelle de Charrière and in the salons of Germaine de Staël, and for which Constant was famous, found a public arena for the advancement of the political ideals to which he was devoted.[1]

### Constant and the Liberal Opposition

Constant was first elected to the Chamber on 25 March 1819 as Deputy for the department of the Sarthe. Briefly sidelined from active politics when the electors did not return him to office in the elections of November 1822, he reentered the Chamber fifteen months later, serving as Deputy for the Seine (Paris) from February 1824 to November 1827, and then as Deputy for Bas-Rhin (Strasbourg) from November 1827 until his death in December

1830. He referred to politics as his "vocation" and clearly enjoyed his new public role.[2] During this period of more than a decade, Constant participated frequently in the debates that took place on the floor of the Chamber[3] and devoted his considerable energy to organizational activities of the Liberal Opposition.[4] Another indication of his engagement with active politics was Constant's outpouring of journal articles—literally numbering in the hundreds—devoted largely to the specific issues facing the Chamber.[5] These first appeared in the *Mercure de France*, which Constant helped to launch in early 1817. Because of censorship problems, the journal's name was changed to *La Minerve française* in 1818. The following year, Constant shifted to *La Renommée*, which later merged with the *Courrier français*, and to which he continued to contribute. In addition, he published articles in the *Constitutionnel* and the *Temps*. Constant's journalism was prolific; his political activity, in the words of Éphraïm Harpaz, "tireless and prodigous."[6]

Robert Alexander has argued persuasively that Constant was central to the Liberal Opposition during the Second Restoration.[7] The Liberal Opposition emerged in 1817 to form committees to coordinate electoral campaigns in both Paris and the departments. Though not a political party in the modern sense of the term, the *parti libérale*, as it came to be known, was able effectively to mobilize local support for popular liberal deputies like Constant, establishing local newspapers devoted to liberal issues, and organizing speeches, musical serenades, private dinners, and banquets. During the 1820s, liberal candidates began giving "patriotic oaths" to highlight their promises to those who had elected them. They introduced the use of electoral "transactions"—agreements that specified that less-popular candidates would throw their support behind better-placed candidates after the first ballot. Liberals interpreted the Charter as a doctrine that installed British-style constitutional government in France. They argued that the Charter provided the framework for the protection of legal rights, and they maintained that the stance of the government ministry should not diverge significantly from that of the majority of elected representatives in the Chamber. They were among those who, during the Restoration, were struggling to put aside the factional struggles that had marked the Revolution, to find an acceptable balance between personal ideological commitments and organized party politics, and to move toward a political order that accepted divergent ideologies and the alternation of power.[8]

Constant was an important member of this Liberal Opposition. He was one of the most effective spokesmen for liberal values and interests, and he was tireless in his efforts to forge unity in Liberal ranks and to arrange tactical alliances with other political groups. In 1817, Constant was one of the founding members of the *Société des Amis de la Presse*, which helped journalists facing persecution by the state. This organization was disbanded in 1819 because of government pressure, but its descendants included informal meetings of journalists and deputies. By late-1819, approximately sixty liberal deputies were meeting weekly during the legislative session.[9] When the second ministry of Richelieu passed new laws in 1820 following the assassination of the Duke de Berry—laws affecting elections, free press, and *habeas corpus*—Constant was at the front of the liberal counter-offensive, attacking preliminary censorship and arguing against infringements of basic legal rights. Constant's speeches, writings, and activities as Deputy during the 1820s touched on a wide range of issues. He argued for the maintenance of the representative system with a legitimate role for a constitutional opposition. He addressed financial matters, foreign policy, educational issues, and, perhaps most centrally, worked to prevent the freedoms guaranteed by law being undermined by the political machinations of ultra royalists. He devoted himself, in short, to defending the constitutional and legal principles supported by the Liberal Opposition's interpretation of the Charter. In the words of Alexander, Constant "played a crucial role in defining the Second Restoration Liberal Opposition. He was a gifted and industrious writer and speaker who addressed all of the leading issues of the period and provided the Opposition with much of their intellectual ammunition, whether in seeking to block reaction or in pushing for fulfillment of the 'representative element' in the Charter. Constant was a leading member of the Left, and the positions he took consistently placed him in the radical wing of the [Liberal] Opposition."[10] He also became involved in campaigns to overturn the condemnation of innocent people.[11]

*Within* the Liberal Opposition, Constant was a pragmatic voice for compromise and moderate change. He was naturally suspicious of ultraroyalists who supported the constitutional powers of parliament only when they controlled the latter (he criticized Chateaubriand's *La monarchie selon la Charte* on this issue[12]), but he believed that compromises with moderate royalists were often necessary. He attempted to avoid aggressive campaigns that would unnecessarily alienate potential future allies or provide the forces of repression with easy causes to exploit. There were times when he believed systematic opposition based on rigid adherence to principles was called for— in 1820, for example, when the Richelieu ministry introduced its repressive legislation; or in 1829, when Constant warned of a pending *coup d'état* by Charles X[13]—but he also maintained that toleration of doctrinal differences within an alliance often was necessary for the adoption of legislation. Constant was worried, for example, when in 1819 some liberals pushed hard for the entry of the abbé Grégoire into the Chamber of Deputies. He supported Grégoire in principle and in public, but correctly feared that this affair would push the *ventue* ("men of the belly," as deputies of the center were uncharitably referred to) to support the ultraroyalists. Constant was to the left of *doctrinaire* liberals (more on this below) and to the right of radical liberals like Voyer d'Argenson and Lafayette (also deputy for the Sarthe), but worked with all of them for common goals. For example, when some liberals, including Lafayette, associated with the Carbonari and flirted with violent insurrection in 1821 and 1822, Constant recommended caution and operating through legal means of opposition to the government.[14] Even in this instance, however, Constant was careful not to condemn his liberal allies publicly, though he suffered politically from the actions of his more intemperate compatriots when the electorate refused to return liberal deputies like Constant to the Chamber in November 1822.[15]

During the crisis leading up to the Revolution of 1830, when it became clear that the last ministry of Villèle and the later ministry of Polignac, to say nothing of the disposition of the King, were opposed to the liberal majority in the Chamber, Constant was careful to articulate repeatedly his loyalty to the Charter and the constitutional monarchy. This loyalty was carefully framed, however, with reference to his understanding of the rules of the game, which included a free press and respect for the prerogative of the Chamber. In 1828, he declared in the Chamber of Deputies: "The ministry is able to advance only with the majority. It is necessary that it knows where [the majority] is, and what it desires." In 1829: "We, the national majority, the immense majority, increasing each day because of all who are becoming enlightened, victorious because the elections are finally the frank expression of popular wishes, victorious because the free press conducts us always to the triumph of reason.... We know that we always have agreed to be loyal to the Charter, always to respect the constitutional King." He also made clear, however, that these loyalties were not extended to the "ministerial crimes" of the Polignac administration.[16]

## Commentaire sur l'ouvrage de Filangieri

During the 1820s, in addition to his political activities for the Liberal Opposition, his legislative work in the Chamber of Deputies, and his composition of articles for the press, Constant arranged for new editions of previous works: a second edition of his *Mémoires sur les Cent-Jours* appeared in March 1829; a collection of other earlier writings, appearing under the title of *Mélanges de littérature et de politique*, was issued in June 1829. And, he continued working on *De la Religion*, published 1824–31 (discussed above). The most impressive political writing of these years, however, was Constant's *Commentaire sur l'ouvrage de Filangieri*,[17] which was written largely during his brief absence from the Chamber (1822–24). This work has been characterized by Kurt Kloocke as "the most complete account of the political doctrine of Constant."[18] Though this is an exaggeration, it is true that the book contains a restatement of Constant's central political concerns.

Constant continued to recommend, for example, the separation and balance of power in the context of a representative system, singling out for special commendation the British parliamentary system, with its loyal opposition, its relatively disciplined political parties, and the "aristocratic principle" that animated its political culture. He was impressed that the British King acted as a "moderator" above political agitation—the role that Constant had previously recommended for a "neutral power"—and he admired the legal protections of property and individual liberties. He also singled out for positive comment the actions of British aristocrats who, he claimed, were able to transcend their personal interests in order to devote themselves to public affairs and, more specifically, to the consecration of an adversary judicial system that protected all members of society regardless of class. Constant expressed some concern that the equilibrium among the different classes in England had become strained during the wars of the revolution era, when a new class of wealthy industrialists and financiers had emerged; but, in general, he was impressed with the stability of a ministerial system that preserved the country from the worst consequences of "industrial and commercial errors."[19]

The attention Constant gave to political institutions, to constitutional guarantees, and to political culture was consistent with his earlier works, and markedly separated him from intellectuals such as Henri de Saint-Simon and Auguste Comte who during these same years gave up on "government" and political institutions in favor of "administration" and social organization.[20] Constant did not. He devoted one of the four parts of the work to judicial procedures, defending *habeas corpus* and, more generally, recommending procedures that would protect individuals from false accusations and excessive punishments.[21] His thoughts on judicial issues continued to be informed by his memories of the abuses of the revolutionary period when, in his own words, "horrible revolutionary tribunals" had "united all the excesses of ignorance with the excesses of ferocity."[22] He devoted a chapter to the injustices and depredations of slavery and the slave trade. This attack was directed at the obvious transgressions of morality and legal norms (he referred to slavers as "speculators in human blood"[23]), but Constant also suggested that the slave trade inevitably would erode cultural mores.

> It is necessary to add that the crimes of the slave trade are not limited to these unbelievable atrocities. To the number of these crimes, and among the acts that weigh on the head of the merchants of slaves, ought to be placed the state in which they push the people who they seduce by their propositions and by their loathsome transactions; they exalt all the vices and the passions of these barbarous nations; they pervert their crude institutions; they empoison their domestic relations.... Slavery corrupts the masters as much as the slaves.[24]

Constant argued in *Commentaire sur l'ouvrage de Filangieri* that legislation should be confined to the two primary responsibilities of government: preventing internal disorders and repelling foreign invasions. These, in turn, required the imposition of taxes. "Thus, legislation ought to punish crimes, organize an armed force against foreign enemies, and impose on individuals a sacrifice of a portion of their property to cover the expenses of these two objects."[25] Beyond this, government action should be severely restricted. Much of the first section of the book is devoted to criticizing Filangieri's confidence in governmental power and his encouragement of state-directed activities. Constant was skeptical of the intentions of government officials and of members of the privileged classes, expressing more faith in individual initiative. He wished not to displace political authority, but to reduce it. He remained, as previously, suspicious of utilitarian justifications of government intervention.[26] And he insisted, as previously, that most actions of individuals should be "by right outside of all social or legislative competence."[27]

> It is surely far from my intention to want to weaken respect for the law, when the law applies itself to objects which are within its competence .... But to pretend, as do Mably, Filangieri, and so many others, to extend the competence of the law over all objects, this is to organize tyranny.[28]

What was new in this book was the extended attention given to economic issues. Constant continued to insist, as he had in his earlier writings, that the modern age was different from the past: commerce had replaced warfare; "interest" was now a more powerful motivator of individuals; equality was growing and "the reign of privilege is finished."[29] But, what the implications of these changes were for government economic policy was now more clearly laid out than in earlier writings. He argued that commerce should be free, meaning that, excepting a few unusual situations, the government should not intervene. The exceptions were important: a small territory might need to protect its economic independence; a sudden and general famine would require extraordinary action by the state; and, in regions where regulation and government intervention had been the historical norm, it might be necessary to introduce free trade incrementally to avoid unnecessary disruptions. But, in general, governments should resist meddling in commercial affairs; the "default" position of governments should be restraint.

Economic improvement would come, according to Constant, through the industry of individuals. Concerning agricultural production, for example, he wrote that it was "necessary to return it to liberty, to individual interest, to the activity that inspires in man the exercise of his own faculties and the absence of all hindrances."[30] Concerning the market in general, he believed that "wealth distributes itself and divides itself in a perfect equilibrium, when the division of property is not hampered and when the exercise of industry does not encounter constraints."[31] Competition, he argued, was one of the major causes of increasing perfection and improvement. Constant even argued that the market would lead to a more equal division of property,[32] a development that he favored because he believed it would have the political benefit of drawing more people into civic involvement. The book ended with a passage celebrating government inaction: "For thought, for education, for industry, the motto of government out to be: *Laissez faire* and *laissez passer.*"[33]

This does not mean that Constant's view of human nature had changed. Consistent with his earlier writings, he believed that an excessive focus on personal interest was limiting; it should be joined with wider concerns if one was to live a fulfilling life and, more broadly, if the community was to survive without tyranny. Economic self-interest was clearly an important motivator in the modern age, but he hoped "that one will not forget that man is not uniquely an arithmetic sign, and that there is some blood in his veins and a need of attachment in his heart."[34]

> It is important not to believe that the earnings of commerce, the profits of industry, the necessities of agriculture alone constitute a motive for action [*un mobile d'activité*] sufficient for men. One often exaggerates the influence of personal interests. Interest is shortsighted in its cares and unrefined in its enjoyments; it works for the present without giving thought to the future. The man in whom opinion languishes is not long excited even by his own interest; a sort of stupor takes hold of him, and as the paralysis spreads from one portion of the body to another, it also extends itself from one to another of his faculties.[35]

Clearly, narrow self-regarding motivations were not sufficient for a full life or for a stable society.

Closely connected to his critique of unqualified self-interest was Constant's appraisal of wider motivations and, more broadly, of human emotional drives. In chapters devoted to a consideration of the population theories of Thomas Malthus, for example, Constant attacked those who counseled the poor to practice abstinence, characterizing it as "continence against nature." While he worried about excessive population growth, he argued that a program founded on a denial of deep-seated instinctual drives was unreasonable.

> [T]o hope that human beings…will be able to deny the attraction of the sexes by the consideration of the evils that come from an excessive population, and that this attraction of the sexes will be subjugated without some shameful vices replacing it; this is to harbor some illusions and some dreams.[36]

He argued that the intimacies of family and friends were central to emotional fulfillment and human happiness. Solitude, he argued, was not a natural state, and it became more and more difficult to endure as one grew older.[37] In several chapters, he repeated his arguments in *De la Religion* concerning the universality of the religious instinct and the unfortunate tendency of sacerdotal religions to redirect this positive instinct in ways that furthered the authoritarian agendas of religious and secular authorities.[38] What he recommended was a balancing of self-regarding motivations—vanity and egoism—with the other-regarding sentiments that bring emotional completeness and support civilization and community. The sentiments of sympathy and compassion, he claimed, were "essential for virtue."[39] Enthusiasm was "the germ of all the successes in the arts and sciences."[40]

> Nature, which has given to man love of himself for his personal preservation, has also given him sympathy, generosity, compassion ….Egoism becomes harmful only when this counterweight is destroyed.[41]

## Liberal Pluralism

It is a cliché, but a true one, that different political theories rest on different conceptions of human nature. Constant and Staël emerged from cultural traditions that emphasized the conflicted nature of the human psyche; moreover, they confronted a revolutionary context that graphically demonstrated the impact of historical change on human responses. These highlighted a problem about human makeup that has remained a central issue of modern political theory: how to create stable political order out of individuals who are self-possessed, self-serving, indolent, or worse. How is it possible for groups to create or sustain a just and enduring polity with individuals who escape from isolation fitfully, find social connections unfulfilling and difficult to sustain, and who share little demonstrable commitment to public principles of justice? And, how are these timeless difficulties negotiated in eras of instability, when human brutalities are more common, when the desire for material goods and for equality are more pronounced, and when general anxiety is growing?

Constant came to the conclusion that human nature was variable, changing in different historical eras. He believed that modern individuals were more drawn to private concerns than their ancient ancestors had been, and that the nature of modern politics must reflect this change. This was part of his anti-utopianism. Modern individuals were pulled in different directions by passions, reason, and sociopolitical forces. He judged modern stability and psychic peace to be difficult because of the agonistic interplay of passions and reason, because of the complexity of interpersonal relations, and because of the instability of revolutionary and post-revolutionary society. It would be foolish, he reasoned, to begin thinking about politics with unrealistic expectations about how individuals would act.

This meant taking man as he is, in contrast to Rousseau's idealized "natural man" independent of other men. Constant believed that modernity was characterized by interdependence. In contrast to Rousseau's depiction of modern society as a corrupt arena where vanity and *amour proper* reign, Constant embraced modern man's desire to obtain the approval of others. Vanity, he argued, is part of our being; the quest for the approval of others encourages moral behavior and helps make up our identity. In Rousseau's world emotional health is to be found in quiet contemplation and isolation from others; in Constant's, emotional health is to be found in intense relationships, in social interaction, in emotional interdependence. Total independence would not define a life worth living; indeed, it would not be a livable life.

Constant was always attentive to how historical context formed character. In his famous 1819 address "De la liberté des Anciens et à celle des Modernes," Constant distinguished individuals in ancient republics from those in modern societies. The former actively participated in public life, while the latter best developed their capacities, and found their greatest satisfactions, in everyday private activities. The thrust of this address was to analyze the type of liberty appropriate for a modern society and to suggest ways to protect "modern liberty" against tyranny, but the analysis was based on an assessment of what Constant referred to as the different "dispositions of mankind"—what we might refer to as the different "selves"—that existed in different historical contexts.[42] As he put it in the 1820s, the changes of modernity "had given man a new nature."[43]

Similarly, when Constant wrote about the Old Regime during the late-1790s, he was critical of how the mores encouraged by the French monarchy had fostered certain unfortunate character traits among the elite.

> A monarchical education, monarchical customs, monarchical souvenirs, monarchical castes besiege us from all sides. Fourteen centuries of royalism have narrowed most souls; enlightenment has gone ahead of sentiment, ideas are too strong for the sensations, characters too small for the human mind. Liberty, which is sliding toward us between anarchy and royalism, encounters a mutilated, fatigued, faded generation.[44]

And, as we have seen, he trenchantly analyzed how the "revolutionary torrent" in France had unleashed violent passions that led to fanaticism, rebelliousness, and the search for vengeance. He was equally upset to see that the chaos of revolutionary violence had led, at the other emotional extreme, to resignation, isolation, and a focus on narrow self-interest. The Revolution, in Constant's view, had accentuated elements of human nature that had weakened the self and consequently undermined stable political relationships.

For a healthy polity to emerge it was necessary to build a legal and institutional framework to protect civil and political liberties; it was equally necessary to foster self-respect, compassion, and enthusiasm needed to sustain character. Though he had faith in progress—in what he termed "perfectibility"—he was not optimistic, because he despaired that modernity had deeply eroded human nature.

> We have lost in imagination what we have gained in knowledge; we are, because of that, even incapable of intense excitement; the ancients were in the full youth of their moral life, we are in its maturity, perhaps in its old age; we are always dragging behind us some sort of afterthought, which is born of experience, and which defeats enthusiasm. The first condition of enthusiasm is not to observe oneself too acutely. Yet we are so afraid of being

fools, and above all of looking like fools, that we are always watching ourselves even in our most violent thoughts. The ancients had complete conviction about all things; we have, about almost everything, only a weak and fluctuating conviction, an incompleteness about which we search in vain to deaden our senses.[45]

Constant's analysis of modernity's impact on human nature was the basis of his rejection of ancient republicanism. He argued that, in the modern age, it was necessary to defend the private sphere against the intrusions of public institutions and public opinion, but at the same time, it was essential to prevent the evacuation of civic commitment. Constant opposed those who wished to impose outdated forms of political organization—like the "ancient liberty" advocated by Rousseau and Robespierre. He was equally opposed to those who wished to impose new forms of domination—like the "conquest and usurpation" advocated by Napoleon. Neither was appropriate for modern humanity, according to Constant, because historical conditions had changed (the rise of commerce and the emergence of larger political entities) and because the dispositions of individuals had changed (the new impulses for independence in the private sphere). Constant was searching for a political order that took into consideration the changes in character that modernity had introduced, that would balance reason and passion, that would recognize the intersubjective nature of self-knowledge and action—that would, in short, take into account the peculiarities, and, therefore, constraints, of the historical context.

This led him to embrace what I have termed political "pluralism." He believed that it was necessary to institutionalize the protection of rights—civil rights, free press, religious freedom—and to establish a constitutional political system based on popular sovereignty, but a popular sovereignty that recognized both its limits and the necessity of dividing the locations of its exercise. Moreover, Constant believed that it was essential to recognize that politics was an ongoing process of accommodation and compromise.

This points to a couple of significant elements of the pluralist tradition that are important to emphasize. Liberals like Constant and Staël believed that political contestation was an inescapable dimension of the modern human condition. There always would be conflicting interests and divergent ideals, and there always would be persistent political divisions. On this issue, liberals like Constant were fundamentally at odds with conservative monarchists who placed faith in an all-powerful king and with Left-wing Saint-Simonians who looked for the leadership of a technocratic elite. It also distinguished Constant's pluralistic liberalism from the state liberalism of Guizot and the Doctrinaires. None of these groups embraced political pluralism.

Constant's pluralist stance was closest to the Doctrinaires, but there was a fundamental divide between these two versions of French liberalism.[46] The Doctrinaires distinguished "tolerance" from "pluralism," accepting the former and rejecting the latter. They were willing to countenance, for example, different aesthetic views and different religious beliefs (differing on this score from Lamennais and religious conservatives), because in their minds aesthetics and religion were essentially affairs of the private sphere. They were also willing to countenance the *expression* of different political beliefs, because they favored "publicity" and encouraged the free expression of ideas. They were not similarly disposed, however, toward differences in political policy. This was the arena of public affairs where they believed reason should command and truth should reign. The Doctrinaires believed that policymakers should not be burdened with reaching a "consensus" with political opponents. Nor should they be slowed down with any process of political negotiation.[47] Doctrinaires identified political pluralism with the pathology of post-revolutionary politics. To Charles de Rémusat, for example, the embrace of pluralism implied an acceptance of equally valid competing political claims, which implied an acceptance that truth and reason were not possible in public affairs. This was unacceptable to him, as it was to other Doctrinaires, because it entailed the renunciation of the possibility of arriving at truth in the political realm. Truth and justice could be recognized; and, in politics, reason must be the ultimate arbiter. Rémusat embraced, in the words of Darío Roldán, an "epistemology of certitude."

The sticky issue, of course, is to determine who has access to general reason: Who determines which individual or individuals speak for general reason? Who is endowed with the authority to distinguish "true" general reason from the "limited" reasoning of any specific individuals? The Doctrinaires assumed that this would be obvious if free discussion and debate were allowed. And in practice, of course, they assumed that they themselves occupied this privileged perspective. For liberals like Constant, on the other hand, politics did not lead to rational truth. There were incommensurable positions that reflected the different interests and perspectives of different groups and regions. Politics, as a consequence, was the hard work of concrete negotiation and compromise. To make politics work, it was necessary to be attentive to the structures that would allow this ongoing negotiation, recognizing that it was often a plodding and ponderous process. This is why the checks and balances of a representative system were important. It was also necessary, according to Constant, to marginalize the effectiveness of verbal-theoretical extravagance and to avoid the temptation to aestheticize politics. Politics was not principally an affair of beautiful phrases or lofty abstractions;[48] it was about protecting liberties and negotiating differences. Liberals like Constant recognized that politics must be brought down to earth and embedded in daily life.

Closely connected with this was Constant's rejection of what we might term the revolutionary mentality: the idea that the past is a slate to be wiped clean, that society could be rebuilt from the ground up, and that "regeneration" was a transparent and rational process. Bronislaw Baczko has argued convincingly that Thermidor led to a cultural shift that included a reevaluation of the temporal dimension upon which the revolutionary mentality rested.[49] Before Thermidor, French revolutionary actors frequently proceeded as if change was a straightforward linear process pointing toward a luminous future that would realize the promises of happiness and regeneration.[50] After Thermidor, the traumas of the Terror had to be integrated into any understanding of revolutionary change, and this made the weight of historical time, now viewed as an agonistic process, more difficult to ignore. This was certainly true for Constant. Constant's insistence that politics must be brought to earth was closely associated with his rejection of the illusion of revolutionary rebirth. This was an extravagant, intemperate, and ultimately dangerous notion, according to Constant, not unlike the biblical dream of a great flood rising to erase an imperfect past. The political implications of such a mentality, he believed, were frequently disastrous, because at its core was an assumption that one could avoid the mundane negotiation of the competing and often incommensurable interests that were legitimately at the center of real politics.

Early nineteenth century French liberals like Constant were not socially progressive—they denied the importance of class; they failed to take seriously the problem of political or economic access; overall, they had at best an anemic concern for social justice. But they were politically progressive: they resisted the revolutionary mentality, and recognized that ongoing political negotiation was an important part of modernity.

\* \* \*

Jacques Julliard has suggested in a recent essay[51] that the legislative and judicial power of the representative system established in Western Europe and North America during the late-eighteenth and early-nineteenth centuries is again under assault. Our modern era, he points out, is marked by the permanent intervention of public opinion, in the form of referendums, opinion polls, and especially the Internet. Moreover, he continues, traditional political theory of the Marxist or liberal variety has discounted the importance of this "public opinion" and has insisted that sovereignty should be exercised by elites—leaders of the workers' movement or elected representatives of the people. This generalization may correctly point to the current frustration of "the people" facing politically powerful individuals and institutions, but it fails to characterize accurately the history of political thought. Constant and his contemporaries were, in fact, extremely sensitive to the importance of "public opinion," indeed of *popular* public opinion,[52] and their political thought took it into account. While no early nineteenth-century political thinkers had any conception of the "information highway" and other peculiarities of current technology, they could hardly ignore the intrusion of the masses into politics.

The famous *journées* of the revolution had demonstrated that the people in the street could claim sovereign political authority and could, at times, overwhelm national institutions, representative or otherwise. The Jacobins frequently appealed to this popular force, claiming that their policies were justified because they represented this ultimate sovereign power. Others, of course, made similar claims, some for the decisions of individuals who spoke for or "represented" the people, others for specific institutions like the Clubs that "represented" the people. As we have seen, pluralistic liberals insisted that this was a precarious basis for politics. It was unclear how to measure the true voice of the people; moreover, the peoples' voice tended to be mercurial in its almost daily fluctuations. Constant insisted that the popular opinion of the moment, even if it *could* demonstrably verify that it represented the majority, should never have a monopoly of power. Liberals like Constant believed that "the people" were the ultimate source of all political authority but also believed that no single person or institution should rule without the checks provided by competing expressions of this will. He insisted, in addition, that politicians should be careful not to run ahead of what the people were prepared to accept. To do so would be to court a revolutionary upheaval, one that in his mind would not be entirely unjustified.

These core issues of Constant's political thinking were closely connected to Constant's pragmatic assessment of the danger of any unified conception of sovereignty. And this, in turn, was directly related to his persistent pluralism. One of the main lessons that Constant took away from the Revolution was that any monopoly of power was dangerous. Sovereign authority *ultimately* always rested with the people, but its expression must take place through a variety of channels. Both public opinion and representative institutions were essential for a balanced liberal politics.

*　*　*

Did liberalism contribute to "the creation of democracy" in France? Was it an important element of *"l'apprentissage de la République,"* to use Maurice Agulhon's phrase?[53] These are perennial questions in modern French history, the answers to which often turn on one's definitions of "democracy" and/or "republic," concepts that are multifaceted. Was the critical period the early period of the Revolution (as claimed by François Furet[54]), the Directory (Jack Livesey[55]), the Restoration (Pierre Rosanvallon[56]), the Second Republic (Agulhon[57]), the Second Empire (Sudhir Harazeesingh[58]), the late-1860s and early–Third Republic (Philip Nord[59]), the end of the nineteenth century (Jean-Fabien Spitz[60]), or was it only with the revision of the Civil Code giving women equal rights in 1965? Is the watershed "le moment Guizot" or "le moment républicain"? Is the critical issue voting (Malcolm Crook[61]), personal autonomy (Carla Hesse[62]), individual rights (Lucien Jaume[63]), social access and economic equality (socialists[64]), or, as this study suggests, the approximations, calculations, and compromises of everyday politics? My endeavor in this study has been to argue that the political liberalism proposed by Benjamin Constant—especially those aspects related to human nature, pluralism, and political culture—have been important constitutive elements of democratic and republican politics in France.

This is not to argue that this idea of political contestation prevailed, even remotely, over opposing strains. Following his death on 8 December 1830, Constant's fame quickly declined, in spite of the fact that he had played an active role in the July Revolution and was named to the *conseil d'état* of the new regime, and in spite of the popularity demonstrated by the huge crowd that attended his funeral. During the July Monarchy, his pluralistic version of liberalism was overwhelmed by the more conservative state liberalism of Guizot and the Doctrinaires, and outflanked on the Left by the new egalitarian doctrines of socialism. Some liberals like Tocqueville and, a bit later, Edouard Laboulaye continued to read and refer positively to his political writings, but his liberalism became a minority strain within French sociopolitical discourse.[65] Constant's reputation reemerged in the late-nineteenth century when literary scholars rediscovered his novel *Adolphe*. But, it is only in the last thirty years, as the French looked to rediscover an indigenous liberal tradition, that his political writings have become the focus of serious scholarly attention.

Several forces worked against the success of pluralistic liberalism in France during the 1790s and subsequent decades. There was, first of all, the robust strain of rationalism in French thought that can be traced back to, at least, Descartes and Malebranche. Its influence on political thinking was considerable, suggesting that clear and distinct ideas about political "truths" were a clear and distinct possibility. The Doctrinaires obviously were descendants of this rationalist discourse. Equally powerful was the political and administrative legacy of absolutism, a system that insisted on a unified vision of political rule and discouraged the development of an opposition.[66] Most important, however, was the political culture generated by the Revolution itself. The turmoil of these years, with its succession of different administrations, often brought to power by violence and purges, cultivated deep suspicions of the intentions of one's opponents. The insistence on national unity faced the ever-present anxiety that conspiracies were lurking, as many were. Such a context did not provide a fertile ground for the growth of a politics that assumed decisions to be the outcome of a process of peaceful disagreement and negotiation; it did not encourage the embrace of a politics devoted to dialogue and compromise.

Closely connected with any analysis of the political volatility of post-revolutionary France is the historiographical debate concerning when French politics shed its instability. Does it date from the 1870s when monarchist hopes fizzled and republicans gained control of the Third Republic; from the early-1960s when DeGaulle consolidated his rule of the new Fifth Republic; or later? Some have argued that a tolerant liberal political culture has emerged in France only during the last few decades. Perhaps this is so, though as recently as 1981 the idea of the *cohabitation* of political parties in the same government was viewed with great anxiety. Many still seemed to assume that if politicians from different parties found themselves riding in the same car, each individual would be happily anticipating the opportunity of shoving members of the other parties out of the car door. Nonetheless, today, stable party politics give all appearances of having settled in.

If one takes the position that political arguments are simply cynical justifications of selfish acts, reflections of deeper socioeconomic forces, or rhetorical cloaks intended to hide operations of brute force, then party politics and the intellectual contribution of early liberals like Constant will be judged of little consequence. This would be the assumption, I assume, of crude Marxists, of Hobbesians, or of anyone who wishes to dismiss liberal stances as inherently naïve and/or rhetorical (i.e., Carl Schmitt). I raise the issue because serious historians have made such charges against the political figures of Thermidor and the Directory. Henri Guillemin, for example, has characterized important figures of the Directory as cynical and duplicitous actors, intent only upon selfish gain.[67] While I do not dismiss the possibility (indeed likelihood) that liberals, like others, had self-interested motives for some of their actions, and while I find compelling the suggestion that these liberals were insufficiently sensitive to socioeconomic issues, especially of the lower classes, I nonetheless reject the assumption that they have nothing of interest for us.

How does one confront the tension between popular sovereignty and political rights? How does one deal with the sociocultural problem of cohesion when uniformity of religious belief is in retreat and secular self-interest is growing? How does one confront the problem of protecting legality when conforming to the rule of law will allow into power those who wish to subvert the system of legality? One of the things that characterized the pluralistic liberalism of Constant was recognition that these are difficult issues, and that any hard-and-fast choice of either side of these various political conundrums will cause problems. In a certain context, the choice of one side (say, of "rights" over "popular sovereignty," or vice versa) likely will have very different consequences than the same choice in a different context.

Constant's pluralistic liberalism confronts central issues of modern politics in an attractive manner because he did not embrace the naive beliefs that are frequently associated with liberalism. Constant did not have a foolishly optimistic view of human nature. He did not believe that utilitarian or rational choice frameworks could or should provide accurate characterizations of how human beings make decisions, as suggested by some market liberals of the late-twentieth and early–twenty-first centuries. Sentiments beyond self-interest were central not only for personal fulfillment and social stability, but also for understanding how individuals moved ahead in economic, social, and political arenas. Constant was sensitive to the modern drive to be autonomous, to be free from fear and from unnecessary constraints—the contentment provided by legal protections; the happiness of individualism in a society that fostered independence. But he was equally insistent that enthusiasm was essential for a full life, and that passionate attachment to values beyond self-interest were defining characteristics of modern individual fulfillment.[68] Respect for these wider values and the negotiation of these individual interests were, he argued, legitimately at the heart of modern politics.

# Notes

## Introduction

1. Kingsley Martin, *French Liberal Thought in the Eighteenth Century: A Study of Political Ideas from Bayle to Condorcet* [1929], 3rd edition, revised (New York: Harper & Row, 1963).
2. André Jardin, *Histoire du libéralisme politique de la crise de l'absolutisme à la constitution de 1875* (Paris: Hachette, 1985).
3. Pierre Manent, *An Intellectual History of Liberalism*, translated by R. Balinski (Princeton: Princeton University Press, 1994).
4. Émile Faguet, though providing a different account of Constant's thought than presented here, is correct to claim that Constant "a inventé le libéralisme." [*Politiques et moralists du dix-neuvième siècle: première série* (Paris: Lucène, Oudin, et Cie, 1891), p. 113.]
5. Pierre Rosanvallon, "François Guizot and the Sovereignty of Reason," in *Democracy Past and Future*, edited by S. Moyn (News York: Columbia University Press, 2006), p. 117.
6. See, for example, Pierre Rosanvallon, *Le Moment Guizot* (Paris: Gallimard, 1985).
7. See, more recently, Pierre Rosanvallon, *The Demands of Liberty: Civil Society in France Since the Revolution*, translated by A.Goldhammer (Cambridge, MA: Harvard University Press, 2007).
8. George Armstrong Kelly, *The Humane Comedy: Constant, Tocqueville, and French Liberalism* (Cambridge: Cambridge University Press, 1992).
9. Lucien Jaume, *L'Individu effacé: ou le paradoxe du libéralisme français* (Paris: Fayard, 1998).
10. Andrew Jainchill, *Reimagining Politics after the Terror: The Republican Origins of French Liberalism* (Ithaca: Cornell University Press, 2008).
11. Annelien de Dijn, *French Political Thought from Montesquieu to Tocqueville: Liberty in a Levelled Society* (Cambridge: Cambridge University Press, 2008).
12. Previous scholars of Constant frequently have argued that Constant did not become a "liberal" until the Empire. The watershed event/text in these accounts is usually taken to be Constant's 1806 version of *Principes de politique*; the watershed change in doctrine is often taken to be Constant's embrace of an agnostic position concerning political institutions—that is, his acceptance that either a republic or a monarchy could be "liberal." See, for example, Etienne Hofmann, *Les "Principes de politique" de Benjamin Constant: la genèse d'une oeuvre et l'évolution de la pensée de leur auteur (1789–1806)*, 2 vols. (Genève: Droz, 1980); Marcel Gauchet, "Constant," in *A Critical Dictionary of the French Revolution*, edited

by F. Furet and M. Ozouf, translated by A. Goldhammer (Cambridge, MA: Harvard University Press, 1989), pp. 924–32; Helena Rosenblatt, *Liberal Values: Benjamin Constant and the Politics of Religion* (Cambridge: Cambridge University Press, 2008). Most recently, Stefano de Luca has argued that Constant's theory did not become "mature" until "the political battle to establish a liberal republic seems lost." ["Benjamin Constant and the Terror," *The Cambridge Companion to Constant*, edited by H. Rosenblatt (Cambridge: Cambridge University Press, 2009), pp. 92–114, this quote, p. 110.]

While Constant's political theory was refined during the Empire, the essential elements were present in his writings of the late-1790s, that is, during the Directory and Consulate. These essential elements, considered in detail in the chapters below, are a critique of absolute power and of a unified (Rousseauean, nonpluralist) conception of political sovereignty; a commitment to the protection of rights and to a representative political system; a pragmatic appreciation of historical context; and, an appreciation of the importance of culture and *moeurs*. The late-1790s is when Constant first used the term "liberal" to refer to his position that included these elements.

Mauro Barberis also claims that the 1790s were the period of the emergence of Constant's liberalism, which he identifies with Constant's theories of the limitation of sovereignty, the neutral power, and the liberty of the moderns. ["Thermidor, le libéralisme et la modernité politique," in *1795 Pour une République sans Révolution*, sous la direction of Roger Dupuy et Marcel Morabito (Rennes: Presses Universitaires de Rennes, 1996), pp. 123–41.]

13. The use of "political pluralism" as an analytical category probably dates from the work of Harold Laski. See his *Studies in the Problem of Sovereignty* (New Haven: Yale University Press, 1917); *Authority in the Modern State* (New Haven: Yale University Press, 1919); and "The Pluralist State," *Philosophical Review* (November 1919), reprinted in *The Foundations of Sovereignty and Other Essays* (New York: Harcourt, Brace, 1921), pp. 232–49.

Only recently has "pluralism" begun again to receive attention in reference to French thought. My thanks to Stuart Jones and Julian Wright for inviting me to the stimulating workshop they organized on "Pluralism and the Idea of the Republic in France, 1789–2006" at Durham University (14–15 April 2007).

Annelien de Dijn [*French Political Thought from Montesquieu to Tocqueville*] recently has written of the importance of a pluralist strain of "aristocratic liberalism," defined as a belief in the importance of intermediary bodies and aristocratic rule. She argues that this tradition had its origins in the thought of Montesquieu and deeply informed liberal thought in the nineteenth century.

While I find De Dijn's rehabilitation of the pluralist strain in French thought refreshing, my argument in this book is quite different. De Dijn, I believe, exaggerates the influence of royalist doctrines on nineteenth-century liberals. The concern of liberals like Constant was to avoid the "despotic" centralization of power in any one institution (executive or legislative), but this did not entail a rejection of popular sovereignty or the embrace of some "new aristocracy," both central elements of De Dijn's "aristocratic liberalism." Constant explicitly embraced the former (popular sovereignty) and rejected the latter (a new aristocracy). Calls for administrative decentralization, in fact, came from anti-authoritarians throughout the political spectrum—royalists, liberals, socialists, and anarchists. Moreover, the desire to create (or recreate) some form of "intermediary powers" or "associations" was similarly widespread, though *which* associations was often hotly contested.

For my own take on the importance of Montesquieuian "liberal republicanism" on French thought on the non-authoritarian Left, see my *Pierre-Joseph Proudhon and the Rise of French Republican Socialism* (New York: Oxford University Press, 1984), pp. 34–41; and my "The Republican Moment(s) in Modern France," *European Journal of Political Theory*, 6.2 (2007): 239–48.

14. There is a new edition of the 1818 English translation of Staël's *Considerations on the Principal Events of the French Revolution*, edited and with an introduction by Aurelian Craiutu (Indianapolis, IN: Liberty Fund Press, 2008).

15. Bronislaw Baczko focuses on this emotional side of politics in the "introduction" to his *Politiques de la Révolution française* (Paris: Gallimard, 2008), pp. 11–40. And, of course, it was not just elites who experienced such emotions. Peter McPhee entitles the chapter on the lived experience of inhabitants of rural France during the early phase of the Revolution "Elation and Anxiety: The Revolutionary Year." Peter McPhee, *Living the French Revolution, 1789–99* (New York: Palgrave, 2006), pp. 35–54.

16. See, especially, Timothy Tackett, *When the King Took Flight* (Cambridge, MA: Harvard University Press, 2003); and Tackett, "Conspiracy Obsession in the Time of Revolution: French Elites and the Origins of the Terror, 1789–1792," *American Historical Review*, 105 (2000): 691–713.

17. Isser Woloch, *The New Regime: Transformations of the French Civic Order, 1789–1820s* (New York: W.W. Norton, 1994), p. 91.

18. Patrice Gueniffey, *La Politique de la Terreur: essai sur la violence révolutionnaire 1789–1794* (Paris: Fayard, 2000).

19. Barry M. Shapiro has recently argued that the experience of the deputies of the Constituent Assembly between 5 May and 14 July 1789 was "traumatic" in a clinical sense. See his *Traumatic Politics: The Deputies and the King in the Early French Revolution* (University Park, PA: Pennsylvania State University Press, 2009).

20. Joseph de Maistre, *Considérations sur la France* (1797), in Joseph de Maistre, *Oeuvres, suivies d'un Dictionnaire Joseph de Maistre*, edited by Pierre Glaudes (Paris: Robert Laffont, 2007), pp. 199–289; these quotes, pp. 200, 207.

21. Bronislaw Baczko, *Ending the Terror: The French Revolution after Robespierre*, translated by M. Petheram (Cambridge: Cambridge University Press, 1994); he emphasizes continuity on p. 34. See also Baszko, *Politiques de la Révolution française*, pp. 165–338.

22. The "law of suspects" of 17 September 1793 was not officially abolished until 4 October 1795. By this time, however, it had ceased being used.

23. The Jacobin Club of Paris was closed in November 1794; in August 1795 all clubs (including Jacobin clubs) were provisionally dissolved by decree. Nonetheless, Jacobins regrouped and Jacobinism survived until Napoleon took power and definitively banned all political clubs. See Isser Woloch, *Jacobin Legacy: The Democratic Movement Under the Directory* (Princeton: Princeton University Press, 1970).
24. This was a recurring conflict during the Revolution. For illuminating accounts of this, see Jon Cowans, *To Speak for the People: Public Opinion and the Problem of Legitimacy in the French Revolution* (New York: Routledge, 2001), and Paul R. Hanson, *The Jacobin Republic Under Fire: The Federalist Revolt in the French Revolution* (University Park, PA: University of Pennsylvania Press, 2003).
25. Baczko refers to this as "controlled unanimity." *Ending the Terror*, p. 42.
26. This has been emphasized, especially, by François Furet, *Interpreting the French Revolution*, translated by E. Forster (Cambridge: Cambridge University Press, 1981); Lucien Jaume, *Le discours Jacobin et la démocratie* (Paris: Fayard, 1989); Keith M. Baker, "Sovereignty," *A Critical Dictionary of the French Revolution*, pp. 844–59; Baczko, *Ending the Terror*.
27. I borrow the phrase from Cowans, *To Speak for the People*, p. 65. Lucien Jaume, similarly, refers to the "*unanimisme mystique*" of the Jacobin conception of the general will (*Le discours Jacobin et la démocratie*, p. 322).
28. Baczko's *Ending the Terror* is about the fifty-six–day period between 9 Thermidor and the end of Year II. He argues forcefully that the conception of unified sovereignty was a thread that connected the different phases of the revolution. "[C]ertain characteristics of the political culture of the Revolution and of revolutionary political *mentalités* remained, beyond all the spectacular changes of direction. In fact, the creation of the democratic arena in 1789 did not entail, and this was the case throughout the Revolution, the *working out of a pluralist political system*. In this sense Jacobinism was both the expression and the perversion of the concept of the political arena as unified" (p. 109, emphasis in original). Constant and Staël, as we see below, broke with this tradition.
29. See, most recently, Renee Winegarten, *Germain de Staël and Benjamin Constant: A Dual Biography* (New Haven: Yale University Press, 2008). My own contribution: "Constant and Women," in *The Cambridge Companion to Constant*, pp. 173–205.
30. Judith N. Shklar, "The Liberalism of Fear," in *Liberalism and the Moral Life*, edited by N.L. Rosenblum (Cambridge, MA: Harvard University Press, 1989), pp. 21–38.

# 1   Benjamin Constant: The Early Years (1767–95)

1. "Préface," to *Mélanges de littérature et de politique* (1829), in Benjamin Constant, *Ecrits politiques*, edited by Marcel Gauchet (Paris: Gallimard, 1997), p. 623.
2. In 1961, the Bibliothèque Nationale in Paris bought some "Oeuvres manuscrites" that date from 1810; in 1974, the Bibliothèque cantonale

et universitaire de Lausanne obtained family archives that contained numerous manuscripts, including political works written during the Directory and the Empire. These works are discussed in more detail below.

3. Paul Bastid, *Benjamin Constant et sa doctrine*, 2 vols. (Paris: Colin, 1967); O. Pozzo di Borgo's notes and commentaries, in Benjamin Constant, *Ecrits et discours politiques*, 2 vols. (Paris: Pauvert, 1964).

4. Benjamin Constant, *Ecrits politiques*, texts choisis, présentés et annotés par Marcel Gauchet (Paris: Hachette, 1980). Gauchet's influential essay in this collection, entitled "Benjamin Constant: L'Illusion lucid du libéralisme," has been translated by A. Goldhammer for *The Cambridge Companion to Constant*, edited by H. Rosenblatt (Cambridge: Cambridge University Press, 2009), pp. 23–46.

   Constant was an important influence for Gauchet's own transition from a supporter of antipolitical *autogestion* to political liberalism. See Samuel Moyn, "Savage and Modern Liberty: Marcel Gauchet and the Origins of New French Thought," *European Journal of Political Theory*, 4.2 (2005): 164–87.

5. Etienne Hofmann, *Les "Principes de politique" de Benjamin Constant: la genèse d'une oeuvre et l'évolution de la pensée de leur auteur (1789–1806)*, 2 vols. (Genève: Droz, 1980). This quote, t. 1, p. 21. Hofmann notes the presence of liberal elements in the first writings, but argues that 1806 is the date of the emergence of the Constant's mature liberalism.

   Mais si certaines pages écrites sous le Directoire proclament, il est vrai, quelques dogmes libéraux—le chapitre sur l'arbitraire dans *Des réactions politiques* par exemple—nous sommes encore loin du penseur qui, sous l'Empire, écrira un véritable traité de philosophie liberale et qui, sous la Restauration, défendra le régime parlementaire comme seul apte à assurer la liberté (t. 1, p. 93)

6. Benjamin Constant, *Oeuvres complètes, série I: Oeuvres* [thirty-six volumes are planned]; *série II: Correspondence* [eighteen volumes are planned]. Comité directeur: Paul Delbouille, Jean-Daniel Candaux, C.P. Courtney, Alain Dubois, Etienne Hofmann, Norman King, Kurt Kloocke, Claude Reymond, François Rosset, Dennis Wood (Tübingen: Max Niemeyer Verlag, 1993–). Most of the volumes containing Constant's major works up to 1820 have appeared. The published volumes of correspondence are currently through t. 8 (1810–1812).

   Each volume of the *Oeuvres complètes* contains a full scholarly apparatus, evidence of an impressive amount of scholarly work. The introductions include textual analyses and discussions of historical context. The notes for both *séries* provide critical details about works cited, individuals mentioned, and Constant's interlocutors.

   Mention should also be made of the publications of L'Association Benjamin Constant, an outgrowth of the Institut Benjamin Constant in Lausanne and the seemingly tireless work of Anne and Etienne Hofmann. See *Annales Benjamin Constant*, which has appeared annually since 1982.

7. For details of Constant's early years, see Gustave Rudler, *La Jeunesse de Benjamin Consant: 1767–1794* (Paris: Colin, 1908); Elizabeth W.

Schermerhorn, *Benjamin Constant: His Private Life and His Contribution to the Cause of Liberal Government in France 1767–1830* (Boston: Houghton Mifflin, 1924); Etienne Hofmann, *Les "Principes de politique" de Benjamin Constant*, t. 1; Kurt Kloocke, *Benjamin Constant: une biographie intellectuelle* (Genève: Droz, 1984); and, Denis Wood, *Benjamin Constant: A Biography* (London: Routledge, 1993).

8. See the discussion in Wood, *Benjamin Constant: A Biography* (London: Routledge, 1993), p. 282, note 75.

9. See Paul Delbouille, "Le dernier procès de Juste de Constant et l'esprit de famille chez Benjamin et chez Marianne Magnin," *Annales Benjamin Constant*, 26 (2002): 89–101.

10. Rosalie de Constant wrote an account of her travels through central Switzerland in 1819, now published as *Un Voyage en Suisse en 1819* (Lausanne: La Bibliothèque des Arts, 1964).

11. See Constant, *Oeuvres complètes: Correspondance générale*. For the later years (not yet published in the *Oeuvres completes*), see *Lettres de Benjamin Constant à sa famille 1775–1830*, edited by Jean H. Menos (Paris: Stock, 1932).

12. There is no record of this discourse. See Benjamin Constant, *Oeuvres complètes, t. 1: Ecrits de jeunesse (1774–1799)* (Tübingen: Max Niemeyer Verlag, 1998), p. 113.

13. It is impossible, given the available evidence, to assess precisely the degree to which the thought of the Scottish political economists influenced Constant while he was a student. But it seems highly likely that his high regard for commerce and commercial societies was influenced by the ideas of the Scottish school—especially the likes of David Hume, Adam Smith, and Dugald Stewart—though he could easily have picked up such notions from French writers like Voltaire and Turgot.

14. Dennis Wood, *Benjamin Constant: A Biography*. In the words of Dan Hofstadter, who agrees with Wood's analysis, Constant "had the orphan's tendency to melancholia, to cramped self-reliance and compulsive nomadism." [*The Love Affair as a Work of Art* (New York: Farrar, Straus and Giroux, 1996), p. 10.]

15. For a more classically Freudian account, see Han Verhoeff, *"Adolphe" et Constant; une étude psychocritique* (Paris: Klincksieck, 1976).

16. *Ma vie (Le Cahier rouge), Oeuvres complètes, t. 3:1, Écrits littéraires (1800–1813)* (Tübingen: Max Niemeyer Verlag, 1995), p. 307.

17. *Ma vie (Le Cahier rouge)*, p. 313. There are three letters from Johannot to Constant in Constant, *Correspondance générale*, t. 1, pp. 67–70.

18. Ibid., pp. 316–17.

19. Ibid., pp. 317–18.

20. Ibid., p. 326.

21. Kloocke, *Benjamin Constant: une biographie intellectuelle*.

22. Benjamin Constant à Isabelle de Charrière (4 juin 1790), *Correspondance générale*, t. 1., p. 256.

23. Benjamin Constant à Isabelle de Charrière (21 janvier 1791), *Correspondance générale*, t. 1., p. 282.

24. Jean Starobinski, "Suicide et mélancholie chez Mme de Staël," in *Madame de Staël et l'Europe*, Colloque de Coppet, 18–24 juillet 1966 (Paris: Klincksieck, 1970), pp. 242–52. See also David J. Denby, *Sentimental Narrative and the Social Order in France, 1760–1820* (Cambridge: Cambridge University Press, 1994), esp. pp. 194–239; and Naomi Schor, *One Hundred Years of Melancholy* (Oxford: Clarendon Press, 1996).

25. Sainte-Beuve was especially censorious, referring to Constant as "un esprit supérieur et fin, uni à un caractère faible et à une sensibilité maladive." This quote is from "Un Dernier mot sur Benjamin Constant," originally published in 1845; reprinted in C.A. Sainte-Beuve, *Portraits contemporains*, t. 5 (Paris: Calmann Lévy, 1889), p. 279. This article shows Sainte-Beuve at his prudish and hypercritical worst.

    For an analysis of Sainte-Beuve's view of Constant, see the discussion by Pierre Deguise, *Benjamin Constant méconnu: le livre De la Religion* (Genève: Droz, 1966), pp. 3–37.

26. Constant's "journaux intimes" were published in an altered, extremely abridged form in 1887. The complete texts have been available only since 1952. The most accessible edition is in *Oeuvres de Benjamin Constant*, edited by Alfred Roulin (Paris: Bibliothèque de la Pléiade, 1957), pp. 221–823. For an account of their publication history, see Roulin's "notice," pp. 1476–82. There is now, however, a wonderful new scholarly edition: Benjamin Constant, *Oeuvres complètes*, t. 6: *Journaux intimes (1804–1807) suivis de Affaire de mon père (1811)* (Tübingen: Max Niemeyer Verlag, 2002). References will be to this new edition.

27. Alison Fairlie, "The Art of Constant's Adolphe: 1. The Stylization of Experience," in *Imagination and Language: Collected Essays on Constant, Baudelaire, Nerval and Flaubert* (Cambridge: Cambridge University Press, 1981), p. 3.

28. Rudler, *La Jeunesse de Benjamin Consant*; Georges Poulet, *Benjamin Constant par lui-même* (Paris: Seuil, 1968).

29. Hofmann, *Les "Principes de politique" de Benjamin Constant*, t. 1, pp. 80, 89, 194, 200.

30. Kloocke, *Benjamin Constant: une biographie intellectuelle*, p. 32.

31. C.P. Courtney, *Isabelle de Charrière (Belle de Zuylen): A Biography* (Oxford: Voltaire Foundation, 1993), pp. 388, 381.

32. Harold Nicolson, *Benjamin Constant* (Garden City, NY: Doubleday, 1949), p. 60.

33. As George Armstrong Kelly has perceptively noted, "his resiliency and fortitude are far more impressive than his malignancy. Deprived of the normal sources of courage, he managed to show great courage amid a life pointed toward tribulation and decomposition." [*The Humane Comedy: Constant, Tocqueville, and French Liberalism* (Cambridge: Cambridge University Press, 1992), p. 8.]

34. Tzvetan Todorov, *A Passion for Democracy: The Life, the Women He Loved and the Thought of Benjamin Constant*, translated from French (New York: Algora, 1999), p. 8.

35. There is now an English edition of this correspondence: *There Are No Letters Like Yours: The Correspondence of Isabelle de Charrière and Constant*

*d'Hermenches*, translated by Janet Whatley and Malcolm Whatley (Lincoln, NE: University of Nebraska Press, 2000).

36. *Ma vie* (*Le Cahier rouge*), pp. 322–23. On Isabelle de Charrière, see especially C. P. Courtney's authoritative biography, *Isabelle de Charrière*. Also see the wonderful short book, originally published in 1925, by Geoffrey Scott, *The Portrait of Zélide* (New York: Helen Marx, 1997). In addition, see Philippe Godet, *Madame de Charrière, d'après de nombreux documents inédits (1740–1805)*, 2 vols. (Genève: Jullien, 1906); Joan Hinde Stewart, *Gynographs: French Novels by Women of the Late Eighteenth Century* (Lincoln, NE: University of Nebraska Press, 1993), pp. 96–132; Mona Ozouf, *Women's Words: An Essay on French Singularity*, translated by Jane Marie Todd (Chicago: University of Chicago Press, 1997), pp. 21–44; Raymond Trousson, *Isabelle de Charrière: Un Destin de femme au XVIIIe siècle* (Paris: Hachette, 1994).

37. See Roland Mortier, "Belle and Benjamin: Political Gradations," *Eighteenth Century Life*, 13.1 (February 1989): 16–25.

38. Rudler, *La Jeunesse de Benjamin Constant*.

39. Courtney, *Isabelle de Charrière*, pp. 384–91.

40. Wood, *Benjamin Constant: A Biography*, pp. 92–3.

41. He visited many times: 10 December 1787–16 February 1788; December 1791; several times between June 1793 and September 1793; August 1794.

42. This correspondence, which is in the various volumes of the *Oeuvres complètes: Correspondance*, is available in its entirety in an edition edited by Jean-Daniel Candaux, *Isabelle de Charrière Benjamin Constant: Correspondance (1787–1805)* (Paris: Desjonquères, 1996).

43. Courtney prefers the latter explanation. See his *Isabelle de Charrière*, pp. 546–84.

44. Isabelle de Charrière to Huber (11 July 1795); cited in Courtney, *Isabelle de Charrière*, p. 581.

45. This is the phrase Constant himself used to describe his flight. [*Ma vie* (*Le Cahier rouge*), p. 333.]

46. For details of this period of Constant's life, see Béatrice W. Jasinski, *L'Engagement de Benjamin Constant: amour et politique (1794–1796)* (Paris: Minard, 1971); Roland Mortier, "Benjamin Constant devant la Révolution française," in *Benjamin Constant et la Révolution française 1789–1799* (Genève: Droz, 1989), pp. 11–21; Henri Grange, *Benjamin Constant: amoureux et républicain 1795–1799* (Paris: Les Belles Lettres, 2004); and the works cited in note 7 above.

47. For recent analyses of the political and ideological dimensions of the relationship between Benjamin Constant and Isabelle de Charrière, see the following: Isabelle Vissière, "Duo épistolaire ou duel idéologique? La correspondance de Madame de Charrière et de Benjamin Constant pendant la Révolution" and Mauro Barberis et Giuseppe Sebaste, "Comment devenir ce que l'on est: Benjamin Constant, Madame de Charrière et la Révolution," both essays are in *Benjamin Constant et la Révolution française 1789–1799*, pp. 23–60.

48. During this period when the marriage with Minna had no future (and after Minna had taken a lover), Constant had an affair with an actress named Caroline (November 1792).
49. Courtney, *Isabelle de Charrière*, p. 489.
50. "Journaux intimes," *Oeuvres complètes*, t. 6, p. 170. She was in fact not two, but nine years older than Constant.
51. There is no record of this discourse. See Constant, *Oeuvres complètes*, t. 1, p. 113.
52. "De la discipline militaire des Romains" (Avril 1786). In *Oeuvres complètes*, t. 1, pp. 117–40.
53. Ibid., pp. 141–97.
54. Ibid., this quote, pp. 184–85.
55. Ibid., pp. 196–97.
56. Isabelle de Charrière, "Observations et conjectures politiques" (1787–1788), *Oeuvres complètes*, X (Amsterdam: Oorschot, 1981), pp. 57–110. Constant continued to discuss these essays in his correspondence with Charrière between December 1787 and March 1788. See Benjamin Constant, *Correspondance générale*, t. 1 (1774–1792), pp. 106, 107, 109, 110, 121, 122, 127, 149–50.
57. No. 3, "Reflexions sur la générosité & sur les Princes," in Isabelle de Charrière, "Observations et conjectures politiques," pp. 70–73; this quote, p. 71.
58. Ibid., pp. 74, 89–92, 95–101; this quote, p. 71.
59. Ibid., pp. 87–89; this quote, p. 89.
60. Ibid., p. 81.
61. Ibid., p. 73.
62. Benjamin Constant à Isabelle de Charrière (ca. 24 décembre 1787), *Correspondance générale*, t. 1, p. 109.
63. Benjamin Constant à Isabelle de Charrière (19–21 mars 1788), *Correspondance générale*, t. 1, p. 150.
64. Benjamin Constant à Isabelle de Charrière (4–5 avril 1788), *Correspondance générale*, t. 1, p. 154.
65. Benjamin Constant, *Recueil d'articles 1820–1824*, edited by Ephraïm Harpaz (Genève: Droz, 1981), pp. 136–37.
66. This phrase, in Benjamin Constant, "A Charles His, rédacteur du *Républicain français*" [juillet 1795], in *Oeuvres complètes*, t. 1, p. 300.
67. Benjamin Constant à Isabelle de Charrière (4 juin 1790), *Correspondance générale*, t. 1, p. 256.
68. Benjamin Constant à Isabelle de Charrière (10 décembre 1790), *Correspondance générale*, t. 1, p. 271.
69. Ibid., t. 1, pp. 271–72. Mirabeau and Barnave were early revolutionaries; Sartine and Breteuil were both identified with the Old Regime (Sartine was ministre de la marine, 1774–1780; Breteuil was ministre de la Maison du Roi, 1783–1788).
70. Constant refers to himself as a "democrat" in letters to Isabelle de Charrière. See the letter of 17 septembre 1792, *Correspondance générale*, t. 1, p. 313; and the letter of 17 mai 1793, *Correspondance générale*, t. 2, p. 90.

71. Benjamin Constant à Isabelle de Charrière (17 mai 1793), *Correspondance générale*, t. 2, p. 90.
72. Benjamin Constant à Salomon de Charrière de Sévery (13 août 1790), *Correspondance générale*, t. 1, p. 260.
73. Benjamin Constant à Isabelle de Charrière (6 juillet 1792), *Correspondance générale*, t. 1, p. 311.
74. Benjamin Constant à Isabelle de Charrière (16 octobre 1793), *Correspondance générale*, t. 2, p. 174. Referring to these frightening spectacles, Constant writes the following: "Quel peuple! Qelle espèce que la nôtre! Il faudra bien en venir à souhaiter que le repos sous le despotisme succède à ces convulsions d'Antropaphages."
75. Benjamin Constant à Isabelle de Charrière (9 novembre 1793), *Correspondance générale*, t. 2, p. 260.
76. Benjamin Constant to his aunt, la comtesse Anne-Marie-Pauline-Andrienne de Nassau (31 janvier 1794); cited by Roland Mortier, "Belle and Benjamin: Political Gradations," *Eighteenth Century Life*, 13.1 (February 1989): 17. Constant talked frequently of writing a book about Mauvillon, a book that he characterized as a biography, a homage, and an introduction to German literature. He never completed this work.
77. Benjamin Constant à Isabelle de Charrière (7 juin 1794), *Correspondance générale*, t. 2, p. 381.
78. Ibid.
79. Benjamin Constant à Isabelle de Charrière (11 novembre 1793), *Correspondance générale*, t. 2, pp. 195–96.
80. See Benjamin Constant à Isabelle de Charrière (20 avril 1794), *Correspondance générale*, t. 2, p. 296.
81. Ibid. Also see Benjamin Constant à Isabelle de Charrière (17 octobre 1793), where Constant writes the following: "Les vertus et les lois reviendront avec la paix." *Correspondance générale*, t. 2, p. 175.
82. Benjamin Constant à Isabelle de Charrière (6 juin 1794), *Correspondance générale*, t. 2, p. 373.
83. Benjamin Constant à Isabelle de Charrière (9 septembre 1794), *Correspondance générale*, t. 2, p. 427.
84. Isabelle de Charrière à Benjamin Constant (10 septembre 1794), *Correspondance générale*, t. 2, p. 429.
85. Benjamin Constant à Isabelle de Charrière (14 octobre 1794), *Correspondance générale*, t. 2, p. 470.
86. The Constant-Staël relationship has been discussed in many sources. For the early years, I have found especially useful: Béatrice W. Jasinski, *L'Engagement de Benjamin Constant: amour et politique (1794–1796)*. For a recent account of the Constant-Staël relationship, see Renee Winegarten, *Germaine de Staël and Benjamin Constant: A Dual Biography* (New Haven and London: Yale University Press, 2008). For the period after January 1804, the essential source is Constant's "journaux intimes."
87. Benjamin Constant à Isabelle de Charrière (25 septembre 1793), *Correspondance générale*, t. 2, p. 142.
88. Jasinski, *L'Engagement de Benjamin Constant*, p. 19.
89. These quotes from Wood, *Benjamin Constant: A Biography*, p. 142.

90. She was, for example, in Paris from May 1797 to January 1798.
91. It is interesting to note that just when Constant's political commitments were becoming more pronounced—his attachment to republicanism becomes definite in 1794—Isabelle de Charrière was moving toward political indifference. She seemed disappointed that Benjamin was giving up the rarified "view from above" that had characterized their personal and epistolary relationship. [See especially Isabelle de Charrière à Benjamin Constant (12 décembre 1794), *Correspondance générale*, t. 2, pp. 506–07.]
92. This is Constant's term, as noted above. See Benjamin Constant à Isabelle de Charrière (21 janvier 1791), *Correspondance générale*, t. 1, p. 256.
93. Madame de Staël, *Des circonstances actuelles qui peuvent terminer la Révolution et des principes qui doivent fonder la République en France*, edited by Lucia Omacini (Genève: Droz, 1979).
94. See Henri Grange, *Les Idées de Necker*, thèse presentée devant l'Université de Paris IV (le 17 décembre 1971) (Lille: Université de Lille III, 1973); and Grange, "De Necker à Benjamin Constant ou du libéralisme ploutocratique au libéralisme démocratique," *Le Groupe de Coppet et la Révolution Française* (Lausanne: Institut Benjamin Constant, 1988), pp. 63–71.
95. Constant's early political writings are in Benjamin Constant, *Oeuvres completes*, t. 1: *Ecrits de jeunesse (1774–1799)* (Tübingen: Max Niemeyer Verlag, 1998). The larger political manuscript was only recently published: Benjamin Constant, *Fragments d'un ouvrage abandonné sur la possibilité d'une constitution républicaine dans un grand pays*, edited by Henri Grange (Paris: Aubier, 1991).

## 2  The Emergence of Liberalism (1795–97)

1. See Mme de Staël, *Considérations sur la Révolution française* [1818]; there is a new edition of the 1818 English translation (Indianapolis: Liberty Fund, 2008).
2. See Lucien Jaume, "'L'esprit de Coppet' et l'organisation du pouvoir exécutif," in *La Constitution de l'an III ou l'ordre républicain*, texts réunis par Jean Bart, Jean-Jacques Clère, Claude Couvoisier, et Michel Verpeaux (Dijon: Editions de l'Université de Dijon, 1998), pp. 121–42.
3. Mme de Staël, "Réflexions sur le procès de la reine," *Oeuvres complètes de Mme. la Baronne de Staël*, t. 2 (Paris: Treuttel et Würtz, 1820), pp. 1–33; these quotes, p. 21.
4. Mme de Staël, "Réflexions sur la paix, adressées à M. Pitt et aux Français," *Oeuvres complètes de Mme. la Baronne de Staël*, t. 2 (Paris: Treuttel et Würtz, 1820), pp. 35–94; these quotes, p. 54.
5. "Réflexions sur la paix intérieure," *Oeuvres complètes de Mme. la Baronne de Staël*, t. 2 (Paris: Treuttel et Würtz, 1820), pp. 95–172; this quote, p. 111.
6. "[D]ans les circonstances actuelles: tous les efforts qu'on tenteroit pour ramener la royauté, n'obtiendroient qu'un résultat, ne causeroient qu'une réaction, le rétablissement de la terreur." [Ibid., p. 134].

7. Ibid., p. 120.
8. Ibid., p. 113.
9. Mme de Staël, *De circonstances actuelles qui peuvent terminer la Révolution et des principes qui doivent fonder la République en France.* Written in the late-1790s, this work was unpublished until 1906 (Paris: Fischbache, 1906). All references are to the new critical edition, edited by Lucia Omacini (Genève: Droz, 1979). For the assessment of 1791, see p. 156.
10. "Cécile," in Benjamin Constant, *Oeuvres*, edited by A. Roulin (Paris: Gallimard/Bibliothèque de la Pléiade, 1957), p. 184.
11. Constant appealed directly to the government of the Directory, and wrote an article about the political rights of exiled French Protestants. See Constant's appeal of 26 July 1796, "Aux citoyens représentans du peuple composant le Conseil des Cinq-cents"; and his article of August 1796, "De la restitution des droits politiques aux descendans des religionnaires fugitifs," in *Oeuvres complètes*, t. 1, pp. 389–411.
12. See Jasinski, *L'Engagement de Benjamin Constant*, pp. 86–106, 232–84, for an analysis of Constant's financial dealings during these years, and for an account of his attempts to obtain French citizenship.
13. See Maurice Déchery, "Benjamin Constant à Luzarches: lettres inédites," *Benjamin Constant et la Révolution française 1789–1799*, pp. 151–68.
14. M.J. Sydenham, *The First French Republic 1792–1804* (Berkeley: University of California Press, 1973), p. 54.
15. Benjamin Constant à la comtesse Anne-Marie-Pauline-Andrienne de Nassau (29 mai 1795), *Correspondance générale*, t. 3, p. 92.
16. Benjamin Constant à la comtesse Anne-Marie-Pauline-Andrienne de Nassau (7 juillet 1795), *Correspondance générale*, t. 3, p. 99.
17. Benjamin Constant à la comtesse Anne-Marie-Pauline-Andrienne de Nassau (7 août 1795), *Correspondance générale*, t. 3, p. 104.
18. Mathiez claimed that the Thermidorians "could do nothing but destroy and disorganize, by placing a jealous parliamentary equality at the service of private appetites and passions." "The Constitution [of 1795]...did not set up a true Republic, but a sort of oligarchy of politicians, the republic of a clique, which called itself the Directory." The Termidorians "had nobody behind them but the purchasers of national property and army-contractors." [Albert Mathiez, *After Robespierre: The Thermidorian Reaction*, translated by Catherine Alison Phillips (New York: Knopf, 1931), pp. 20, 236, 260.] Furet, similarly, wrote that "Compared with the heros of the Committee of Public Safety and the legendary genius of Napoleon, they present a picture of corrupt intermediaries clinging on to power with no scruples about their methods.... those regicide representatives, those former servants of the revolutionary government, those generals risen from the ranks, those men grown rich in the business of war and the state...." [François Furet, *Revolutionary France 1770–1880*, translated by Antonia Nevill (Oxford: Blackwell, 1992), p. 155.]
19. See, for example, *1795 Pour une République sans Révolution*, sous la direction de Roger Dupuy et Marcel Morabito (Rennes: Presses Universitaires de Rennes, 1996); Daniel Hollander Colman, "The Foundation of the

French Liberal Republic: Politics, Culture and Economy after the Terror," Ph.D. Dissertation, Stanford University (1997); *La Constitution de l'an III ou l'ordre républicain*; and *La Constitution de l'an III: Boissy d'Anglas et la naissance du libéralisme constitutionnel*, sous la direction de Gérard Conac et Jean-Pierre Machelon (Paris: PUF, 1999).

20. The Commission charged with drawing up the new constitution included, most importantly, a group of ex-Girondins (Pierre-Claude-François Daunou, Jean-Baptiste Louvet, Louis-Marie La Révellière-Lépeaux, and Pierre-Charles-Louis Baudin des Ardennes), moderates (Jean-Denis Lanjuinais and François-Antoine Boissy d'Anglas), and one Jacobin (Théophile Berlier). Most scholars see Daunou as the main architect of the constitution. See André Douteribes, "Daunou et le modèle du régime représentatif," in *La Constitution de l'an III: Boissy d'Anglas et la naissance du libéralisme constitutionnel*, pp. 111–38.

21. See Romuald Szramkiewicz, "Boissy d'Anglas, la Constitution de l'an III et la politique religieuse," in *La Constitution de l'an III: Boissy d'Anglas et la naissance du libéralisme constitutionnel*, pp. 153–65.

22. Gérard Conac has suggested that this division reflected a belief that younger men were naturally more creative and imaginative, while older men were naturally more sensible and reasonable. See Conac's "La convention thermidorienne: épisode réactionnaire ou transition novatrice?" in *La Constitution de l'an III: Boissy d'Anglas et la naissance du libéralisme constitutionnel*, pp. 274–81.

23. See the discussions by Lucien Jaume, "Necker: examen critique de la Constitution de l'an III," and by Henri Grange, "Mme de Staël et la Constitution de l'an III: avant et après." Both articles are in *La Constitution de l'an III: Boissy d'Anglas et la naissance du libéralisme constitutionnel*, pp. 167–82; 183–99. Also see Jaume, " 'L'esprit de Coppet' et l'organisation du pouvoir exécutif."

24. See, for these two arguments, Michel Troper, "La séparation des pouvoirs dans la Constitution de l'an III," in *La Constitution de l'an III: Boissy d'Anglas et la naissance du libéralisme constitutionnel*, pp. 51–71; and Marcel Morabito, "Les nouveautés constitutionnelles de l'an III," in *1795 Pour une République sans Révolution*, pp. 167–77.

25. See Chapter 3 for discussion of the various crises of the Directory period.

26. See Mona Ozouf, "Les décret des deux-tiers ou les leçons de l'Histoire," in *1795 Pour une République sans Révolution*, pp. 193–209.

27. Benjamin Constant, "Lettres à un député de la Convention," in *Nouvelles politiques nationals et étrangères*, 6, 7, 8, messiror, an 3 (24, 25, and 26 juin 1795). These are in *Oeuvres complètes*, t. 1, pp. 277–88.

28. Benjamin Constant, *Mémoires inédits*, in *Portraits mémoires souvenirs*, edited by Ephraïm Harpaz (Paris: Librairie Honoré Champion, 1992), pp. 58–59.

29. These are the words of Jean-Baptiste Louvet, as reported by Henri Grange, *Benjamin Constant: amoureux et républicain 1795–1799* (Paris: Les Belles Lettres, 204), p. 66.

230 *Notes to Pages 48–52*

30. Benjamin Constant, "A Charles His, rédacteur du *Républicain français*," in *Oeuvres complètes*, t. 1, pp. 295–300, this quote, p. 299.
31. For discussions of Constant's views of the Two-Thirds Decree, see the note by Ephraïm Harpaz in Benjamin Constant, *Recueil d'articles 1795–1817*, edited by Ephraïm Harpaz (Genève: Droz, 1978), p. 33; and Jasinski, *L'Engagement de Benjamin Constant*, pp. 107–54.
32. He wrote to his aunt in August 1795 that he was hopeful that the Republic would succeed. "Je crois que tous les jours malgré quelques petites tentatives Jacobines, quelque divisions dans l'assemblée, & autres petits mouvements, la Répubique s'affermit." Benjamin Constant à la comtesse Anne-Marie-Pauline-Andrienne de Nassau (7 août 1795), *Correspondance générale*, t. 3, p. 103.
33. These are reprinted in *Oeuvres complètes*, t. 1, pp. 309–18.
34. See Jeremy D. Popkin, *The Right-Wing Press in France, 1792–1800* (Chapel Hill: University of North Carolina Press, 1980) for an analysis of the royalist and moderate press during these years.
35. Julie Talma was the former wife of a celebrated actor. She and Constant would remain close friends until her death in 1805.
   Staël indicated in her correspondence that she disagreed with the aggressive tone of some of Constant's early publications. On 17 July 1796, for example, she responded to Roederer's criticisms of Constant's *De la force du governement actuel* (discussed below in this chapter), in the following way: "[L]'ouvrage de Benjamin n'est pas le mien. Je suis, il est vrai, très enthousiaste de son talent.... Quant à ce qui vous en a deplu, je suis a beaucoup d'égards de votre avis. La raillerie de *mémoire implacable*, etc., n'était pas de mon opinion; je trouve que les honnêtes gens ont fait des fautes, mais c'est avec plus de respect que j'approcherais de leur examen." [cited by Hofmann, *Les "Principes de politique" de Benjamin Constant: la genèse d'une oeuvre et l'évolution de la pensée de leur auteur (1789–1806)*, t. 1, p. 112].
36. Constant was arrested with François de Pange (1764–96), who was a moderate publicist who had been close to the Chénier brothers and to Condorcet, and was now close to Staël.
37. Constant was released from prison because of the intervention of Jean-Baptiste Louvet and Marie-Joseph Chénier. For accounts of Constant's actions during May–October 1795, see Grange, *Benjamin Constant: amoureux et républicain 1795–1799*, pp. 61–87; and Jasinski, *L'Engagement de Benjamin Constant*, pp. 157–73.
38. Benjamin Constant à la comtesse Anne-Marie-Pauline-Andrienne de Nassau (16 octobre 1795), *Correspondance générale*, t. 3, p. 128.
39. Benjamin Constant à la comtesse Anne-Marie-Pauline-Andrienne de Nassau (21 octobre 1795), *Correspondance générale*, t. 3, p. 131.
40. Ibid.
41. Benjamin Constant à la comtesse Anne-Marie-Pauline-Andrienne de Nassau (29 octobre 1795), *Correspondance générale*, t. 3, pp. 134–5.
42. Grange, *Benjamin Constant: amoureux et républicain 1795–1799*, p. 89.
43. Benjamin Constant à la comtesse Anne-Marie-Pauline-Andrienne de Nassau (10 décembre 1795), *Correspondance générale*, t. 3, p. 141.

44. Benjamin Constant, *De la force du gouvernement actuel de la France et de la nécessité de s'y rallier*, in *Oeuvres complètes*, t. 1, pp. 319–80; *Des réactions politiques*, in *Oeuvres complètes*, t. 1, pp. 447–506.
45. *De la force du gouvrnement actuel*, p. 328.
46. Ibid., p. 336.
47. Ibid., p. 346.
48. Ibid., pp. 346–55.
49. Ibid., p. 338.
50. This phrase is in Constant's article "A Charies His, rédacteur de *Républicain français*," in *Le Républicain français* (24 juillet 1795), in *Oeuvres complètes*, t. 1, pp. 295–300; this quote p. 300.
51. *De la force du gouvernement actuel*, pp. 328, 375.
52. Ibid., pp. 377–78.
53. Ibid., p. 338.
54. This quote is from *Des réactions politiques*, *Oeuvres complètes*, t. 1, p. 506. He repeats this phrase, slightly altered, in "Discours prononcé au Cercle constitutionnel, le 9 ventôse an VI [27 février 1798]," in *Oeuvres complètes*, t. 1, p. 598: "l'espèce humaine s'égalise, en même tems et par cela même qu'elle s'élève."
55. *De la force du gouvernement actuel*, p. 341. These, of course, are all famous days of the Revolution: 14 July 1789 = the taking of the Bastille; 10 August 1792 = the fall of the monarchy; 9 Thermidor an II (July 27, 1794) = the end of the Terror; 4 Prairial an III (23 May 1795) = the repression of the last Jacobin uprising.
56. Ibid., p. 379.
57. Etienne Hofmann discusses some of these responses in his excellent chapter on Constant during the Directory. *Les "Principes de politique" de Benjamin Constant: la genèse d'une oeuvre et l'évolution de la pensée de leur auteur (1789–1806)*, esp. t. 1, pp. 104ff.
58. See the discussion by Jasinski, *L'Engagement de Benjamin Constant*, pp. 195–203; and Grange, *Benjamin Constant: amoureux et républicain 1795–1799*, pp. 120–21.
59. Adien de Lezay-Marnésia, *De la foiblesse d'un gouvernement qui commence, et de la nécessité où il est de se rallier à la majorité nationale* (Paris: Matthey, an IV [1796]). The title itself is obviously a parody of Constant's article.
60. *De la force du gouvrnement actuel*, p. 358.
61. Ibid.
62. Ibid., p. 341.
63. Louis-François Bertin de Vaux (1771–1842) was a journalist of the Right-center. He attacked Constant for being a Jacobin because Constant in *De la force du gouvernement actuel* criticized moderate republicans for not agreeing with the policies of the government. In *Feuille de jour* (15 juin 1796), he wrote: "Carnot [President of the Directory] feroit sagement de mettre à la porte ce petit Suisse incivil qui abuse de l'imprudente hospitalité qu'on a eu la bonté de lui donner, et de le renvoyer dans son pays, cacher sa honte et ses remords, avec un écriteau sur son dos: Bassesse inutile."
64. Constant's published letter to Bertin de Vaux is in *Oeuvres complètes*, t. 1, p. 387. Bertin de Vaux's retraction was published in *Feuille de jour*

(16 juillet 1796). For a thorough account of this affair, see Béatrice W. Janinski, *L'Engagement de Benjamin Constant*, pp. 219–31.

65. Benjamin Constant à Samuel de Constant (16 juin 1796), *Correspondance générale*, t. 3, p. 187.

66. Benjamin Constant à la comtesse Anne-Marie-Pauline-Andrienne de Nassau (11 juin 1796), *Correspondance générale*, t. 3, p. 188.

67. On 17 September 1796, Constant wrote to his aunt about the "Affaire du camp de Grenelle," a failed attempt by Parisian Jacobins to provoke an uprising of soldiers camped at Grenelle. The ensuing struggle led to 20 deaths and 132 taken as prisoners. Subsequently, thirty-three individuals were condemned to death. See Benjamin Constant à la comtesse Anne-Marie-Pauline-Andrienne de Nassau (17 septembre 1796), *Correspondance générale*, t. 3, p. 223.

On 4 October 1796, he wrote to his aunt: "Il parait que les Jacobins s'agitent, que les Royalistes espèrent profiter de leurs tentatives, mais que les Républicains sont sur leurs gardes." [Benjamin Constant à la comtesse Anne-Marie-Pauline-Andrienne de Nassau (4 octobre 1796), *Correspondance générale*, t. 3, p. 227.]

68. Benjamin Constant à Isabelle de Charrière (10 décembre 1790), *Correspondance générale*, t. 1, pp. 271–72. Mirabeau and Barnave were early revolutionaries; Sartine and Breteuil were both identified with the Old Regime. See note 69, on page 225 above

69. Constant, *De la force du gouvernement actuel*, p. 332.

70. Ibid., p. 337.

71. Ibid., p. 358.

72. This was especially pronounced in Constant's *De réactions politiques* [1797], in *Oeuvres complètes*, t. 1, p. 468.

73. Charles Walton recently has argued, much like Constant, that the Old Regime culture of calumny and honor made it difficult to establish a politics of tolerance and compromise during the Revolution. This culture, he suggests, reinforced "a polarizing dynamic at the heart of revolutionary politics—one that began by exacerbating enmities between revolutionaries and counterrevolutionaries and continued by exacerbating enmities among revolutionaries themselves." [Charles Walton, *Policing Public Opinion in the French Revolution: The Culture of Calumny and the Problem of Free Speech* (New York: Oxford University Press, 2009), this quote, p. 9.]

74. Constant, "Discours pour la plantation de l'arbre de la liberté" [16 septembre 1797], *Oeuvres complètes*, t. 1, p. 553.

75. *De la force du gouvernement actuel*, p. 343.

76. Constant, *Des effets de la Terreur* [mai–juin 1797], *Oeuvres complètes*, t. 1, p. 524.

77. This is a reference to counter-revolutionary émigré activities at this time. The most famous was the landing of royalists at Quiberon; they were defeated by Republican forces, but raised Republican anxieties.

78. "A Charles His, rédacteur de *Républicain français*," p. 296.

79. Ibid., p. 297.

80. "Discours prononcé au Cercle constitutionnel pour la plantation de l'arbre de la liberté" [16 septembre 1797], in *Oeuvres complètes*, t. 1, this quote, p. 553.

81. *De la force du gouvernement actuel*, p. 344.
82. "Nécrologie de Louvet" [originally published in *La Sentinelle* (28 août 1797)], in *Oeuvres complètes*, t. 1, pp. 535–44; this quote p. 541.
83. "Des suites de la contre-révolution de 1660 en Angleterre" [juin 1799], in *Oeuvres complètes*, t. 1, p. 679.
84. Constant, *De la force du gouvernement actuel*, pp. 367–68.
85. Constant, "A Charles His, rédacteur du *Républicain français*," p. 295.
86. *De la force du gouvernement actuel*, pp. 367–68.
87. Ibid., p. 368.
88. Ibid., p. 370.
89. *Des effets de la Terreur*, p. 515.
90. "Comte rendu de *De l'influence des passions sur le bonheur des individus et des nations* de Germaine de Staël," *Gazette nationale, ou le Moniteur universel* (26 octobre 1796); in *Oeuvres complètes*, t. 1, pp. 419–27.
91. Ibid., p. 422.
92. *De la force du gouvernement actuel*, pp. 339–42.
93. This phrase, ibid., p. 358.
94. Ibid., p. 376.
95. *Des réactions politiques*, p. 458.
96. Ibid.
97. *De la force du gouvernement actuel*, pp. 341-42. See also the discussion by Brigitte Sändig, "Entre liberté et puissance. Réflexions sur l'activité intellectuelle dans les écrits politiques de Benjamin Constant," *Les Valenciennes*, no. 18 (1995), pp. 119–28.
98. *Des effect de la Terreur*, pp. 523–26 (emphasis in original).
99. Ibid., p. 519.
100. Some journals attacked Constant as a Jacobin. In *Le Véridique ou Courrier universel*, for example, there were two such negatives articles. In the first (16 avril 1797), Constant was accused of having developed "la doctrine du 'plus pur jacobinisme'.... Entre cet écrit et ceux de Babeuf, il n'y a d'autre différence que celle du style." Cited in Constant, *Correspondance générale*, t. 3, p. 259, note 9.
101. See, on this issue, Etienne Hofmann, *Les "Principes de politique" de Benjamin Constant*, t. 1, pp. 146–49; François Furet, "Une polémique thermidorienne sur la Terreur. Autour de Benjamin Constant," *Passé Présent*, 2 (1983), pp. 44–55; Philippe Raynaud, "préface," *De la force du gouvernement actuel* (Paris: Flammarion, 1988), pp. 14–20; Grange, *Benjamin Constant: amoureux et républicain 1795–1799*, pp. 168–74; and de Luca, "Benjamin Constant and the Terror," *The Cambridge Companion to Constant*, pp. 92–114.
102. *Des effets de la Terreur*, p. 519.
103. Ibid., p. 526.
104. Staël petitioned the Directory in December 1796, and Constant raised the issue with Merlin de Douai, the Minister of Justice, and with Barras, one of the Directors, in Paris in January 1797.
105. There is a good discussion of the issue of Staël's "nationality" by Claude Reymond in Constant's *Oeuvres complètes*, t. 1, pp. 431–36.
106. Germaine de Staël in *Nouvelles politiques* (3 juin 1795); cited by Hofmann, *Les "Principes de politique" de Benjamin Constant*, t. 1, p. 111, note 104.

107. *Emigrés* who take up arms against France are "criminals," according to Staël, and should be banished from France. *Réflexions sur la paix intérieure*, pp. 101–2 note.
108. *Réflexions sur la paix intérieure*, p. 100.
109. Ibid., p. 139.
110. Ibid., pp. 140–41, 169–72.
111. Ibid., p. 165.
112. Ibid., p. 170.
113. *De l'influence des passions sur le bonheur des individus et des nations*, published with *Essai sur les fictions*, présenté par Michel Tournier (Paris: Ramsay, 1979), pp. 53–256; this quote, p. 67.
114. Staël's first publication was on Rousseau: *Lettres sur les ouvrage et le caractère de J.-J. Rousseau* [1788], in *Oeuvres de Jeunesse* (Paris: Desjonquères, 1997), pp. 33–98.
115. The introduction and conclusion of *De l'influence des passions* discuss the context of the revolution. This quotation p. 252.
116. There is an excellent discussion of this in Baczko, *Politiques de la Révolution française*, pp. 379–84.
117. Mme de Staël, *Des circonstances actuelles qui peuvent terminer la Révolution*, p. 146.
118. See *De l'influence des passions*, pp. 156–59 for a discussion vengeance and of "*l'héroïque oubli.*"
119. "Compte rendu de *De l'influence des passions sur le bonheur des individus et des nations* de Germaine de Staël," in *Oeuvres complètes*, t. 1, pp. 419–27.
120. Mme de Staël, *Considérations sur la Révolution française*, deuxième partie, chapter XVII (Paris: Charpentier, 1862), t. 1, p. 299.
121. See Isser Woloch, *Jacobin Legacy: The Democratic Movement Under the Directory* (Princeton: Princeton University Press, 1970), pp. 27–32.
122. See, especially, Steven Kale, *French Salons: High Society and Political Sociability from the Old Regime to the Revolution of 1848* (Baltimore and London: Johns Hopkins University Press, 2004). See also my "Elite Culture in Early Nineteenth-Century France: Salons, Sociability, and the Self," *Modern Intellectual History*, 4.2 (2007): 327–51.
123. Baczko, *Politiques de la Révolution française*, p. 372.
124. I draw here from ibid., pp. 387–401
125. These quotes are from *De la littérature considérée dans ses rapports avec les institutions socials* (Paris: Garnier, 1998), pp. 288, 285. Cited by Baczko, *Politiques de la Révolution française*, pp. 397.
126. Ibid., pp. 308–09; cited in Baczko, *Politiques de la Révolution française*, p. 399.
127. Germaine de Staël à Benjamin Constant (27 octobre 1815); cited by Kale, *French Salons*, p. 100.
128. Benjamin Constant, *Mémoires inédits*, in *Portraits Mémoires Souvenirs*, edited by Ephraïm Harpaz (Paris: Librairie Honoré Champion, 1992), p. 48.
129. Constant, *Des réactions politiques* [1797], p. 484.
130. Constant, "Discours pronouncé au Cercle constitutionnel, pour la plantation de l'arbre de la Liberté, le 30 fructidor an 5" [16 septembre 1797], in *Oeuvres complètes*, t. 1, p. 556.

131. The French adjective *liberal* previously referred to individuals who gave generously; or to individuals who did not impose on others or accept being imposed on oneself; or to careers and professions that were relatively independent of the state. See *Trésor de la langue français*, 10 (Paris, 1983): 1156–57.

The first use by Constant of "liberal" to refer to his position is, I believe, in his article "A Charles His, rédacteur de *Républicain français*," which appeared in *Le Républicain français* (24 juillet 1795), in *Oeuvres complètes*, t. 1, pp. 295–300. He uses the phrase "principes libéraux" on p. 297.

In subsequent writings he referred to "des idées libérales" (*Des réactions politiques*, p. 469), to "les opinions libérales" (p. 472); to those who were "libéraux dans leurs principes abstraits" (p. 474). Constant used "liberal" as an adjective; I am unaware of any use of the term "liberal" as a noun at this time. Germaine de Staël used the term (also as an adjective) in *De l'influence des passions sur le bonheur des individus et des nations*, see p. 74.

The editors of the *Oeuvres complètes* refer to Constant in the late 1790s as a defender of "une politique libérale avant la lettre." [*Oeuvres completes*, t. 4, p. 19]. I wish to argue that he advocated "une politique libérale."

132. *Des réactions politiques*, p. 479.

133. Philippe Raynaud makes this point in the "préface" to his edition of Constant's *De la force du gouvernement actuel* (Paris: Flammarion, 1988), p. 14.

134. I borrow the phrase, as mentioned above, from Judith N. Shklar, "The Liberalism of Fear," *Liberalism and the Moral Life*, edited by N.L. Rosenblum (Cambridge, MA: Harvard University Press, 1989), pp. 173–205.

It is a characterization that others have made about the politics of the Directory. François Luchaire has suggested, correctly I think, that "fears"—of the mob, of dictatorship by an Assembly, of the monarchy, of dictatorship by one man, of reaction, and so on—deeply informed the agenda of those who wrote the Constitution of 1795. ["Boissy d'Anglas et la Constitution de l'an III," in *La Constitution de l'an III: Boissy d'Anglas et la naissance du libéralisme constitutionnel*, pp. 43–50.] It is also a theme raised by Gérard Conac. ["La convention thermidorienne: épisode réactionnaire ou transition novatrice?" in the same collection, pp. 201–86.]

135. Kloocke, *Benjamin Constant: une biographie intellectuelle*, p. 39.

136. Hofmann, Les "*Principes de politique*" de Benjamin Constant, t. 1, pp. 93, 100, 119, 161.

137. Ibid., pp. 155–56.

138. Helena Rosenblatt, *Liberal Values; Benjamin Constant and the Politics of Religion*. These quotes, pp. 49, 63, 122.

139. This is discussed by Grange, *Benjamin Constant: amoureux et républicain 1795–1799*, pp. 135–41. Grange sees this as an example of Constant's "machiavelianism." I see it as an example of his pragmatism.

140. *Des réactions politiques*, p. 473.
141. In his "Nécrologie de Louvet," published in *La Sentinelle* (11 Fructidor, anV [28 août 1797]), Constant leveled perhaps his fiercest criticism of "l'opinion publique": "cette opinion qui se compose des mensonges de quelques-uns, de la malignité de plusieurs, de la sottise de presque tous." In *Oeuvres complètes*, t. 1, p. 543.
142. *Des réactions politiques*, pp. 457–58.
143. See ibid., pp. 489–95, for Constant's discussion of midrange principles. Immanual Kant wrote an essay responding to this section of *Des réactions politiques*, published in *Berlinischer Blätter* (6 September 1797). Kant disputed Constant's claim (on p. 493) that one could tell a lie in order to save a human life.
144. Andrew Jainchill, *Reimagining Politics After the Terror: The Republican Origins of French Liberalism* (Ithaca: Cornell University Press, 2008), pp. 10–11, 60–61.
145. *De la force du gouvernement actuel*, p. 360.
146. Ibid., p. 356.

## 3 Liberal Dilemmas (1797–1802)

1. See, especially, Isser Woloch, *Jacobin Legacy: The Democratic Movement Under the Directory* (Princeton: Princeton University Press, 1970); Denis Woronoff, *La République bourgeoise de Thermidor à Brumaire,, 1794–1799* (Paris: Seuil, 1972); M.J. Sydenham, *The First French Republic 1792–1804* (Berkeley: University of California Press, 1974); Martyn Lyons, *France Under the Directory* (Cambridge: Cambridge University Press, 1975); Lynn Hunt, David Lansky, and Paul Hanson, "The Failure of the Liberal Republic in France 1795–1799: The Road to Brumaire," *Journal of Modern History*, 51 (December 1979): 734–59; Jeremy D. Popkin, *The Right-Wing Press in France, 1792–1800* (Chapel Hill: University of North Carolina Press, 1980); Isser Woloch, *The New Regime: Transformations of the French Civic Order, 1789–1820s* (New York: W.W. Norton, 1994); Bernard Gainot, *1799, un nouveau Jacobinisme?: la démocratie représentative, une alternative à brumaire* (Paris: CTHS, 2001); James Livesey, *Making Democracy in the French Revolution* (Cambridge, MA: Harvard University Press, 2001); Howard G. Brown and Judith A. Miller, eds., *Taking Liberties: Problems of a New Order from the French Revolution to Napoleon* (Manchester: Manchester University Press, 2002); and Howard G. Brown, *Ending the French Revolution: Violence, Justice and Repression from the Terror to Napoleon* (Charlottesville: University of Virginia Press, 2006).
2. There were 260 seats contested; royalists won 180. As a consequence, royalists controlled about 330 seats (of the 750) in the two Councils. If moderates leaned their way, they would control the Councils. These figures are from D.M.G. Sutherland, *The French Revolution and Empire: The Quest for a Civic Order* (Malden, MA: Blackwell, 2003), p. 284.
3. François Barbé-Marbois was elected President of the Council of Ancients and Charles Pichegru was elected President of the Council of Five-Hundred. Both were royalists.

4. Acquitted of the charge of conspiracy, they were condemned to death for advocating the restoration of the Constitution of 1793, which had become a capital offence by the Law of 27 Germinal (16 April 1796).

5. Constant wrote his Aunt on April 14, 1797 (i.e., between the first and second stage of the elections): "Les choix pour le renouvellement du corps législatif sont presque tous royalistes; l'esprit public se précipite dans cette direction avec une impétuosité qui dépasse tous les interêts. Les Républicains sont insulté partout...." [Benjamin Constant à la comtesse Anne-Marie-Pauline-Andrienne de Nassau (14 avril 1797), in *Correspondance générale*, t. 3, p. 252.]

6. See *Des réactions politiques*, especially chapters 8 and 9, pp. 489–504.

7. These quotes from an article in *Le Véridique ou Courrier universel* (16 avril 1797), cited in *Correspondance générale*, t. 3, p. 259 note 9.

8. See Béatrice W. Jasinski, "Constant et le Cercle constitutionnel," and Gérard Gengembre "Le Cercle constitutionnel: un laboratoire du libéralisme?" in *Benjamin Constant et la Révolution française 1789–1799*, edited by Verry and Delacrétez (Genève: Droz, 1989), pp. 119–49. For the relationship of this club to Jacobinism at this time, see Isser Woloch, *Jacogin Legacy: Democratic Movement Under the Directory*, pp. 63–70.

9. The Directors Barras, Reubell, and La Réveillière-Lépeaux imposed on the other two Directors, Carnot and Barthélemy (who was a new Director, elected on 26 May), to nominate five new ministers, of which Talleyrand was one.

10. Benjamin Constant à Samuel de Constant (1 août 1797). *Correspondance générale*, t. 3, pp. 286–87. "Si d'ici a deux mois il n'arrive pas je ne sai quel envenement qui remette la République à flot, il n'y a plus aucune espérance a avoir, & cet evenement même peut être une calamité par ses conséquences."

11. There is also an ambiguous reference to "ce que nous ferons dans la suite" in a letter of 2 September 1797 (two days before the coup), which suggests that Constant might have been involved in discussions and activities leading up to the coup. See Constant à Jean Debry (2 septembre 1797), *Correspondance générale*, t. 3, pp. 291–92.

12. Benjamin Constant à Samuel de Constant (9 août 1797). *Correspondance générale*, t. 3, pp. 290–91.

13. There was a second meeting on August 15. See the discussion by Hofmann, *Les "Principes de politique" de Benjamin Constant*, t. 1, p. 151; and Baczko, *Politiques de la Révolution française*, pp. 441–44. Both authors rely on Thibaudeau's *mémoires* (written many years after these events). Antoine Clair Thibaudeau, *Mémoires sur la Convention et le Directoire* (Paris: Baudouin frères, 1824), t. 2, pp. 242–50.

14. There is a good discussion in Howard G. Brown, "The Search for Stability," in *Taking Liberties: Problems of a New Order from the French Revolution to Napoleon*, pp. 20–50.

15. Georges Lefebvre, *The Directory*, translated by Robert Baldick (New York: Vintage Books, 1967), p. 102. D.M.G. Sutherland's recent assessment is similar. The coup "saved the republican form of government but at the expense of the integrity of the legislature." [*The French Revolution and Empire*, p. 264.]

16. Sydenham, *The First French Republic*, pp. 144–75; this quote pp, 156–57.
17. Brown, "The Search for Stability," in *Taking Liberties: Problems of a New Order from the French Revolution to Napoleon*, p. 25.
18. Henri Grange, *Benjamin Constant: amoureux et républicain 1795–1799* (Paris: Belles Lettres, 2004), p. 205.
19. Staël wanted constitutional revision that would strengthen the executive Directory and, also, make the Conseil des Anciens a more powerful legislative and quasi-judicial body. Constant also would focus, as we shall see, on constitutional details.
20. Madame de Staël, *Des circonstances actuelles qui peuvent terminer la Révolution et des principes qui doivent fonder la République en France*, edited by Lucia Omacini (Genève: Droz, 1979), pp. 179–80.
21. Isser Woloch offers a similar assessment of the Fructidor coup: "in a surprisingly effective yet bloodless way—the coup d'état overturned the disloyal majority of reactionaries and royalists that had come to power in the elections of 1797." [Woloch, *Jacobin Legacy*, p. 77.]
22. Constant's speech "Discours prononcé au Cercle constitutionnel pour la plantation de l'arbre de la liberté, le 30 fructidor an V [16 Septembre 1797]" is reprinted in Constant, *Oeuvres complètes*, t. 1, pp. 551–62; this quote, p. 561.
23. Ibid., pp. 552–53.
24. Ibid., p. 553.
25. See the discussion by Béatrice W. Jasinski, "Constant et le Cercle constitutionnel," *Benjamin Constant et la Révolution française 1789–1799*, p. 129. Albert Mathiez has argued that Constant's support of the coup of 18 Fructidor indicates a willingness to support a powerful executive if such an executive would protect property. Etienne Hofmann effectively refutes this interpretation. See Albert Mathiez, "Saint-Simon, Lauraguais, Barras, Benjamin Constant etc. et la réforme de la Constitution de l'an III, après le coup d'Etat du 18 fructidor an V," *Annales historiques de la Révolution française*, t. VI (1929), pp. 5–23; Hofmann, *Les "Principes de politique" de Benjamin Constant: la gènese d'une oeuvre et l'évolution de la pensée de leur auteur (1789–1806)* (Genève: Droz, 1980), t. 1, pp. 156–61.
26. Others have judged Staël's and Constant's support of the coup more severely. Henri Grange accuses Staël of supporting "despotisme et dictature." ["Mme de Staël et la Constitution de l'an III: avant et après," in *Constitution de l'an III: Boissy d'Anglas et la naissance du libéralisme constitutionnel*, sous la direction de Gérard Conac et Jean-Pierre Machelon (Paris: PUF, 1999), pp. 183–99; this quote, p. 193.]
    Olivier Pozzo di Borgo has accused Constant of "duplicity." [See Pozzo di Borgo's edition of Benjamin Constant, *Ecrits et discours politiques* (Paris: Pauvert, 1964), t. 1, p. 128.] Etienne Hofmann judges Constant to be not yet a "liberal" because he does not insist on the absolute liberty of individuals against the government. [Hoffman, *Les "Principes de politique" de Benjamin Constant*, t. 1, pp. 155–56.]
    I wish to argue that their pragmatic judgment of what, given the context, was appropriate action was central to their liberalism.

27. In his "Souvenirs historiques," première letter [in *Portraits Mémoires Souvenirs*, edited by Ephraïm Harpaz (Paris: Librairie Honoré Champion, 1992), p. 73], Constant wrote: "les causes du 18 brumaire remontent au 18 fructidor, journee á laquelle des amis peu éclairés de la république avaient coopéré. La voyant menacée par un parti actif et puissant, ils avaient cru qu'on pouvait sauver une constitution par un coup d'Etat, c'est-à-dire par la violation de la constitution même." Cited in *Oeuvres complètes*, t. 1, p. 548.

28. Constant, "Discours prononcé au Cercle constitutionnel, le 9 ventôse an VI [27 février 1798]," in *Oeuvres complètes*, t. 1, pp. 585–601. Neo-Jacobin journalists attacked Constant's speech for defending property and for supporting the restriction of active politics to the wealthy class. They accused Constant of being a "fauteur d'une olygarchie française." See the discussion by Woloch, *Jacobin Legacy*, pp. 155–59; this quote (p. 156) is from *Journal des homes libres*.

29. Constant, "Discours prononcé au Cercle constitutionnel, le 9 ventôse an VI [27 février 1798]," *Oeuvres complètes*, t. 1, see esp. pp. 595–96.

30. Constant, "Discours prononcé au Cercle Constitutionnel, le 9 ventôse an VI," see esp. p. 597. Constant remained critical of many journalists, who he believed irresponsibly attacked individuals, unnecessarily stirred up political passions, and thereby undermined *moeurs*. See, for example, Benjamin Constant à Ludwig Ferdinand Huber (16 août 1798), *Correspondance générale*, t. 3, p. 359.

31. He took office on 13 November 1797. See Constant, "Discours d'installation prononcé à Luzarches le 23 brumaire an VI [23 novembre 1797]," in *Oeuvres complètes*, t. 1, pp. 575–77. Also see Maurice Déchery, "Benjamin Constant à Luzarches: Lettres inédites," *Benjamin Constant et la Révolution française*, pp. 151–68.

32. The Second Directory supported Théophilanthropie and *le culte décadaire*. Théophilanthropie was not an official cult, but was supported by important political figures like La Révellière-Lépeaux. It consisted of simple beliefs like the existence of God, immortality of the soul, tolerance, and social obligation. *Le culte décadaire* was briefly the official civic religion of the state. Founded on 3 February 1798, it was strongly supported by Merlin de Douai and François de Neufchâteau, both hostile to Théophilanthropie. It celebrated, as the name indicates, the day of "decadi" on the revolutionary calendar, and was to inspire people to moral and patriotic action. It was clearly intended to ween people away from the Catholic church.
    Neither survived very long. Théophilanthropie was undercut by the Corcordat of 1801 and definitively extinguished by the Organic Articles of 1802. *Le culte décadaire* was opposed by supporters of both the Catholic and constitutional churches, and quickly lost support.

33. This is the period of the foundation of the various national institutions devoted to education, and to the ascendancy of the Idéologues who viewed themselves as "organic intellectuals" who incarnated reason and, therefore, should lead the people. The Idéologues had great faith

in instruction from the top down. They also believed that while the people were the *source* of power, they need not necessarily *exercise* power. Lucien Jaume has perceptively referred to Cabanis' stance as "democracy purged of all its inconveniences." [Jaume, *L'Individu effacé: ou le paradoxe du libéralisme français*, pp. 32–34.] A similar elitist and rationalist view would inform the politics of François Guizot and the Doctrinaires. Constant seemed to share some of these notions about an elite educating the people at this time. He would abandon them ca. 1800, when he explicitly rejected the idea that the people could be "educated" into supporting a political regime. Moreover, he always interpreted popular sovereignty to mean that people should not only be the *source* of political power; they should also *exercise* power.

34. Constant uses this phrase in his letter to Nicolas-Louis François de Neufchâteau (9 octobre 1798), *Correspondance générale*, t. 3, p. 376. Neufchâteau was, at this time, Interior Minister.

35. "Benjamin Constant à ses collègues de l'Assemblée électorale du département de Seine et Oise" (10 avril 1798), in *Oeuvres complètes*, t. 1, pp. 613–25; this quote, p. 613.

36. In his correspondence, Constant referred to his opponents in the departmental assembly as "anarchists." See Benjamin Constant à la comtesse Anne-Marie-Pauline-Andrienne de Nassau (28 avril 1798), *Correspondance générale*, t. 3, p. 330. More generally, see the discussion in *Correspondance générale*, t. 3, p. 330 note 2. And, also, see Hofmann, *Les "Principes de politique" de Benjamin Constant*, t. 1, pp. 166–78.

37. Woloch judges the election of 1798 as the point at which the Directory "lapsed into authoritarianism." [Woloch, *Jacobin Legacy*, pp. 239–343; this quote, p. 287.] Hunt, Lansky, and Hanson, similarly but more generally, suggest that the republicans supporting the Directory governments "wanted to establish a liberal republic without accepting the imperatives of liberal politics." [Hunt, Lansky, and Hanson, "The Failure of the Liberal Republic in France 1795–1799: The Road to Brumaire," p. 736.]

Woloch argues that the purge of 22 Floréal, An VI [29 March 1798] "affirmed [the Directory government's] unwillingness to tolerate organized opposition or to legitimize public division among republicans over certain issues.... In fact their own constitution [of 1795] was suited neither to their political objectives nor their elitist style. The conservatism (relative to the advanced state of French public life) proved increasingly irreconcilable with their constitutional liberalism" (pp. 347–48). Woloch points out, however, that there were numerous reports of disorders in the primary assemblies that affected the Directory's perceptions.

Woloch argues that the neo-Jacobin rejection of the Directory emerged after the Floréal purge: "Indeed, the Directorys' [sic] repressive policies of the Year VI operated like a veritable self-fulfilling prophecy. The conspiratorial faction whose existence it had fabricated and denounced gradually came into being" (p. 352). Constant, like other moderates, believed that the danger to the Republic represented by the electoral actions of the Jacobin clubs was great *during* the 1798 elections. He was not convinced that, at this time, the neo-Jacobins were as "embracing of the constitution" as Woloch suggests (p. 348). Many members of the reinvigorated Jacobin clubs had been closely associated with the regime of 1793–94. Knowledge of this, combined with accounts of the disruptive actions of the neo-Jacobins during the primary assemblies in 1798, reanimated memories of the Terror and, not surprisingly, fostered dread of similar actions if the Jacobins carried the election.

38. Such charges of opportunism are raised by Henri Guillemin, *Benjamin Constant muscadin, 1795–1799* (Paris: Gallimard, 1958).

39. Kurt Kloocke has characterized Constant's thought during this period as "une idéologie de la bourgeoisie aisée." See Kloocke, *Benjamin Constant: une biographie intellectuelle*, p. 73.

40. The retraction appeared in *L'Ami du Lois* (6 Floréal, an VI [25 avril 1798]).

41. The debate among Swiss natives over the intervention of the French into Switzerland was closely tied up with the tensions between the *pays de Vaud* and Berne, which had a grip on political power. Marie-Claude Jequier has argued convincingly that Constant's opposition to French intervention into Switzerland was not all that strong. It probably reflected his attachment to Germaine de Staël and her father Necker, both of whom opposed French intervention. [Marie-Claude Jequier, "Frédéric-César Laharpe, Benjamin Constant et Mme de Staël face à la Suisse (1797–1814)," *Société vaudoise d'histoire*, 86 (1978): 39–56.]

Once the French had established a new regime that gave the Vaudois more power vis-à-vis the Bernois, all three (Staël, Necker, and Constant) enjoyed good relations with the new government in spite of their previous opposition to French intervention. Moreover, Constant prudently avoided any public criticism. In 1814, he explained to his cousin Rosalie that while he had disapproved of the revolutionary change in Switzerland in 1798, he was opposed to upsetting the new stability. [Benjamin Constant à Mademoiselle Rosalie de Constant (29 janvier 1814), in *Lettres de Benjamin Constant à sa famille 1775–1830*, edited by Jean-H. Menos (Paris: Stock, 1931), p. 512.]

42. This is the suggestion of Grange, *Benjamin Constant: amoureux et républicain 1795–1799*, p. 217.

43. Constant, "Discours prononcé au Cercle constitutionnel, le 9 ventôse an VI [27 février 1798]"; this quote p. 596.

44. In 1799, Constant explored the possibility of seeking election to the Council of Five Hundred as the representative of Léman, which had recently become part of the French Republic. But, he stepped aside in favor of one Frarin, who had been president of the departmental administration.

45. See, for example, Benjamin Constant à Carl Gustav von Brinkman (8 juillet 1799), *Correspondance générale*, t. 3, p. 432.

46. Benjamin Constant à la comtesse Anne-Marie-Pauline-Adrienne de Nassau (1er avril 1799), *Correspondance générale*, t. 3, p. 413.

47. Benjamin Constant à Emmanuel-Joseph Sieyès (18 mai 1799), *Correspondance générale*, t. 3, p. 421.

48. Benjamin Constant, *Souvenirs historique, deuxième lettre* (1830), in *Portraits Mémoires Souvenirs*, edited by Ephraïm Harpaz (Paris: Librairie Honoré Champion, 1992), p. 100.
    Constant's opinion of Sieyès would change dramatically in later years. In 1828, Constant told Jean-Jacques Coulmann that "Sieyès est un des hommes qui ont fait le plus de bien à la France en 89, et qui depuis, à deux ou trios époques, lui ont fait le plus de mal." [Constant, *Mémoires inédits*, in *Portraits Mémoires Souvenirs*, p. 55.]
49. Anatoine-Jacques-Claude-Joseph Boulay de la Meurthe, *Essai sur les causes qui, en 1649, amenèrent en Angleterre l'établissememt de la République, sur celles qui devaient l'y consolider et sur celles qui l'y firent périr* (Paris: Baudouin, 1799).
50. Joseph de Maistre, *Considérations sur la France* (London [Bâle], 1797).
51. See F. Vermale, "Les Origines des "Considérations sur la France" de Joseph de Maistre," *Revue d'Histoire Littéraire de la France*, 33 (1926): 521–29. "Pour se défendre contre la nouvelle campagne de ralliement [à la Republic] qui partit de Lausanne et de Coppet au début de 1796, J. de Maistre composa, en réponse à la brochure de Benjamin Constant, les *Considérations fur la France*. Telle est l'origine des *Considérations*" (p. 525).
52. Letter of Joseph de Maistre to comte d'Avaray (30 août 1796). Cited by Pierre Glaudes, "introduction" to *Considérations sur la France*, in Joseph de Maistre, *Oeuvres, suivies d'un Dictionnaire Joseph de Maistre* [henceforth, *Oeuvres*], edited by Pierre Glaudes (Paris: Robert Laffont, 2007), p. 184.
    There are clear references to Constant's position in Maistre's text. For example, Constant had written that people in the modern age (unlike their ancient predecessors) were looking for "repose," and that this could best be achieved in a constitutional regime. Maistre countered that those who rejected the monarchy "veulent follement *le repos et la constitution*, qu'ils n'auront ni le repos ni la constitution. Il n'y a point de sécurité parfaite pour la France dans l'état où elle est [en 1797]. Le roi seul, et le roi légitime, . . . peut éteindre ou désarmer toutes les haines, tromper tous les projets sinistres, classer les ambitions en classant les hommes, calmer les esprits agités, et créer subitement autour du pouvoir cette enceinte magique qui en est la véritable gardienne." (*Considérations sur la France*, p. 266, emphasis in original).
53. Maistre, *Considérations sur la France*, in *Oeuvres*, p. 260.
54. Constant relied on Clarendon, Hume, Gilbert Burnet, and Edmund Ludlow. There are excellent notes referring to the historians and texts utilized in the new edition of "Des suites de la contre-révolution de 1660 en Angleterre," in *Oeuvres complètes*, t. 1, pp. 643–79.
55. Benjamin Constant à Samuel de Constant (1er octobre 1799), *Correspondance générale*, t. 3, p. 445.
56. "Nécrologie de Baudin des Ardennes" (17–18 octobre 1799), in *Oeuvres complètes*, t. 1, p. 687.
57. Benjamin Constant à Samuel de Constant (3 septembre 1799), *Correspondance générale*, t. 3, p. 444.
58. Benjamin Constant à Samuel de Constant (1er octobre 1799), *Correspondance générale*, t. 3, p. 445.

59. *De suites de la contre-révolution de 1660 en Angleterre*, in *Oeuvres complètes*, t. 1, pp. 643–79; this quote, p. 675.
60. Ibid. On religion, see pp. 662–67; on property, p. 668.
61. Ibid., p. 660.
62. This sentence, ibid., p. 672.
63. Ibid., pp. 661–62.
64. This phrase, ibid., p. 669.
65. Ibid., p. 676.
66. See *De suites de la contre-révolution de 1660 en Angleterre*, p. 677, note a: "J'ai tâché d'y établir le système qui me paroît seul propre à consolider la liberté, et à l'entourer des moyens d'application qui lui manquent parmi nous."
67. Denis Wood characterizes *Des suites de la contre-révolution de 1660 en Angleterre* as "one of [Constant's] most effective and, in the circumstances, courageous works." *Benjamin Constant: A Biography*, p. 152.
68. See Constant's letters of 1798 in *Correspondance générale*, t. 3, pp. 330–62.
69. Benjamin Constant à Isabelle de Charrière (26 mars 1796), Constant, *Correspondance générale*, t. 3, p. 169. Constant probably read the translation of *Caleb Williams* attributed to Samuel de Constant, published in Lausanne in 1796.
70. Benjamin Constant à la comtesse Anne-Marie-Pauline-Andrienne de Nassau (autour de 12 octobre 1798), *Correspondance générale*, t. 3, p. 376.
71. Benjamin Constant à Ludwig Ferdinand Huber (27 novembre 1798), *Correspondance générale*, t. 3, pp. 383–84.
72. See Benjamin Constant à la comtesse Anne-Marie-Pauline-Andrienne de Nassau (6 décembre 1798), *Correspondance générale*, t. 3, pp. 387–88; Benjamin Constant à Samuel de Constant (14 mars 1799), p. 406; Benjamin Constant à Samuel de Constant (31 mai 1799), p. 426; Benjamin Constant à la comtesse Anne-Marie-Pauline-Andrienne de Nassau (11 juillet 1799), p. 434; Benjamin Constant à Samuel de Constant (3 septembre 1799), pp. 443–44.
73. There is a new critical edition. Benjamin Constant, *Oeuvres complètes*, t. 2 (Tübingen: Niemeyer Verlag, 1998).
74. Benjamin Constant, "De Godwin, de ses principes, et de son ouvrage sur la Justice politique" [1810], in *Oeuvres completes*, t. 2:2, p. 1418.
75. Hofmann, *Les "Principes de politique" de Benjamin Constant*, t. 1, p. 175.
76. William Godwin, *Enquiry Concerning Political Justice* (London: Penguin Classics, 1976), p. 253.
77. Ibid., p. 283. See also the "introduction" by Isaac Kramnick, pp. 47–48.
78. "De Godwin, de ses principes, et de son ouvrage sur la Justice politique" [1810], p. 1415.
79. Ibid., pp. 1416–17.
80. The New Annual Register for 1788 (1789), p. 108; cited in Peter H. Marshall, *William Godwin* (New Haven: Yale University Press, 1984), p. 76.
81. *Enquiry Concerning Political Justice*, pp. 144–45. Godwin's belief was connected with his belief that truth and reason would, if faced with error

and weakness, always triumph. "Truth," he wrote in *Political Justice*, "includes in it the indestructible germ of ultimate victory." "Truth is omnipotent. The vices and moral weakness of man are not invincible: Man is perfectible, or in other words susceptible of perpetual improvement." These quotes, from *Political Justice*, pp. 142, 140.

82. Ibid., p. 448.
83. This phrase, ibid., p. 283.
84. Godwin's relationship to Sandemanian Protestantism and, more broadly, to radical religious dissent is a common theme in Godwin scholarship. See, for example, W. Stafford, "Dissenting Religion translated into Politics: Godwin's *Political Justice*," *History of Political Theory*, 1.2 (June 1980): 279–99; Mark Philp, *Godwin's Political Justice* (Ithaca: Cornell University Press, 1986); Gregory Claeys, "The Concept of 'Political Justice' in Godwin's *Political Justice*," *Political Theory*, 11.4 (November 1983): 565–84.
85. Quoted in Barbara Taylor, *Mary Wollstonecraft and the Feminist Imagination* (Cambridge: Cambridge University Press, 2003), p. 54.
86. *Enquiry Concerning Political Justice*, pp. 136–37.
87. Ibid., p. 139.
88. D.H. Monro, *Godwin's Moral Philosophy: An Interpretation of William Godwin* (London: Oxford University Press, 1953), p. 33.
89. William Godwin, *Caleb Williams* (New York: W.W. Norton, 1977), p. 340.
90. Ibid., p. 339.
91. Ibid., p. 109.
92. "De Godwin, de ses principes, et de son ouvrage sur la Justice politique" [1810], p. 1415.
93. I analyze this in detail in "Benjamin Constant, the French Revolution, and the Problem of Modern Character," *History of European Ideas*, 20 (2004): 5–21.
94. William Godwin, *Uncollected Writings (1785–1822)*, edited by J.H. Marken and B.R. Pollin (Gainesville, Forida, 1968), p. 1; cited by Kramnick, "Introduction," p. 47.
95. Godwin, *Enquiry Concerning Political Justice*, p. 251–52.
96. Ibid., p. 269.
97. Ibid., p. 261.
98. Ibid., pp. 274–81.
99. Benjamin Constant, "De Godwin, et de son ouvrage sur la justice politique" [1817], published in Mercure de France (avril 1817); reproduced in *Oeuvres complètes*, t. 2:2, pp. 1421–28, this quote, p. 1421.
100. Benjamin Constant à Samuel de Constant (3 septembre 1799), *Correspondance générale*, t. 3, p. 444.
101. Constant, *Fragments d'un ouvrage abandonné sur la possibilité d'une constitution républicaine dans un grand pays*, edited by Henri Grange (Paris: Aubier, 1991) [henceforth *Fragments d'un ouvrage abandonné*]. Constant worked on this manuscript from 1798 to 1807; parts of it were clearly completed before Napoleon's coup in 1799, others clearly after the coup but before the proclamation of the Empire in 1804.

There are two versions of the manuscript, one in Paris and one in Lausanne, but the differences are not significant. There is a thorough discussion of the different texts and Constant's revisions in *Oeuvres complètes*, t. 4 (Max Niemeyer Verlag: Tübingen, 2005), pp. 355–96. The editors of the *Oeuvres complètes* decided to entitle the work *De la possibilité d'une constitution républicaine dans un grand pays: fragments d'un ouvrage abandonné* because this title occurred in a manuscript of some of Constant's additions to the text(s). Both of the complete manuscripts, however, have the title *Fragments d'un ouvrage abandonné sur la possibilité d'une constitution républicaine dans un grand pays*, which is the title under which the work was first published in 1991. I have chosen to retain the original title. References will be to the 1991 edition of Henri Grange.

102. As he put it at the time: "Ce qui doit aujourd'hui fixer tous nos regards, absorber toutes nos attentions, ce sont les mesures de garantie, les institutions préservatrices; elles seules nous dispenseront de recourir à des violences toujours affligeantes." "Discours prononcé au Cercle constitutionnel pour la plantation de l'arbre de la Liberté" (le 30 fructidor an V). In Constant, *Oeuvres complètes*, t. 1, p. 552.

103. See Henri Grange, *Les Idées de Necker*, thèse presentée devant l'Université de Paris IV (le 17 décembre 1971) (Lille: Université de Lille III, 1973), pp. 552–64; and Lucien Jaume, "Necker: examen critique de la Constitution de l'an III," in *Constitution de l'an III: Boissy d'Anglas et la naissance du libéralisme constitutionnel*, pp. 167–82.

104. See the discussion of these works in chapter 2 above.

105. Germaine de Staël, *De l'influence des passions sur le bonheur des individus et de nations* [1797] (Paris: Ramsay, 1979), p. 67.

106. Germaine de Staël, *Des circonstances actuelles qui peuvent terminer la Révolution et des principes qui doivent fonder la République en France*, edited by Lucia Omacini (Genève: Droz, 1979). Omacini suggests that Staël did not publish the work for the following reasons: because of her own precarious situation in France; because she feared she might compromise Constant's political career; and, because the message of the manuscript had become anachronistic due to political changes ("Introduction," p. lxiv).

107. Henri Grange, "introduction," *Fragments*, pp. 14–16. A similar point is made by Edouard Herriot, *Un Ouvrage inédit de Mme de Staël: les fragments d'écrits politiques (1799)* (Paris: Plon, 1904), p. 75. See also Biancamaria Fontana, "The Thermidorian republic and its principles," in *The Invention of the Modern Republic*, edited by Biancamaria Fontana (Cambridge: Cambridge University Press, 1994), pp. 118–38; and Henri Grange, "Mme de Staël et la Constitution de l'an III: avant et après," in *La Constitution de l'an III: Boissy d'Anglas et la naissance du libéralisme constitutionnel*, pp. 183–99.

108. For Constant's immediate reaction, see Benjamin Constant à Emmanuel-Joseph Sieyès (10 novembre 1799), *Correspondance générale*, t. 3, pp. 455–56. We discuss Constant's reaction in chapter 5.

109. This point is made by Henri Grange, "introduction," *Fragments d'un ouvrage abandonné*, pp. 21–22.

110. In *De la force du gouvernement actuel de la France* [1796], Constant had already raised the issue of whether a republic was possible in a large country of 25 million. He argued that it was possible, contrary to those who believed it was not because a republic had never previously existed in such a populous country. See *De la force du gouvernement actuel de la France*, pp. 364–66.
111. *Fragments d'un ouvrage abandonné*, p. 210.
112. Ibid., p. 400.
113. *Des reactions politiques* [1797], in *Oeuvres complètes*, t. 1, pp. 470–72. Constant was alluding to the second part of Necker's *De la Révolution française*, where he argued that the stability of the monarchy had been undermined by the elimination of hereditary nobility by the Constitution of 1791. Constant clearly wished to separate himself from this position, and from Necker.
114. *Fragments d'un ouvrage abandonné*, p. 113.
115. Ibid., p. 115.
116. Ibid., p. 111.
117. Ibid., p. 116.
118. Ibid., p. 142.
119. Ibid., p. 187.
120. Ibid., p. 196.
121. Ibid., pp. 161–80.
122. Ibid., p. 204.
123. Ibid., p. 127.
124. This quote, ibid., p. 141. But, also see pp. 197–200.
125. Ibid., p. 134; in the text, Constant indicates that this passage was written in 1800.
126. Ibid., pp. 131–33, 158, 189–93.
127. See, for example, ibid. pp. 291–96.
128. Ibid., pp. 179–80.
129. Ibid, p. 151.
130. Constant argued that "the sentiment of liberty" was encouraged by participation in elections. Ibid., p. 319.
131. Ibid. p. 151.
132. Constant refers to five executives on p. 233; to seven on p. 400.
133. Ibid. Book V: "De la complexité du pouvoir executive," pp. 229–52.
134. This phrase, p. 246.
135. Constant repeated this criticism of the 1795 constitution in 1828. [*Mémoires inédits* in *Portraits Mémoires Souvenirs*, ed by Ephraïm Harpaz (Paris: Librairie Honoré Champion, 1992), p. 56.]
136. This phrase, *Fragments d'un ouvrage abandonné*, p. 247.
137. Ibid., p. 247. Interestingly enough, he does not provide a specific date when the threshold of "legality" is breached.
138. Ibid., pp. 246–47. Constant discussed the Fructidor coup also on pp. 423–24, calling it a "violation of the republican constitution" that "unleashed" "arbitrary government."
139. Ibid. p. 151.

140. Jacques Necker, *De la Révolution française*, in *Oeuvres complètes de M. Necker* (Paris: Treuttel et Würtz, 1821), t. X, pp. 133–34; cited by Henri Grange, "introduction," p. 35. Necker also used the term "*entremêlement*" to refer to the interrelationship he favored between legislative and executive powers. [Noted by Jaume, "Necker: Examen critique de la Constitution de l'an III," p. 168.]

141. *Fragments d'un ouvrage abandonné*, p. 436. Similarly, on p. 390, he refers to the "pouvoir préservateur" as "le pouvoir judiciaire des autres pouvoirs."

142. Ibid., livre VIII, pp. 359–453. Henri Grange points to the similarity of Constant's "pouvoir préservateur" and Sismondi's discussion of the Venetian Counsel of Ten in his *Histoire des républiques italiennes du Moyen Age* (published in 1809). See Grange, "introduction," pp. 46–47.

143. Ibid., pp. 354–55.

144. Constant, following Montesquieu, referred to the judiciary as "*une puissance nulle politiquement*." Ibid., p. 149.

145. See, for example, the note, ibid. p. 338, where Constant criticizes the special tribunals of the previous decade.

146. Ibid., p. 264.

147. Ibid., p. 225.

148. Ibid., p. 210.

149. Ibid., p. 389.

150. Constant referred favorably to the "federalism" of the American system. Ibid., pp. 182–83.

151. Ibid., p, 408. The connection with Necker is explored by Henri Grange, "introduction," pp. 76–81.

152. *Fragments d'un ouvrage abandonné* , p. 416.

153. This phrase, ibid., p. 148.

154. Ibid.

155. Benjamin Constant à Isabelle de Charrière (10 décembre 1790), *Correspondance générale*, t. 1, p. 271.

156. *Des réactions politiques* [1797], in *Oeuvres complètes*, t. 1, p. 496.

157. Ibid., p. 493.

158. Ibid., pp. 489–504.

159. Ibid., p. 498.

160. Ibid., p. 487.

161. Benjamin Constant à Isabelle de Charrière (12 octobre 1793), *Correspondance générale*, t. 2, p. 163.

162. Etienne Hofmann, *Les "Principes de politique" de Benjamin Constant*, t. 1, p. 61.

163. *Fragments d'un ouvrage abandonné*, p. 434.

164. Ibid., Livre VIII, chapitre 11: "Des Moyens de perfectionnement nécessaries à toutes les institutions politiques," pp. 419–27.

165. Immanual Kant, "What is Enlightenment?" in *Kant's Political Writings*, translated by H.B. Nisbet, edited by Hans Reiss (Cambridge: Cambridge University Press, 1970), p. 55.

166. Immanual Kant, "The Contest of Faculties," *Kant's Political Writings*, p. 187 (emphasis in original); cited by Gareth Stedman Jones, "Kant, the

French revolution and the definition of the republic," in *The Invention of the Modern Republic*, edited by B. Fontana (Cambridge: Cambridge University Press, 1994), p. 159.

See also the classic discussion of Kant's political thought by Leonard Krieger, *The German Idea of Freedom* (Chicago: University of Chicago Press, 1957), pp. 86–125.

167. Constant would be even more critical of German idealism. After meeting Schlegel in April 1804, he wrote in his journal the following about *la nouvelle philosophie allemande*: " il est difficile de le comprendre, sans être initié à ce systeme. je crois l'avoir compris: mais si je ne me trompe, tout ce systême n'est autre chose qu'un rechauffé de subtilités Scholastiques, un composé de négations d'idées prises pour des réalités, et d'arrangemens de mots pris pour des choses." [Benjamin Constant, *Journaux intimes* (24 avril 1804), in *Oeuvres complètes*, t. 6 (Tübingen: Max Niemeyer Verlag, 2002), p. 114.

168. *Fragments d'un ouvrage abandonné*, p. 137.

169. Ibid., p. 138.

170. Ibid., p. 137

171. Ibid., pp. 415–16.

172. Ibid., p. 426.

173. Germaine de Staël, *Des circonstances actuelles*, p. 32.

174. Benjamin Constant à Emmanuel-Joseph Sieyès (10 novembre 1799), *Correspondance générale*, t. 3, p. 455. Constant would later judge Sieyès more harshly. In his"Souvenirs historique" [1830] he mentioned that Sieyès' actions had, on some occasions, "a donné des preuves déplorables de faiblesse." Benjamin Constant, *Portraits Mémoires Souvenirs*, edited by Ephraïm Harpaz (Paris: Librairie Honoré Champion, 1992), p. 78.

175. See Benjamin Constant à Emmanuel-Joseph Sieyès (15 novembre 1799), *Correspondance générale*, t. 3, p. 457.

176. For an good summary, see Irene Collins, *Napoleon and his Parliaments 1800–1815* (New York: St. Martin's Press, 1979), pp. 8–27.

177. These are the words of Alain Laquièze, "introduction générale" to Benjamin Constant, *Discours au Tribunat*, in *Oeuvres complètes*, t. 4 (Tübingen: Max Niemeyer Verlag, 2005), p. 37.

178. See Béatrice Jasinski, "Benjamin Constant tribun," *Benjamin Constant, Madame de Staël et le Groupe de Coppet* (Oxford: The Voltaire Foundation, 1982), pp. 64–88. Jasinski dismantles the arguments of those, like Henri Guillemin, who have suggested that Constant was a zealous servant of Bonaparte. Constant was critical of the government from his first intervention.

179. "Discours prononcé par Benjamin Constant, sur le projet concernant la formation de la loi, proposé au Corps législatif par le Gouvernement le 12 nivose, an VIII" (séance du 15 Nivose an VIII – 5 janvier 1800), *Oeuvres complètes*, t. 4, p. 74.

180. "Opinion de Benjamin Constant sur le projet de loi relatif à la faculté de tester" (séance du 29 ventôse an VIII—20 mars 1800), *Oeuvres complètes*, t. 4, pp. 151–62.

181. "Intervention de Benjamin Constant au Tribunat sur une petition de citoyens détenus à Perpignan" (séance du 4 ventôse an VIII – 23 février 1800), *Oeuvres complètes*, t. 4, p. 109.

182. "Opinion de Benjamin Constant, sur le projet de loi concernant l'établissement de Tribunaux criminals spéciaux" (séance du 5 Pluviose an IX–21 janvier 1801), *Oeuvres complètes*, t. 4, pp. 209–46.

183. Ibid., p. 237.

184. Ibid., p. 242.

185. Henri Grange argues that with this shift, Constant finally embraced "liberalism." Grange, *Benjamin Constant: amoureux et républicain 1795–1799*.

186. For a discussion of the context of civil justice at this time, see Isser Woloch, *The New Regime*, pp. 297–320.

187. Robert Alexander has convincingly argued that Constant was an effective practicing politician during the Restoration. See his *Re-Writing the French Revolutionary Tradition: Liberal Opposition and the Fall of the Bourbon Monarchy* (Cambridge: Cambridge University Press, 2003), and his "Benjamin Constant as a Second Restoration Politician," *The Cambridge Companion to Constant*, pp. 146–70.

188. Isabelle de Charrière à Louis-Fernand Huber (4 mars 1801); cited by Jasinski, "Benjamin Constant tribun," p. 81.

189. Isabelle de Charrière à Benjamin Constant (20 février 1801), *Correspondance générale*, t. 4, p. 222.

190. Etienne Hofmann argues that the critical years are the Consulate and early Empire, and that the crucial document is the 1806 version of Constant's *Principles de politique*. [See *Les "Principes de politique" de Benjamin Constant*, infra]. Other scholars have followed Hofmann's lead. For example (to mention only the most recent works), Stefano de Luca, "Benjamin Constant and the Terror," p. 110; Helena Rosenblatt, *Liberal Values: Benjamin Constant and the Politics of Religion* (Cambridge: Cambridge University Press, 2008).

## 4 Liberal Culture: *Sensibilité* and Sociability

1. Benjamin Constant à la comtessa Anne-Marie-Pauline-Adrienne de Nassau (15 mai 1798), Benjamin Constant, *Correspondance générale*, t. 3 (1795–1799) (Tübingen: Max Niemeyer Verlag, 2003), p. 335.

2. In 1797, passing several days in Coppet with only her father and Constant in residence, she wrote to a friend: "il faut du monde pour avoir de l'esprit, du monde pour s'animer, du monde pour tout." Cited in Grange, *Benjamin Constant: amoureux et républicain 1795–1799*, p. 134.

3. This is a direct translation of the *code chiffré du journal abrégé*—that is, of the numerical code that Constant himself devised to refer to his shifting emotional states for the abridged version of his *Journaux intimes*. 2 = "Désire de romper mon éternel lien dont il est si souvent question." 3 = "Retours à ce lien par des souvenirs ou quelque charme momentané."

[Benjamin Constant, *Oeuvres complètes*, t. 4: *Journaux intimes (1804–1807)* (Tübingen: Max Niemeyer Verlag, 2002), p. 44.]

4. Jean Starobinski has suggested that Staël struggled with melancholy and was preoccupied with thoughts of suicide. Constant suffered from a similar inquietude. See Starobinski, "Suicide et mélancolie chez Mme de Staël," in *Madame de Staël et l'Europe* (Paris: Klincksieck, 1970), pp. 242–52.

5. I have examined Constant relationships with women in more detail in "Constant and Women," *The Cambridge Companion to Constant*, edited by Helena Rosenblatt (Cambridge: Cambridge University Press, 2009), pp. 173–205; and in "Character, Sensibilité, Sociability and Politics in Benjamin Constant's *Adolphe*," *Historical Reflections/Réflexions Historiques*, 28.3 (2002): 361–83.

6. In a letter to Isabelle de Charrière (28 April 1794), Constant referred to his "chastes amours" with Charlotte. Constant, *Correspondance générale*, t. 2 *(1793–1794)*, p. 313.

7. Constant's letters have not survived, but thirty-two of Charlotte's letters of 1793–94 are in *Correspondance générale*, t. 2. In *Cécile*, Constant mentions receiving in late December 1795 a letter from Charlotte dated June 1795. See *Oeuvres complètes*, t. 3:1, *Ecrits littéraires (1800–1813) (Tübingen: Max Niemeyer Verlag, 1995)*, p. 259.

8. *Journaux intimes* (4 May 1805), p. 387.

9. Constant's diary records that after "thirteen years of resistance," they became lovers on 20 October 1806. *Journaux intimes* (19–20 October 1806), p. 467.

10. There is a good account of this final period in Renee Winegarten, *Germaine de Staël and Benjamin Constant: A Dual Biography* (New Haven: Yale University Press, 2008), pp. 247–87.

11. *Journaux intimes* (4 May 1805), p. 387.

12. During the stormy period of his breakup with Staël, Constant records that her "impetuosity, egoism, and constant preoccupation with herself," compares unfavorably with Charlotte's "gentle, calm, humble, modest manner of being. . . . I am tired of the man-woman whose iron hand has enchained me for ten years; a truly feminine woman is intoxicating and enchanting me." *Journaux intime* (26 October 1806), pp. 468–69.

13. Benjamin Constant, *Principes de politique applicables à tous les gouvernements*, edited by Etienne Hofmann (Genève: Droz, 1980), t. 2, p. 443.

14. Textual reference to *Adolphe* will be to the new *Oeuvres complètes*, t. 3:1; this quote, p. 100.

15. My analysis of Staël's novels draws from numerous secondary sources. See especially Christopher Herold, *Mistress of an Age: A Life of Madame de Staël* (New York: Bobbs-Merrill, 1958); Madelyn Gutwirth, *Madame de Staël, Novelist: The Emergence of the Artist as Woman* (Urbana: University of Illinois Press, 1978); Simone Balayé, *Madame de Staël: lumières et liberté* (Paris: Klincksieck, 1979); Balayé, *Madame de Staël: écrire, lutter, vivre* (Genève: Droz, 1994).

16. Rousseau's sexual politics have gotten a lot of attention recently. For recent measured assessments, see Helena Rosenblatt, "On the 'Misogyny'

of Jean-Jacques Rousseau: The *Letter to d'Alembert* in Historical Context," *French Historical Studies*, 25.1 (Winter 2002): 91–114; and Mary Seidman Trouille, *Sexual Politics in the Enlightenment: Women Writers Read Rousseau* (Albany: State University of New York Press, 1997).

On the relationship of this scholarship to Constant, see Helena Rosenblatt, "Interpreting *Adolphe*: The Sexual Politics of Benjamin Constant," *Historical Reflections/Réflexions Historiques*, 28.3 (2002): 341–60.

17. Staël, "Quelques réflexions sur le but moral de Delphine." Cited in Gutwirth, *Madame de Staël, Novelist: The Emergence of the Artist as Woman*, p. 142.

18. Naomi Schor, "The Portrait of a Gentleman: Representing Men in (French) Women's Writing," *Representations*, 20 (1987): 113–33; this quote, p. 120.

19. For a feminist analysis of the significance of gender in *Adolphe*, see Margaret Waller, *The Male Malady: Fictions of Impotence in the French Romantic Novel* (New Brunswick, NJ: Rutgers University Press, 1993), pp. 93–113.

20. On the question of the genesis of *Adolphe*, see the introduction in *Oeuvres complètes*, t. 3:1, by Françoise Tilkin, pp. 83–96; Paul Delbouille, *Genèse, structure et destin d' "Adolphe"* (Paris: Les Belles Lettres, 1971); and Paul Delbouille's introduction to the edition of *Adolphe* (Paris: Les Belles Lettres, 1977), pp. 7–96.

21. *Journal intime* (30 octobre 1806), *Oeuvres complètes*, t. 6, p. 471.

22. The secondary literature devoted to *Adolphe* is very extensive. I have found especially useful the essays by Alison Fairlie, collected in *Imagination and Language: Collected Essays on Constant, Baudelaire, Nerval and Flaubert* (Cambridge: Cambridge University Press, 1981), pp. 3–125; Timothy Unwin, *Constant: Adolphe* (London: Grant & Cutler, 1986); Dennis Wood, *Benjamin Constant: Adolphe* (Cambridge: Cambridge University Press, 1987); Patrick Coleman, *Reparative Realism: Mourning and Modernity in the French Novel 1730–1830* (Genève: Droz, 1998), pp. 79–101.

23. *Adolphe*, p. 132.

24. Fairlie, "The Art of Constant's *Adolphe*: 1. The Stylization of Experience" [originally published in 1967], in *Imagination and Language*, pp. 3–27; this quote p. 3.

25. Ibid., p. 6.

26. *Adolphe*, p. 109.

27. Ibid., pp. 157–58.

28. "Fragments de la préface de la second édition," p. 196.

29. "Préface de la second édition," p. 102.

30. Ibid.

31. "Fragments de la préface de la second édition," pp, 196–97. There are numerous variations for these fragments. The text in Delbouille's 1977 edition is slightly different: "La fidélité en amour est une force comme la croyance religieuse, comme l'enthousiasme de la liberté" (pp. 246–47).

32. Benjamin Constant, "Lettre sur Julie," *Oeuvres complètes*, t. 3:1, p. 213. First published in 1829, this portrait of Julie Talma was probably written in 1806.

33. *Adolphe*, p. 148.
34. Joan DeJean, *Ancients against Moderns: Culture Wars and the Making of a Fin de Siècle* (Chicago: University of Chicago Press, 1997), this phrase, p. 78.
35. See James H. Johnson, *Listening in Paris: A Cultural History* (Berkeley: University California Press, 1995), esp. pp. 51–95.
36. See Anne Vincent-Buffault, *Histoire des larmes: XVIIIe–XIXe siècles* (Paris: Editions Rivages, 1986).
37. In his "Discours sur l'origine et les fondements de l'inégalité parmi les hommes" Rousseau claimed that self-respect [*amour-de-soi-même*] and compassion [*pitié*] were the "two principles prior to reason" and the basis of all social interaction. *Oeuvres compètes*, t. 3 (Paris: Gallimard, Bibliothèque de la Pléiade, 1964), pp. 125–26.
38. Germaine de Staël, *Lettres sur les ouvrages et le caractère de J.-J. Rousseau* in *Oeuvres de Jeunesse* (Paris: Desjonquères, 1997), p. 60.
39. On this issue, see Dennis Wood, "Le Rousseauisme de Constant," *Rousseau and the Eighteenth Century* (Oxford: Voltaire Foundation), pp. 325–34.
40. I have found several recent works useful for thinking about how sentiment informed social and political thinking. David J. Denby, *Sentimental Narrative and the Social Order in France, 1760–1820* (Cambridge: Cambridge University Press, 1994); Martin S. Staum, *Minerva's Message: Stabilizing the French Revolution* (Montreal: McGill-Queens University Press, 1996), pp. 95–135; William M. Reddy, *The Navigation of Feeling: A Framework for the History of Emotions* (Cambridge: Cambridge University Press, 2001), part 2; James Livesey, *Making Democracy in the French Revolution* (Cambridge, MA: Harvard University Press, 2001).

   For a discussion of these themes in English novels, see John Mullan, *Sentiment and Sociability: The Language of Feeling in the Eighteenth Century* (Oxford: Clarendon Press, 1988); and G.J. Barker-Benfield, *The Culture of Sensibility: Sex and Society in Eighteenth-Century Britain* (Chicago: University of Chicago Press, 1992).
41. See Pierre Deguise, *Benjamin Consant méconnu: le livre De la Religion* (Genève: Droz, 1966), pp. 82–86; Alix Deguise, *Trois Femmes: le monde de Madame de Charrière* (Genève: Slatkine, 1981); and Carla Hesse, "Kant, Foucault, and Three Women," in *Foucault and the Writing of History*, edited by Jan Goldstein (Cambridge, MA: Harvard University Press, 1994), pp. 81–98.
42. Benjamin Constant, *Des réactions politiques* [avril 1797], *Oeuvres complètes*, t. 1: *Ecrits de jeunesse (1774–1799)* (Tübingen: Verlag, 1998), pp. 489–95.

   Kant wrote an essay responding to this section of *Des réactions politiques*, published in *Berlinischer Blätter*, 6 September 1797. See the discussions by Robert J. Benton, "Political Expediency and Lying: Kant vs. Benjamin Constant," *Journal of the History of Ideas*, 43.1 (1982): 135–44; and Jules Vuillemin, "On Lying: Kant and Benjamin Constant," *Kant-Studien*, 73.4 (1982): 413–24.
43. Benjamin Constant, "Fragmens d'un essai sur la perfectibilité de l'espèce humaine," in *Oeuvres complètes*, t. 3:1, p. 450.
44. Germaine de Staël, *De l'influence des passions sur le bonheur des individus et des nations*. References are to the edition with *Essai sur les fictions* (Paris: Editions Ramsay, 1979); this quote, p. 248.

45. Benjamin Constant, "Discours pronouncé au Cercle constitutionnel, le 9 ventôse an VI" (27 février 1798), in *Oeuvres completes*, t. 1, p. 589.

46. Germaine de Staël, *De l'Allemagne* (Paris: Firmin Didot Frères, 1854), p. 579.

47. Staël and Constant rehabilitated "enthusiasm" from the negative associations it had had in the thought of writers like Bayle, Locke, and Voltaire. For more detail, see my "Benjamin Constant, the French Revolution, and the Origins of French Romantic Liberalism," *French Historical Studies*, 23:4, 628–32.

48. I have examined the places where Constant believed these sentiments were most likely to be encouraged and refined (in literature, the arts, conversation, and salons) in "Character, Sensibilité, Sociability, and Politics in Benjamin Constant's *Adolphe*," *Historical Reflections/Réflexions Historiques*, 28.3 (2002): 361–83.

49. Benjamin Constant, "Fragments d'un essai sur la littérature dans ses rapports avec la liberté," *Oeuvres complètes*, t. 3:1, p. 496. These fragments were probably written around 1805.

50. *De la force du gouvernement actuel*, pp. 367–68.

51. Jean-Jacques Rousseau, "Discours sur l'origine et les fondements de l'inégalité parmi les hommes," in *Oeuvres complètes*, t. 3, pp. 125–26.

52. I have found two recent works useful here: John Claiborne Isbell, *The Birth of European Romanticism: Truth and Propaganda in Staël's 'De l'Allemagne', 1810–1813* (Cambridge: Cambridge University Press, 1994); Denby, *Sentimental Narrative and the Social Order in France, 1760–1820*.

53. Madame de Staël, *De l'Allemagne*, part IV, chapters X–XII (Paris: Firmin Didot Frères, 1854), pp. 574–89; this quote p. 574.

54. Ibid., pp. 578–89.

55. *Lettres sur les ouvrages et le caractère de J.- J. Rousseau*, p. 43.

56. Ibid., p. 48.

57. *Des circonstances actuelles*, pp. 289–90.

58. *De la littérature considérée dans ses rapports avec les institutions sociales* [1800] (Paris: Classiques Garnier, 1988), p. 322. See also Staël's critical comments concerning "l'amour de la gloire" in *De l'Influence des passions sur le bonheur des individus et des nations*, pp. 83–99.

59. On this issue, I follow the lead of Jasinski, *L'Engagement de Benjamin Constant*, pp. 200–04.

60. *De la force du gouvernement actuel*, p. 342.

61. *Principes de politique applicables à tous les gouvernements répresentatives et particulierement à la Constitution actuelle de la France*, in *Oeuvres complètes*, t. 9:2, p. 822.

62. See, for example, Pierre Deguise, *Benjamin Constant méconnu: la livre De la Religion* (Genève: Droz, 1966); Tzvetan Todorov, "Un chef-d'oeuvre oublié," in Benjamin Constant, *De la religion* (Paris: Actes Sud, 1999) [reference will be to the English-language translation "Religion According to Constant," in *The Cambridge Companion to Constant*, pp. 275–85]; Kurt Kloocke, "Religion et société chez Benjamin Constant," in *Coppet, Creuset de l'esprit libéral*, pp. 121–33; Etienne Hofmann, "Histoire, politique et religion: essai d'articulation

de trios composantes de l'oeuvre et de la pensée de Benjamin Constant," *Historical Reflections/Réflexions Historiques,* 28.3 (2002): 397–418; Helena Rosenblatt, *Liberal Values: Benjamin Constant and the Politics of Religion;* Bryan Garsten, "Constant on the Religious Spirit of Liberalism," in *The Cambridge Companion to Constant,* pp. 286–312.

63. Constant, *De la religion considérée dans sa source, ses formes et ses développements,* présenté par Tzvetan Todorov et Etienne Hofmann (Paris: Actes Sud, 1999). Constant first contemplated writing a religious work in 1785, and though nothing was published until 1824 he devoted a great deal of effort to his religious investigations, especially during 1794 (while in Brunswick), but also in 1804 (while in Weimar), 1806–8, and 1811–13 (while in Göttingen).

64. See, especially, Klooke, "Religion et société chez Benjamin Constant" and Rosenblatt *Liberal Values: Benjamin Constant and the Politics of Religion.* Rosenblatt has argued that Constant's thought was "indebted to a distinctly Protestant *way of thinking"* [p. 127, my emphasis]. I think this exaggerates the influence of Protestantism on Constant's thought and underestimates the importance of *sensibilité,* a European-wide cultural movement that was broader than religiosity and that had other roots than religious piety.

65. These quotes come from Laurence Dickey, "Constant and Religion: Theism Descends from Heaven to Earth," in *The Cambridge Companion to Constant,* pp. 313–48. Dickey claims that "Constant was certainly religious" and that *"his liberalism* can be shown to have deep roots in theism and late eighteenth-century Protestant (mainly, though not exclusively German) religious thinking" [pp. 315, 317, my emphasis]. I believe that this interpretation mistakenly reduces the moral dimension of Constant's thought to religion, and it more generally mistakenly suggests that we can collapse his liberalism into a variant of religious thought.

66. Pierre Deguise, *Benjamin Constant méconnu: le livre "De la Religion"* (Genève: Droz, 1966).

67. Constant, *Ma vie (Le Cahier rouge),* in *Oeuvres complètes,* t. 3:1; p. 314.

68. Wilde wrote: "an Athiest professed, he maintains at the same time the cause of Paganism, and while he spurns Jehovah cringes before Jupiter, while he execrates the bigotry and laughs at the follies of superstitious Christians, yet makes the vices of adulterous Deities the subject of his panegyric and prostitutes his genius to support the ridiculous mummeries of its Priests." Cited by C.P. Courtney, "Isabelle de Charrière and the 'Character of H.B. Constant': A False Attribution," *French Studies,* 36.3 (1982): 282–89.

69. I rely here on the discussion of Kloocke and Rosenblatt, who have analyzed an unpublished manuscript that Constant worked on during the 1790s "D'une nouvelle espèce de rapports que les Théologiens modernes voudroient introduire dans la Religion" that is in the Fonds Constant, Bibliothèque cantonale et universitaire de Lausanne. See Kloocke, "Religion et société chez Benjamin Constant" and Rosenblatt, *Liberal Values: Benjamin Constant and the Politics of Religion,* esp. pp. 29–32.

70. "Je travaille fort a mon grand ouvrage, & il avance. Il y en a trente sept chapitres de faits, desquels je ne suis point mécontent, mais c'est d'une difficulté Diabolique." [Benjamin Constant à Isabelle de Charrière, 23 mai 1794, *Correspondance générale*, t. 2, p. 359.]

71. See Albert Mathiez, *La Théophilanthropie et le culte décadaire: essai sur l'histoire religieuse de la Révolution 1796–1801* (Paris: Alcan, 1903).

72. Rosenblatt has argued that Constant went through a Deistic period during the late-1790s, and that by 1799 was advocating the replacement of Catholicism with Protestantism. [*Liberal Values*, pp. 37–75.] While Constant clearly preferred Protestantism to Catholicism, I have found no indication that Constant recommended any state-supported church, Protestant or otherwise. He briefly supported Theophilanthropy, I believe, because it encouraged religiosity without bringing with it an institutional shell.

73. Pierre Deguise, *Benjamin Constant méconnu*, p. 227.

74. Benjamin Constant, *Journaux intimes* (5 sepbembre 1804), in *Oeuvres complètes*, t. 6, p. 204.

75. Benjamin Constant, "Comte rendu de *Détails historiques et Recueil de pieces sur les divers projets de réunion de toutes les communions chrétiennes, de M. Rabaut le jeune*" [originally published in *Gazette de France* (10 février 1807)], *Oeuvres complètes*, t. 3:2, p. 1032.

76. Benjamin Constant, *Journaux intimes* (19 février 1805), p. 330.

77. Benjamin Constant, *De l'ésprit de conquête et de l'usurpation*, in *Oeuvres complètes*, t. 8:2, p. 781.

78. Benjamin Constant, *Principes de politique* [1815], in *Oeuvres complètes*, t. 9:2, p. 823.

79. Rosenblatt, *Liberal Values*, pp. 186–88.

80. *De la Religion*, p. 581.

81. Deguise, *Benjamin Constant méconnu*, p, 228.

82. *Principes de politique* [1815], p. 821.

83. Ibid.

84. *De la Religion*, pp. 41–2.

85. During his final months, facing debilitating health problems ("La vieillesse s'annonce de tous côtés, elle envahit mes yeux, mon estomac, mes reins, mes entrailles, mes pieds"), Constant nonetheless resisted his cousin's religious prodings, writing that "je n'ai que des doutes, et je suis trop sceptique pour être incrédule." [Benjamin Constant à Mademoiselle Rosalie de Constant (7 octobre 1829 and 15 novembre 1829), *Lettres de Benjamin Constant à sa famille 1775–1830*, edited by Jean H. Menos (Paris: Stock, 1932), pp. 579, 581.]

86. Volume one appeared in 1824; volumes 4 and 5 appeared posthumously in 1831.

87. Benjamin Constant, "A M. le Rédacteur du Constitutionnel" (24 juin 1824), in *Receuil d'articles, 1820–1824*, edited by Ephraïm Harpaz (Geneva: Droz, 1981), pp. 342, 344.

88. Constant, *Principes de politique* [1806], Hofmann edition, t. II, pp. 158–60.

89. Constant, "Lectures on Religion" (1818); cited by Garsten "Constant on the Religious Spirit of Liberalism," p. 292.

90. Scholars have suggested different intellectual sources for Constant's belief that there is fundamental difference between religious sentiment and religious form. Kloocke suggests that the source is Kant ["Réligion and société chex Benjamin Constant," p. 124]. James Lee argues that the source is Christoff Martin Wieland ["An Answer to the Question: What Is Liberalism? Benjamin Constant and Germany," *Annales Benjamin Constant*, 29 (2005): 127–41]. Rosenblatt has argued sensibly that the idea was widespread during this historical period [*Liberal Values*, p. 107; and "The Christian Enlightenment," in T. Tackett and S. Brown, eds, *The Cambridge History of Christianity*, vol. 7 (Cambridge: Cambridge University Press, 2006), pp. 283–301].
91. Cited in Pierre Deguise, *Benjamin Constant méconnu*, p. 94.
92. Todorov, "Religion According to Constant," pp. 276–79.
93. *Principes de politique* [1806], t. II, p. 160.
94. *Du polythéisme romain, considéré dans ses rapports avec la philosophie grecque et la religion chrétienne* [1833], II, pp. 91–92.
95. *Principes de politiques* [1806], t. II, p. 163.
96. Cited in Deguise, *Benjamin Constant méconnu*, p. 147. While this statement comes from a manuscript that Deguise claims was written after the French Revolution, it is entirely consistent with what Constant wrote in the late-1790s, and with what Staël wrote after 1796. It is very difficult to date precisely the manuscript fragments in which Constant discussed the "religious passions." Pierre Deguise dates them 1804–5 and 1813. [Deguise, pp. 59–64, 147–52.] Patrice Thompson dates them from 1794. [Patrice Thompson, *La religion de Benjamin Constant: les pouvoirs de l'image* (Paris: Touzot, 1978), pp. 543–50.]
97. "Fragments de la préface de la second édition," p. 197.
98. Ibid., pp. 196–98.
99. Lucien Jaume has also emphasized the importance for liberalism of a moral and political culture. See *L'Individu effacé* (Paris: Fayard, 1997); and "Coppet, Creuset du libéralisme comme 'culture morale,'" in *Coppet, Creuset de l'esprit libéral*, edited by Lucien Jaume (Aix-en-Provence: Presses Universitaires d'Aix-en-Provence, 2000), pp. 225–239.
100. This was especially pronounced in *Des réactions politiques*.
101. This passage is from *De la force du gouvernement actuel*, p. 368.
102. Ibid., p. 367.
103. Constant, reputation notwithstanding, did not advocate an unqualified embrace of "negative liberty" *à la* Isaiah Berlin. Cecil Courtney's analysis corrects this one-sided interpretation of Constant's stance. He writes that Constant "is aware that the moral solitude of the individual and the decadence of society are two complementary aspects of the same problem and that it is for this reason that it is necessary not to separate his personal writings from his political writings." [Cecil P. Courtney, "La Pensée politique de Benjamin Constant," *Actes de Congrès Benjamin Constant* (Geneva: 1968), p. 33.]
104. These are analyzed in chapter 5 below.

105. Benjamin Constant, "Fragments d'un essai sur la littérature dans ses rapports avec la liberté," *Oeuvres complètes*, t. 3:1: *Ecrits littéraires (1800–1813)*, p. 496.

106. Staël also favored sympathy and enthusiasm, and expressed reservations about isolation. In *Corinne*, for example, she wrote the following: "Et quand elle [Corinne] se releva…, elle semblait animé par un enthousiasme de vie, de jeunesse et de beauté, qui devait persuader qu'elle n'avait besoin de personne pour être heureuse. Hélas! Il n'en était pas ainsi" (VI:1, p. 115). And, "l'émulation, l'enthousiasme, tous ces moteurs de l'âme et du génie, ont singulièrement besoin d'être encouragés, et se flétrissent comme les fleurs sous un ciel triste et glacé" (XIV:1, p. 308). Page references to *Corinne ou l'Italie* (Paris: Charpentier, 1853).

107. For a perceptive analysis of "lucidity" in *Adolphe*, see Coleman, *Reparative Realism*, pp. 89–101.

108. "Fragmens d'un essai sur la perfectibilité de l'espèce humaine," *Oeuvres complètes*, t. 3:1, p. 448.

109. "De la perfectibilité de l'espèce humaine," *Oeuvres complètes*, t. 3:1, pp. 456–75. He wrote the following: "Les passions mêmes peuvent et doivent être les instruments de la volonté. Elles peuvent être comme les liqueurs fortes, des moyens à l'aide desquels lorsque nous avons besoin de telle impulsion, nous la donnons à nos organes, en observant toujours de ne pas la donner telle que nous ne puissions la diriger" (p. 464).

110. The phrase "sociable communication" comes from Daniel Gordon's excellent analysis of sociability in French thought of the Enlightenment. See *Citizens Without Sovereignty: Equality and Sociability in French Thought, 1670–1789* (Princeton: Princeton University Press, 1994); this phrase, p. 129.

111. See chapter 2 above. Also Steven Kale, *French Salons: High Society and Political Sociability from the Old Regime to the Revolution of 1848* (Baltimore: Johns Hopkins University Press, 2004); and my article "Elite Culture in Early Nineteenth-Century France: Salons, Sociability, and the Self," *Modern Intellectual History*, 4.2 (2007): 327–51.

112. Albert Sorel, *Mme De Staël* (Paris: Hachette, 1890), p. 6.

113. Madame de Staël, *Considérations sur la Révolution Française*, [IIème partie; lettre XVII], nouvelle édition (Paris: Charpentier, 1862), t. 1, p. 301.

114. Linda Orr, "Outspoken Women and the Rightful Daughter of the Revolution: Madame de Staël's *Considérations sur la Révolution Française*," in *Rebel Daughters: Women and the French Revolution*, edited by Sara E. Melzer and Leslie W. Rabine (New York: Oxford University Press, 1992), pp. 121–36.

115. Constant becomes more critical of the nobility and their salons during the late-1790s. See, for example, Constant's attack in "Discours prononcé au Cercle constitutionnel pour la plantation de l'arbre de la Liberté" (16 septembre 1797), in *Oeuvres complètes*, t. 1, p. 556.

116. William M. Reddy has suggested that there was a radical change in emotional repertoire after 1794. See "Sentimentalism and Its Erasure: The Role of Emotions in the Era of the French Revolution," *Journal of Modern History*, 72.1 (March 2000): 109–152.

117. Staël to Constant (27 octobre 1815); in *Lettres de Mme de Staël à Benjamin Constant* (Paris: 1926), p. 261; cited by Steven Kale, *French Salons*, p. 100.
118. *Le Publiciste*, 12 mai 1807, in Constant , *Oeuvres complètes*, t. 3:2, p. 1061. See also Simone Balayé,"Benjamin Constant, lecture de *Corinne*," in *Madame de Staël, écrire, lutter, vivre*, pp. 265–78.
119. Ibid., pp. 1061–62.
120. "Fragmens d'un essai sur la littérature dans ses rapports avec la liberté," *Oeuvres complètes*, t. 3:1, p. 497.
121. Ibid., pp. 513–14.
122. *De la force du gouvernement actuel*, p. 343.
123. See Staum, *Minerva's Message*.

## 5  Liberal Pluralism and the Napoleonic Empire (1802–15)

1. *Principes de politique applicable à tous les gouvernements*, texte établi par Etienne Hofmann (Genève: Droz, 1980). In this chapter, references to the 1806 version of *Principles of Politics Applicable to All Governments* will be to the translation by Dennis O'Keeffe (Indianapolis: Liberty Fund, 2003). [Henceforth referred to as *Principles of Politics* (1806)]. However, at times I have modified the translation.
2. *De l'esprit de conquête et de l'usurpation, dans leurs rapports avec la civilization Européenne*, *Oeuvres complètes*, t. 8:1-2 (Tübingen: Max Niemeyer Verlag, 2005), pp. 527–822. In this chapter, references to *The Spirit of Conquest and Usurpation and Their Relation to European Civilization* will be to the translation by Biancamaria Fontana, in Benjamin Constant, *Political Writings* (Cambridge: Cambridge University Press, 1988). [Henceforth referred to as *The Spirit of Conquest and Usurpation*.] However, at times I have modified the translation.
3. *Réflexions sur les constitutions, les distributions des pouvoirs, et les garanties, dans une monarchie constitutionnelle*, in *Oeuvres complètes*, t. 8:2, pp. 929–1283. [Henceforth referred to as *Réflexions sur les constitutions*.]
4. *De la responsabilité des ministres*, in *Oeuvres complètes*, t. 9:1 (Tübingen: Max Niemeyer Verlag, 2001), pp. 413–96.
5. *Principes de politique applicables à tous les gouvernements représentatives et particulièrement à la Constitution actuelle de la France*, *Oeuvres completes*, t. 9:2, pp. 653–858. In this chapter, references to the 1815 published version of *Principles of Politics Applicable to All Representative Governments* will be to the translation by Biancamaria Fontana, in Constant, *Political Writings*. [Henceforth referred to as *Principles of Politics* (1815)]. However, at times I have modified the translation.
6. Hofmann emphasizes the more abstract and systematic nature of Constant's writings beginning with the 1806 *Principes de politique*. Andreas Kalyvas and Ira Katznelson recently have argued that there is an intellectual evolution in Constant's political thought from a "republican origins" in the *Fragments*, through a "pure" liberalism in the 1806

version of *Principes*, to a "moderated" and "syncretic" liberalism in the 1815 version of *Principes*. [See Kalyvas and Katznelson, *Liberal Beginnings: Making a Republic for the Moderns* (Cambridge: Cambridge University Press, 2008), pp. 146–75.] The argument in this chapter is that there is more substantive continuity than evolution.

7. This point is made convincingly by Olivier Devaux and Kurt Kloocke in the various introductions to the works in t. 9:1-2 of the *Oeuvres complètes*.

8. "Des Révolutions de 1660 et de 1688 en Angleterre, et de celle de 1814 en France," *Journal de Débats* [21 avril 1814]; in *Oeuvres complètes*, t. 8:2, pp. 915–23.

9. Ibid., p. 921.

10. The Declaration of Saint-Ouen, announcing a new constitution, was made on 2 May 1814; the Charter was promulgated on 4 June 1814. Constant's *Réflexions sur les constitutions* appeared between these two dates (though probably too late to influence decisions).

Relevant here are other details of the historical context. Louis XVIII, having returned from exile, refused to adhere to the so-called *Constitution sénatoriale* adopted by the Imperial Senate on 6 April 1814. This constitution had specified that it was a contract between the King and the people (similar to the formulation in the Constitution adopted in 1830). The Charter that Louis XVIII finally "offered" to the people of France on 4 June 1814 retained the traditional legitimacy and prerogatives of the King. It noted the continuity of the new regime with the Old Regime, though, of course, interrupted by the "parenthesis" of the Revolution.

11. Béatrice Fink, "Introduction," *Réflexions sur les constitutions, Oeuvres complètes*, t. 8:2, p. 933.

12. See Lucien Jaume's "introduction" to *De la responsibilité des ministres* for an excellent discussion of the continuities and differences of function of the "neutral power" as presented in the *Fragments* and of the constitutional monarch as presented in the works of the First Restoration. *Oeuvres complètes*, t. 9:1, pp. 415–38.

13. *Réflexions sur les constitutions, Oeuvres complètes*, t. 8:2, pp. 1054–55.

14. *De la responsibilité des ministres, Oeuvres complètes*, t. 9:1, p. 458.

15. Cited in "Introduction" to *Principes de Politique* [1815], *Oeuvres complètes*, t. 9:2, p. 656.

16. *Act additionnel aux Constitutions de l'Empire*, in *Oeuvres complètes*, t. 9:2, pp. 561–623.

17. Not all contemporaries were so severe on Constant. Montlosier, for example, wrote to Prosper de Barante on 22 April 1814: "Notre conseiller d'Etat n'a pas tout à fait le certitude de l'avenir, mais il en a l'espérance. Ses anciens articles contre [Napoléon], ne font rien, il est populaire." [cited in *Oeuvres completes*, t. 9:1, p. 10.]

18. Benjamin Constant, *Mémoires sur les Cent-Jours, Oeuvres complètes*, t. 14 (Tübingen: Max Niemeyer Verlag, 1993).

19. *Mémoires sur les Cent-Jours, Oeuvres complètes*, t. 14, p. 116.

20. A good general history is M.J.C. Vile, *Constitutionalism and the Separation of Powers* (Oxford: Clarendon Press, 1967). For an account of the influence

of these traditions on the 1789 "Declaration of Rights of Man and of the Citizen," see J.K. Wright, "National Sovereignty and the General Will: The Political Program of the Declaration of Rights," *The French Idea of Freedom: The Old Regime and the Declaration of Rights of 1789*, edited by Dale Van Kley (Stanford: Stanford University Press, 1994), pp. 199–233.

21. The use of "pluralism" to refer to a politics probably dates from the work of Harold Laski. See his *Studies in the Problem of Sovereignty* (New Haven: Yale University Press, 1917); *Authority in the Modern State* (New Haven: Yale University Press, 1919); and "The Pluralist State," *Philosophical Review* (November 1919), reprinted in *The Foundations of Sovereignty and Other Essays* (New York: Harcourt, Brace, 1921), pp. 232–49.

22. But, there is new interest in the issue. Pierre Rosanvallon recently has argued that pluralism in modern France, while absent in the theories and policies of government, prospered in civil society. [*The Demands of Liberty: Civil Society in France since the Revolution*, translated by A. Goldhammer (Cambridge, MA: Harvard University Press, 2006).] J.A.Q. Gunn, on the other hand, finds evidence of attempts to think clearly about pluralistic politics during the Restoration. [*When the French Tried to Be British: Party, Opposition, and the Quest for Civil Disagreement 1814–1848* (Montreal: McGill-Queen's University Press, 2009).] Annelien de Dijn traces a distinctive strain of pluralist political thought. [*French Political Thought from Montesquieu to Tocqueville* (Cambridge: Cambridge University Press, 2009).]

23. There is an ongoing debate concerning the causes of the anti-pluralist nature of revolutionary political culture. François Furet and Keith Michael Baker highlight the deep ideological causes. [Furet, *Interpreting the French Revolution*, translated by E. Forster (Cambridge: Cambridge University Press, 1981); Baker, *Inventing the French Revolution: Essays on French Political Culture in the Eighteenth Century* (Cambridge: Cambridge University Press, 1990)]. Timothy Tackett focuses on the political radicalization of revolutionary actors between 1788 and 1791. [*Becoming a Revolutionary: The Deputies of the French National Assembly and the Emergence of a Revolutionary Culture 1789–1790* (Princeton: Princeton University Press, 1996); *When the King Took Flight* (Cambridge, MA: Harvard University Press, 2003); "Paths to Revolution: The Old Regime Correspondence of Five Future Revolutionaries," *French Historical Studies*, 32:4 (2009), pp. 531–54]. Barry M. Shapiro traces it to the experience of trauma experienced by representatives in the National Assembly during June and July 1789. [*Traumatic Politics: The Deputies and the King in the Early French Revolution* (University Park, PA: Pennsylvania State University Press, 2009).]

24. Lucien Jaume, *Le discours Jacobin et la démocratie* (Paris: Fayard, 1989), this phrase p. 322.

25. See William J. Bouwsma, *Concordia Mundi: The Career and Thought of Guillaume Postel (1510–1581)* (Cambridge, MA: Harvard University Press, 1957); and Quentin Skinner, *The Foundations of Modern Political Thought*, vol. 2: *The Age of Reformation* (Cambridge: Cambridge University Press, 1978), pp. 239–54; and Joseph Lecler, *Histoire de la tolérance au siècle de la réforme* (Paris: Aubier, 1955). Bodin's tolerant religious attitude is stated

in his *Colloquium of the Seven*, completed in 1588 (but unpublished at the time).

26. Of course, it is necessary to distinguish this early phase of Catherine de Medici's religious policy from her stance after 1572. In August 1572, she abandoned attempts at religious conciliation and sanctioned the mass-murder of the Huguenot leadership in the St. Bartholmew Day's massacre.

27. On the strains of religious coexistence during this era, see Keith P. Luria, *Sacred Boundaries: Religious Coexistence and Conflict in Early-Modern France* (Washington D.C.: The Catholic University of America Press, 2005); and idem., "France: An Overview," in *Multiconfessionalism in the Early Modern World*, edited by Thomas Max Safley (Leiden: Brill, forthcoming).

28. See Dale Van Kley, *The Religious Origins of the French Revolution: From Calvin to the Civil Constitution, 1560–1791* (New Haven: Yale University Press, 1996).

29. For an analysis of the historical background of the changes of the revolutionary period, see Raymond Birn, "Religious Toleration and Freedom of Expression," in *The French Idea of Freedom: The Old Regime and the Declaration of Rights of 1789*, pp. 265–99.

30. This was the argument advanced to justify refusing political rights to Jews. These arguments did not prevail, and Jews were granted citizenship. See Gary Kates, "Jews into Frenchmen: Nationality and Representation in Revolutionary France," in *The French Revolution and the Birth of Modernity*, edited by Ferenc Fehér (Berkeley: University of California Press, 1990), pp. 103–16.

31. Bodin, *Les six livres de la république;* as cited by Keith Baker, "Sovereignty," in *Critical Dictionary of the French Revolution*, edited by F. Furet and M. Ozouf, translated by A. Goldhammer (Cambridge, MA: Harvard University Press, 1989), p. 845. The scholarship on Bodin is voluminous. I have relied on J.W. Allen, *A History of Politiccal Thought in the Sixteenth Century* (London: Methuen, 1928), pp. 394–444; and Skinner, *The Foundations of Modern Political Thought*, vol. 2, pp. 284–301.

32. See Julian H. Franklin, "Introduction," in *Constitutionalism and Resistance in the Sixteenth Century* (New York: Pegasus, 1969), pp. 11–46.

33. There are wide divergences of opinion concerning the exact date of the emergence of national consciousness in France. Bernard Guenée summarizes the problem of provenance as follows:

> What do we really know about national sentiment in France at the end of the Middle Ages? First of all, when did it appear? Did it exist all through the Middle Ages, as claimed by J. Huizinga? Did it originate only at the end of the Hundred Years' War, as suggested by H. Hauser? Or was it only later still, in the sixteenth century, that it can be unmistakably recognized as such, as is the view of F. Chabod? But the answer to our initial question brings up, or rather follows, a whole series of others. Above all, what precisely should we call "national sentiment?"

Bernard Guenée, "The History of the State in France at the End of the Middle Ages as Seen by French Historians," in *The Recovery of France in* the *Fifteenth Century*, edited by P.S. Lewis, translated by G.F. Martin (New York: Macmillan, 1971), p. 341.

On the emergence of French national consciousness and "nationalism," see my "National Consciousness, Nationalism, and Exclusion: Reflections of the French Case," *Historical Reflections/Réflexions Historique*, 19.3 (1993): 433–49; and David A. Bell, *The Cult of the Nation in France: Inventing Nationalism, 1680–1800* (Cambridge, MA: Harvard University Press, 2001).

34. French became the only language of the political and cultural elite after the conquest of Languedoc. In 1539, François I made Parisian French the sole official language of the realm, an act that reduced the importance of *langue d'oc* of the south of France, Breton of Brittany, and Basque of the western Pyrennes. The creation of the Académie Française by Cardinal Richelieu in 1634 led to further codification of the language and hence unification of the realm, though there would remain movements, active still today, demanding linguistic and regional autonomy.

35. William F. Church sees this as "the first step in the gradual elimination of the king from the concept of the *patrie*." See his "France," in *National Consciousness, History, and Political Culture in Early-Modern Europe*, edited by Orest Ranum (Baltimore: Johns Hopkins University Press, 1975), pp. 43–66.

36. French disagreements over the nature of political sovereignty and over the form the constitution should assume did not create any serious crises over the existence of the state qua state. This was because France had a long history of linguistic uniformity and administrative-political centralization that everyone took for granted. Even when reformers criticized the power of the monarchy, for example, they did not question the existence of a linguistically unified nation-state. This was in sharp contrast with the metaphysically and historically hyperconscious nationalists in central and eastern Europe, who during the late-eighteenth century began agonizing over the conflicts among languages, states, and nations. French reformers and revolutionaries, decrying oppression and despotism, made frequent complaints against the king and about despotism, but they perceived no need to demand national unification, national independence, or national liberation. For excellent discussions of the distinction between "old continuous nations" like France, which enjoyed a slowly emerging national consciousness uninterrupted by external blows, and "new nations" that emerged largely in the nineteenth century is central to many analyses of nationalism, see Hugh Seton-Watson, *Nations and States: An Enquiry into the Origins of Nations and the Politics of Nationalism* (Boulder, CO: Westview Press, 1977) and Benedict Anderson, *Imagined Communities: Reflections on the Origins and Spread of Nationalism* (London: Verso, 1983).

37. Roger Chartier, *The Cultural Origins of the French Revolution*, translated by L.G. Cochrane (Durham, NC: Duke University Press, 1991), pp. 111–35; this quote, p. 122.

38. Keith Michael Baker, *Inventing the French Revolution* (Cambridge: Cambridge University Press, 1990); Baker, "Sovereignty," in *Critical*

*Dictionary of the French Revolution*, pp. 844–59; Van Kley, *The Religious Origins of the French Revolution: From Calvin to the Civil Constitution, 1560–1791*; Van Kley, "The Religious Origins of the French Revolution, 1560–1791," in *The Origins of the French Revolution*, edited by Peter R. Campbell (New York: Palgrave, 2006), pp. 160–90. More generally, see *The Cambridge History of Eighteenth-Century Political Thought*, edited by M. Goldie and R. Wokler (Cambridge: Cambridge University Press, 2006).

39. See the synthetic article by Dale Van Kley, "From the Lessons of French History to Truths for All Times and All People: The Historical Origins of an Anti-Historical Declaration," in *The French Idea of Freedom*, pp. 72–113.

40. Ibid., p. 109.

41. Montesquieu, *De l'Esprit des Lois*, Book V, section 19. I have used the translation of Thomas Nugent (New York: Hafner, 1949), p. 68.

42. Sudhir Hazareesingh notes that the term "centralization" dates from the Revolutionary era. [*From Subject to Citizen: The Second Empire and the Emergence of Modern French Democracy* (Princeton, NJ: Princeton University Press, 1998), pp. 13–14.] For the revolutionary era, see the excellent article by Yann Fauchois, "Centralization," *Critical Dictionary of the French Revolution*, pp. 629–39.

43. Pierre Rosanvallon, *Le Moment Guizot* (Paris: Gallimard, 1985).

44. Pierre Rosanvallon, "Political Rationalism and Democracy in France" [originally pub. 1994], in *Democracy Past and Future*, edited by S. Moyn (New York: Columbia University Press, 2006), p. 130.

45. Recently, Rosanvallon has represented French ideas since the Revolution as a tradition that "emphasizes the centralizing tradition as well as the permanent antiliberal temptation stemming from the 'absolutization' of popular sovereignty and the states' claim to institute and instruct society." Rosanvallon contrasts this ideology with a social history that highlights the importance of the concrete existence of "intermediary bodies." This is an important contrast, but the ideological landscape is more varied than this suggests. Pierre Rosanvallon, *The Demands of Liberty: Civil Society in France since the Revolution*, translated by A. Goldhammer (Cambridge, MA: Harvard University Press, 2007), this quote, p. 3.

46. Lucien Jaume is a good guide here. See his *Individu effacé: ou le paradoxe du libéralisme français* (Paris: Fayard, 1998).

47. Book VII and Book IX of *Principles of Politics* [1806] focus, respectively, on rights and the legal safeguards necessary to protect them. Chapter VII of *Réflexions sur les constitutions* focuses on individual rights. Chapters 16, 18, and 19 of *Principles of Politics* [1815] focus, respectively, on liberty of the press, the liberty of the individual, and judicial guarantees.

48. *Principles of Politics* [1806], this quote, p. 13. Rousseau is the focus of the five of the first six chapters of Book I, pp. 6–21.

49. Ibid., pp. 20–21.

50. *Principles of Politics* [1815], this quote, p. 180.

51. *Principles of Politics* [1806], p. 31. There is an identical passage in *Principles of Politics* [1815], p. 177.

52. *Principles of Politics* [1806], p. 27.

53. *Principles of Politics* [1815], p. 180.

54. Ibid., pp. 261–305.
55. See Annabel Herzog, "Hobbes and Corneille on Political Representation," *The European Legacy*, 14.4 (2009): 379–89.
56. *Principles of Politics* [1806], pp. 21–22.
57. Ibid., pp. 39–42, 47–49.
58. Ibid., p. 40.
59. Ibid., pp. 48–49.
60. "A positive, general, unrestricted duty, every time a law seems unjust, is to avoid becoming its executor. This passive resistance does not carry with it any upheavals, revolutions or disorders. Nothing justifies the man who lends his assistance to a law which he believes iniquitous." *Principles of Politics* [1815], p. 181.
61. *Principles of Politics* [1806], p. 401.
62. Ibid., p. 407.
63. Ibid., p, 408.
64. Ibid., p. 410.
65. Ibid., p. 412.
66. *The Spirit of Conquest and Usurpation*, pp. 96–97.
67. *Principles of Politics* [1806], pp. 327–28.
68. Ibid. p. 328.
69. "De la liberté des brochures, des pamphlets et des journaux, considérée sous le rapport de l'intérêt du Gouvernement," [1814], *Oeuvres complètes*, t. 9:1, p. 78.
70. Bryan Garsten points out that Constant cited the influence of Aristotle and Machiavelli on this point. See "Behind the Nostalgia for Ancient Liberty," *European Journal of Political Theory*, 8.3 (2009): pp. 401–11. See also Giovanni Paoletti, *Benjamin Constant et les anciens: politique, religion, histoire*, translated (from Italian into French) by Marie-France Merger (Paris: Champion, 2006).
71. *De la responsabilité de ministres*, *Oeuvres complètes*, t. 9:1, pp. 439–96.
    As Lucien Jaume points out, Constant wished to separate the "responsibility" which members of government have to conduct policy, from the "power" to dominate. To control the latter, Constant looked to legal prosecution for illegal acts. To control the former, he looked in 1815 to the power vested in the "neutral power" (of the monarch) to dismiss governments and Assemblies that overstepped their authority. See Jaume's "introduction" to *De la responsabilité de ministres*, *Oeuvres complètes*, t. 9:1, pp. 415–38.
72. See *Principles of Politics* [1815], pp. 227–50; this quote, p. 235; and *De la responsabilité de ministres*.
73. *De la responsabilité de ministres*, *Oeuvres complètes*, t. 9:1, p. 450.
74. Mary S. Hartman has suggested that Constant did not believe in 1814–1815 that France was ready for an English-style parliamentary government. Moreover, she argues that Constant's "constitutional schemes for France reveal him to be more sympathetic to the executive power, which is consistently granted far more authority than the legislative." ["Benjamin Constant and the Question of Ministerial Responsibility in France, 1814–1815." *Journal of European Studies*, 6 (1976): 248–61; this

quote p. 258.] Constant did worry about an overly powerful legislative branch, no doubt because of his assessments of the Constitutions of 1791 and 1795 and of the revolutionary regimes of the 1790s. He also, however, worried about an overly powerful executive branch.

75. *Principles of Politics* [1815], pp. 221–25; this quote, p. 222.

76. Constant wrote the following of the "need to impress":

This need, which degenerates into a kind of fury, is the more dangerous in so far as it does not originate in the nature of man, but is a social creation.... Consequently, it does not restrain itself, like those natural passions which are exhausted by their own duration. Sentiment does not stop it, as it has nothing in common with sentiment. Reason is impotent against it, for it is not a question of being convinced, but of convincing. Even fatigue does not calm it; as he who experiences it fails to note his own sensations, but observes only those it produces in other people...

[O]ur vanity is humble, as well as unrestrained: it aspires to everything but is contented with very little. By looking at the pretensions it displays, one would think it insatiable. But watching it clinging to the smallest achievements, one admires its frugality. [*Principles of Politics* (1815), p. 223].

77. *Principles of Politics* [1806], p. 31.

78. Ibid., p. 54.

79. Ibid., p. 384.

80. Ibid., p. 332.

81. Madame de Staël, *Des circonstances actuelles qui peuvent terminer la Révolution et des principes qui doivent fonder la République en France* [1798], edited by Lucia Omacini (Genève: Droz, 1979), p. 39.

82. Ibid., pp. 155–207.

83. There were different opinions among liberals at this time concerning *how much* separation of power there ought to be. Staël and her father Jacques Necker opposed too much separation, arguing that the executive should have a role in the discussion of laws and that he should have a suspensive (though not an absolute) veto. The essential work here is Henri Grange, *Les Ideés de Necker* (Lille: Université de Lille III, 1973), pp. 552–82.

84. Madame de Staël, *Considérations sur la Révolution Française* [1818] (Paris: Charpentier, 1862), t. 1, p. 12.

85. *Des circonstances actuelles*, p. 255.

86. *Considérations sur la Révolution Française*, t. 1, pp. 453–54.

87. Ibid., t. 2, p. 22.

88. Ibid., t. 2, p. 151.

89. *Principles of Politics* [1815], chapter 19: "On Judicial Guarantees," pp. 295–302.

90. Ibid., pp. 334–35.

91. Ibid., p. 183.

92. *Des circonstances actuelles*, p. 223.

93. Ibid., p. 232.

94. See *Considérations sur la Révolution Française*, t. 2, pp. 437–50: "du mélange de la religion avec la politique."

95. On this issue, see the recent article by Helena Rosenblatt, "Madame de Staël, the Protestant Reformation, and the History of 'Private Judgement'," *Annales Benjamin Constant*, 31–32 (2007): 143–54.
96. *De la force du gouvrenement actuel*, in *Oeuvres complètes*, t. I, p. 374.
97. "De la restitution des droits politiques aux descendans des religionnaires fugitives," in *Oeuvres complètes*, t. 1, p. 410.
98. Ibid.
99. Benjamin Constant à Nicolas-Louis François de Neufchâteau (17 mai 1799), *Correspondance générale*, t. 3, p. 418.
100. *Principles of Politics* [1815], p. 281.
101. Ibid., p. 275.
102. Stanislas-Marie de Clermont-Tonnerre, *Réflexions sur le fanatisme*, cited by Constant, *Principles of Politics* [1806], pp. 145–46.
103. Ibid., p. 255. Similar attacks of "fanaticism" are in *Considérations sur la Révolution Française*; for example, the attack on "philosophical fanaticism" (t.1, p. 50); and the chapter "du fanatisme politique," t. 1, pp. 427–31.
104. *Principles of Politics* [1806], p. 415.
105. "La maladie de la Révolution française, c'est de porter le fanatisme dans le raisonnement et d'admettre la cruauté, non seulement par violence, mais par théorie." Staël, *Des circonstances actuelles*, p. 297.
106. *Principles of Politics* [1806], p. 416.
107. It is famous in part because of Isaiah Berlin's influential essay "Two Concepts of Liberty" [1958], republished in Isaiah Berlin, *The Proper Study of Mankind* (New York: Farrar, Straus and Giroux, 1998), pp. 191–242. Unfortunately, Berlin exaggerated Constant's attachment to "modern" liberty at the expense of "ancient" liberty.

    For more balanced analyses, see James Mitchell Lee, "Doux Commerce, Social Organization, and Modern Liberty in the Thought of Benjamin Constant," *Annales Benjamin Constant*, 26 (2002): 117–49; and Jeremy Jennings, "Constant's Idea of Modern Liberty," *The Cambridge Companion to Constant*, pp. 69–91.
108. Benjamin Constant, "De la liberté des anciens comparée à celle des modernes," [1819] in *Ecrits politiques*, edited by Marcel Gauchet (Paris: Gallimard, 1997). In this chapter, references to "The Liberty of the Ancients compared with that of the Moderns" will be to the translation by Biancamaria Fontana in *Political Writings*, pp. 307–28.
109. See, especially, *Principles of Politics* [1806], pp. 349–80; *The Spirit of Conquest and Ururpation*, pp. 105–14.
110. *Principles of Politics* [1806], p. 351.
111. Ibid., p. 355.
112. Ibid., p. 358.
113. Ibid., p. 364.
114. Ibid., p. 365.
115. Ibid., pp. 386–87.
116. Ibid. p. 393.
117. "The Liberty of the Ancients compared with that of the Moderns," pp. 310–11.
118. *Principles of Politics* [1806], p. 387.
119. *Principles de Politics* [1815], p. 239.

## Conclusion: *Une Philosophie Engagée*

The phrase "une philosophie engagée" comes from Éphraïm Harpaz, "Introduction," Benjamin Constant, *Recueil d'articles 1820–1824* (Genève: Droz, 1981), p. 10.

Constant often remarked in his correspondence that his political writings and actions were the result of his being "engaged," and not driven by naive hopes that his campaigns would necessarily be successful. [See, for example, Benjamin Constant à Mademoiselle Rosalie de Constant (1822), *Lettres de Benjamin Constant à sa famille 1775–1830*, edited by Jean H. Menos (Paris: Stock, 1932), p. 557.]

1. The connection between Constant's precocious rhetorical skills and his later parliamentary career is made by Fernand Baldensperger, "Preface," to Elizabeth W. Schermerhorn, *Benjamin Constant: His Private Life and His Contribution to the Cause of Liberal Government in France 1767–1830* (Boston: Houghton Mifflin, 1924), pp. viii–x. He quotes a contemporary who observed Constant in action:

   Always epigrammatic, he discussed the deepest political questions with lucid, concise and forcible logic, his argument tinged with sarcasm. When, with marvelous but subtle skill, he led his adversary into the snare he had laid for him, he left him there confounded and helpless, under the blow of an epigram from which there was no recovery. No one ever understood so well the art of overthrowing an opponent in conversation.

2. Constant, in a characteristic statement, wrote to his cousin Rosalie: "Ma mission est de faire, si faire se peut, triompher un gouvernement constitutionnel." [Benjamin Constant à Mademoiselle Rosalie de Constant (7 novembre 1820), *Lettres de Benjamin Constant à sa famille 1775–1830*, p. 552.]

3. *Discours de M. Benjamin Constant à la Chambre des Députés*, 2 vols. (Paris: Ambroise Dupont et Compagnie, 1827 et 1828).

4. The essential secondary scholarship for Constant during this period is the recent work by Robert Alexander, *Re-Writing the French Revolutionary Tradition: Liberal Opposition and the Fall of the Bourbon Monarchy* (Cambridge: Cambridge University Press, 2003); and idem., "Benjamin Constant as a Second Restoration Politician," *The Cambridge Companion to Constant*, edited by Helena Rosenblatt (Cambridge: Cambridge University Press, 2009), pp. 146–70. Also see Schermerhorn, *Benjamin Constant*, pp. 310–67; Paul Bastid, *Benjamin Constant et sa doctrine*, vol. 1 (Paris: Colin, 1966); and Ephraïm Harpaz, *L'Ecole libérale sous la Restauration, le "Mercure" et la "Minerve," 1817–1820* (Genève: Droz, 1968).

5. Ephraïm Harpaz has edited numerous volumes of Constant's articles. Benjamin Constant, *Recueil d'articles 1795–1817*, introduction, notes et commentaries par Éphraïm Harpaz (Genève: Droz, 1978); Constant, *Recueil d'articles: Le Mercure, La Minerve et La Renommée*, 2 v., introduction, notes et commentaries par Éphraïm Harpaz (Genève: Droz, 1972); Constant, *Recueil d'articles 1820–1824*, introduction, notes et commentaries par Éphraïm Harpaz (Genève: Droz, 1981); Constant, *Recueil d'articles 1825–1829*, texte établi, introduit, annoté et commenté par

Éphraïm Harpaz (Paris: Champion, 1992); Constant, *Recueil d'articles 1829–1830*, texte établi, introduit, annoté et commenté par Éphraïm Harpaz (Paris: Champion, 1992). The number of articles is overwhelming, especially given Constant's other engagements. In the compilation of Constant's articles from the end of December 1816 to early May 1820, there are 188 articles (more than one article/week). [Constant, *Recueil d'articles: Le Mercure, La Minerve et La Renommée*, 2 v.] Robert Alexander points out that in the three months of April, May, and June 1829, Constant published 24 articles (approximately 2 articles/week). ["Benjamin Constant as a Second Restoration Politician," p. 150.]

6. Éphraïm Harpaz, "Introduction," Constant, *Recueil d'articles 1820–1824*, p. 10.

7. Much of the following discussion of the Liberal Opposition draws from Alexander, *Re-Writing the French Revolutionary Tradition: Liberal Opposition and the Fall of the Bourbon Monarchy.*

8. On the hesitancy of French political writers to embrace pluralistic politics, and their reluctance to accord legitimacy to their political opponents, see J.A.W. Gunn, *When the French Tried to Be British: Party, Opposition, and the Quest for Civil Disagreement 1814–1848* (Montreal: McGill-Queens University Press, 2009).

9. Alexander, "Benjamin Constant as a Second Restoration Politician," pp. 162–63.

10. Ibid., p. 169.

11. On Constant's role in a campaign to overturn an unjust legal verdict, see Etienne Hofmann, *Une erreur judiciaire oubliée: L'Affaire Wilfrid Regnault (1817–1818)* (Genève: Slatkine, 2009).

12. In his pamphlet *De la doctrine politique qui peut réunir tous les parties en France* [1816], Constant wrote the following:

    "A more appropriate title for such books would be, not *The Monarchy According to the Charter*, but *The Charter According to the Aristocracy*, and they should be like the Vedas, written in a sacred language, to be read only by the favored caste, and remain unknown to the profane.... A certain bishop, finding himself on a ship that was about to sink, said his prayers. 'My God!' he cried, 'save me, save only me; I do not want to overtax Thy mercy!' Let us not invoke liberty as this bishop invoked Providence." [cited by Schermerhorn, *Benjamin Constant: His Private Life and His Contribution to the Cause of Liberal Government in France 1767–1830*, p. 311.]

13. On the latter period, see Jean-Pierre Aguet. "À la veille de 1830: Benjamin Constant, journaliste et député dans le feu de l'action," in *Coppet, Creuset de l'esprit libéral*, edited by Lucien Jaume (Aix-en-Provence: Presses Universitaires d'Aix-Marseille, 2000), pp. 99–120.

14. On the Carbonari, see Alan B. Spitzer, *Old Hatreds and Young Hopes: The French Carbonari against the Bourbon Restoration* (Cambridge, MA: Harvard University Press, 1971); and Sylvia Neely, *Lafayette and the Liberal Ideal, 1814–1824: Politics and Conspiracy in the Age of Reaction* (Carbondale, IL: Southern Illinois University Press, 1991), pp. 149–242. On Constant's

actions at this time, see Alexander, *Re-Writing the French Revolutionary Tradition,* pp. 135–86; and Bastid, *Benjamin Constant et sa doctrine,* t. 1, pp. 346–84.

15. Constant did not participate in the uprising, but he was cited by one of the rebels as part of the planned provisional government. He also fought a duel with an ultraroyalist who attacked him in the press. He subsequently lost his bid for reelection in 1822, largely because of the reactionary backlash among the electorate after the insurrections.

16. These passages from Constant's speeches in the Chamber of Deputies, as reported in the *Archives parlementaires,* are cited by Aguet, "À la veille de 1830: Benjamin Constant, journaliste et député dans le feu de l'action," pp. 103, 106.

17. Reference will be to the new edition: Benjamin Constant, *Commentaire de l'ouvrage de Filangieri,* edited by Alain Laurent (Paris: Les Belles Lettres, 2004).

18. Kurt Kloocke, *Benjamin Constant: une biographie intellectuelle* (Genève: Droz, 1984), p. 361.

19. *Commentaire sur l'ouvrage de Filangieri,* pp. 86–102; this phrase, p. 90.

20. On the contrast with Saint-Simon, see Helena Rosenblatt, *Liberal Values: Benjamin Constant and the Politics of Religion* (Cambridge: Cambridge University Press, 2008), pp. 158–68. On Comte's intellectual evolution during these years, and his disagreements with liberals, see Mary Pickering, *Auguste Comte: An Intellectual Biography,* vol. 1 (Cambridge: Cambridge University Press, 1993), pp. 245–75.

21. *Commentaire sur l'ouvrage de Filangieri,* Part 3, pp. 227–77.

22. Ibid., p. 265.

23. Ibid., p. 108.

24. Ibid., pp. 115–18.

25. Ibid., pp. 56–57.

26. L'on peut trouver des motifs d'utilité pour tous les commandements et pour toutes les prohibitions. Défendre aux citoyens de sortir de leurs maisons serait utile; car on empêcherait ainsi tous les délits qui se commettent sur les grandes routes. Obliger chacun de se présenter tous les matins devant les magistrates serait utile; car on découvrirait plus facilement les vagabonds et les brigands qui se cachent pour attendre les occasions de faire le mal. C'est avec cette logique qu'on avait, il y a vingt années, transformé la France en un vaste cachot." [Ibid. p. 68.]
There is an almost identical passage in *Les "Principes de politique" de Benjamin Constant* (1806), t. 2, p. 67.

27. *Commentaire sur l'ouvrage de Filanbieri,* p. 59.

28. Ibid., p. 54.

29. This phrase, ibid., p. 43.

30. Ibid., p. 31.

31. Ibid., p. 53.

32. "Quand la disposition de la propriété est libre, elle tend au morcellement; les lois seules pourraient l'arrêter." [Ibid. p. 164.]

33. Ibid., p. 332.

34. Ibid., p. 135.
35. Ibid., p. 77.
36. Ibid., pp. 133–34.
37. In a passage that obviously reflected his own sentimental calculus as he grew older, Constant wrote about the aged that "A cette période de son existence, l'homme ne peut plus supporter la solitude; car l'illusion seule l'embellit, et l'illusion lui est devenue étrangère. L'entourage, les soins de l'amitié, et au défaut de la realité l'apparence, tout devient précieux pour des êtres que la nature sévère se plaît à dépouiller chaque jour." [Ibid. p. 166.]
38. Concerning the positive aspects of religion, he wrote that it "adoucit les moeurs, elle élève l'âme, elle donne à l'ensemble de la vie humanine une tendance plus pur et plus morale; mais elle ne saurait se mettre en lutte contre la puissance de l'intérêt ne contre l'evidence du calcul." [Ibid. p. 121.]
39. Ibid., pp. 130–31.
40. Ibid., p. 192.
41. Ibid., p. 320.
42. Benjamin Constant, "De la Liberté des anciens comparée à celle des modernes," in *Ecrits politiques*, edited by Marcel Gauchet (Paris: Gallimard, 1997), pp. 589–619; this quote, p. 604.
43. Constant, *Commentaire de l'ouvrage de Filangieri*, this phrase, p. 28.
44. Benjamin Constant, "Discours pronouncé au Cercle constitutionnel pour la plantation de l'arbre de la liberté" (16 septembre 1797), in *Oeuvres complètes*, t. 1, p. 553.
45. Benjamin Constant, "De l'Esprit de conquête et de l'ursurpation dans leurs rapports avec la civilization européenne," in *Oeuvres complètes*, t. 8:2, pp. 687–801; this quote, p. 755.
46. Upon his return to Paris in 1816, Constant frequented the salon of Madame Davillier, where Liberals, but also former Jacobins and Bonapartists, gathered.
47. Darío Roldán captures the essential contradiction of the Doctrinaires.
    La position des doctrinaires recèle ainsi un paradoxe. D'une part, elle défend la raison individuelle contre le sens commun et contre l'Aurorité; de l'autre comme elle n'est pas prête à renoncer à toute idée de transcendance, elle postule, en même temps, la priorité légitime de la raison générale sur la raison individuelle. La question est donc de savoir ce qui fait la différence entre le sense commun et la raison générale car on peut affirmer qui la raison générale est déjà l'Autorité. Si l'Autorité est déjà la raison générale, la raison individuelle et sa capacité au doute sont un facteur disruptif dans la société.
    [*Charles de Rémusat: certitudes et impasses du libéralisme doctrinaire* (Paris: Harmattan, 1999), p. 107.]
    Lucien Jaume's *L'individu effacé: ou le paradoxe du libéralisme français* (Paris: Fayard, 1997) explores this division among French liberals.
    Aurelian Craiutu, in a recent book on the Doctrinaires, has referred to Guizot as a "pluralist," meaning that he believed modern society required providing the conditions for "a free competition for power

between rival ideas, principles, forces, modes of life, and social interests." [*Liberalism Under Siege: The Political Thought of the French Doctrinaires* (Kabgan, Maryland: Lexington Books, 2003), this quote pp. 110–11]. Guizot, however, was not a political pluralist. He believed that sovereignty was a question of "reason, truth, and justice," not political negotiation. Guizot further believed that he had privileged access to "reason, truth, and justice"—as he demonstrated during his tenure as head of the French government administration (1840–48), when he practiced an elitist politics that undermined individual rights and blocked reform. See my review of Craiutu's book, "Doctrinaire Liberalism," *European Legacy*, 10.3 (2005): 211–13.

48. I'm thinking of the aesthetic and rationalistic orientation of much German "political" thinking of this period. See my discussion above in chapter 3, pp. 120–24.

49. Bronislaw Baczko, "Le tournant culturel de l'an III," in *1795 Pour une République sans Révolution*, sous la direction de Roger Dupuy et Marcel Morabito (Rennes: Presses Universitaires de Rennes, 1996), pp. 17–37.

50. Discussions of revolutionary "transparency" are relevant here. The classic analysis of its importance in political thought is Jean Starobinski, *Jean-Jacques Rousseau: la transparence et l'obstacle* (Paris: Gallimard, 1971). For its importance for the revolutionary mentality, see Lynn Hunt, *Politics, Culture, and Class in the French Revolution* (Berkeley: University of California Press, 1984), esp. pp. 19–51.

51. Jacques Julliard, *La reine du monde: essai sur la démocratie d'opinion* (Paris: Flammarion, 2009).

52. I distinguish "popular public opinion" from the "public opinion" referred to by Habermas, Baker, and others. These scholars are concerned with the emergence of rational "public opinion" among an educated elite (Habermas) or the manner in which elite actors appealed to "public opinion" as a rhetorical device to justify a given political stance (Baker).

53. Maurice Agulhon, *1848 ou l'apprentissage de la république 1848–1852* (Paris: Seuil, 1973).

54. François Furet, *Interpreting the French Revolution* [1978], translated by E. Forster (Cambridge: Cambridge University Press, 1981).

55. James Livesey, *Making Democracy in the French Revolution* (Cambridge, MA: Harvard University Press, 2001).

56. Pierre Rosanvallon, *Le moment Guizot* (Paris: Gallimard, 1985).

57. Maurice Agulhon, *1848 ou l'apprentissage de la république*; and, Agulhon, *La Republique au village* (Paris: Plon, 1970).

58. Sudhir Hazareesingh, *From Subject to Citizen: The Second Empire and the Emergence of Modern French Democracy* (Princeton: Princeton University Press, 1998).

59. Philip Nord, *The Republican Moment: Struggles for Democracy in Nineteenth-Century France* (Cambridge, MA: Harvard University Press, 1995).

60. Jean-Fabien Spitz, *Le moment républicain en France* (Paris: Gallimard, 2005).

61. Malcolm Crook, *Elections in the French Revolution: An Apprenticeship in Democracy 1789–1799* (Cambridge: Cambridge University Press, 1996).

62. Carla Hesse, *The Other Enlightenment: How French Women Became Modern* (Princeton: Princeton University Press, 2001).

63. Lucien Jaume, *L'Individu effacé: ou le paradoxe du libéralisme français*; and, Jaume, *La liberté et la loi: les origins philosophiques du libéralisme* (Paris: Fayard, 2000).

64. See my *Pierre-Joseph Proudhon and the Rise of French Republican Socialism* (New York: Oxford University Press, 1984); and *Between Marxism and Anarchism: Benoît Malon and French Reformist Socialism* (Berkeley: University of California Press, 1992).

65. Robert Gannett, Jr. found manuscript evidence that Tocqueville had read of some of Constant's writings of the late-1790s. [*Tocqueville Unveiled: The Historian and His Sources for The Old Regime and the Revolution* (Chicago: University of Chicago Press, 2003), pp. 32–37.] Most Tocqueville scholars, however, have failed to recognize any influence. Hugh Brogan, for example, in his otherwise excellent new biography of Tocqueville, makes no reference to Constant or to liberalism of the Directory or the Consulate and, therefore, incorrectly refers to the *doctinaires* as the first liberals. [Hugh Brogan, *Alexis de Tocqueville: A Life* (New Haven: Yale University Press, 2006).]

    For the best recent accounting of Constant's influence on subsequent thought, see Helena Rosenblatt, "Eclipses and Revivals: Constant's Reception in France and America, 1830–2007," *The Cambridge Companion to Constant*, pp. 351–77.

66. Lucien Jaume has recently argued that the strength of anti-federalism and anti-pluralism in France during this era came largely from "l'esprit monarchique et catholique." [*Tocqueville: les sources aristocratiques de la liberté: biographie intellectualle* (Paris: Fayard, 2008), p. 40.

67. Henri Guillemin, *Benjamin Constant muscadin 1795–1799* (Paris: Gallimard, 1958).

68. Gerald Izenberg has referred to this aspect of Constant's thought as "individuality." ["Individualism and Individuality in Constant," *The Cambridge Companion to Constant*, pp. 206–24.] While I agree with the thrust of Izenberg's argument, I'm reluctant to use the term "individuality" (though Constant used it at least once [in the "préface" to *Mélanges de littérature et de politique* (1829), in *Ecrits politiques*, p. 623]). I am reluctant because the concept of "individuality" is so strongly associated with German *bildung*. Constant's concerns were less contemplative, less aesthetic, as well as more intersubjective, than were those of his German contemporaries. And, of course, compared to them, Constant was more focused on how self-development was associated with political action within a constitutional and parliamentary order. He was primarily concerned, that is, not with the philosophical roots of "individuality," but rather with the practical realization of a framework that would protect individual liberty and moral autonomy.

    On this issue, see the probing articles of Kurt Kloocke: "Benjamin Constant et l'Allemagne: Individualité—Religion—Politique," *Annales Benjamin Constant*, 27 (2003): 127–71; and "L'Idée de l'individualité dans les écrits politiques de Benjamin Constant," *Annales Benjamin Constant*, 29 (2005): 143–58.

# Index

Printed in Great Britain
by Amazon

57517228R00165